The
FEMALE
CYCLIST

*Gearing up
a level*

by Gale Bernhardt

Foreword by
Linda Jackson

VELO
press

BOULDER, COLORADO USA

The Female Cyclist
Copyright © 1999 Gale Bernhardt

International Standard Book Number: 1-884737-58-7

Library of Congress Cataloging-in-Publication Data

Bernhardt, Gale, 1958 — The female cyclist: gearing up a level/Gale Bernhardt.
p.cm.—(Ultimate training series from VeloPress; 3)Includes
bibliographical references and index. ISBN 1-884737-58-7 1.Cycling for women.
2.Women athletes—Health and hygiene. 3.Sports for women. I.Title. II.Series.
GV1057.B47 1999
796.6'082—dc21
99-18666
CIP

PRINTED IN THE USA

Photography: Norman Rehme
Cover design: Erin Johnson
Interior layout/production: Daisy Bauer

1830 N. 55th Street • Boulder, Colorado • 80301-2700 • USA
303/440-0601 • FAX 303/444-6788 • E-MAIL velopress@7dogs.com

To purchase additional copies of this book or other Velo products,
call 800/234-8356 or visit us on the Web at www.velogear.com

To my mother, Margie,
the strongest woman I know

TABLE OF CONTENTS

FOREWORD

In 1994, at the age of 34, I gave up my career as an investment banker to pursue my dream of becoming a world-class cyclist. I didn't know where my dream would take me. I only knew that I wanted to give myself every chance I had to become the best that I could be. Due to my age, I was faced with a lot of skepticism from the cycling federation, as well as others in the sport. I ignored the negativity and started training in earnest. I devoted a lot of time, money and energy acquiring training knowledge. I consulted with various experts on nutrition, weight training, altitude training, and the psychological aspect of sport. By the age of 39 I had realized my dream and had won several major international stage races.

Although very difficult and time consuming, the knowledge that I obtained was critical to my ability to perform at the world-class level. Gale Bernhardt has just made the acquisition of training knowledge a lot easier. Her book *The Female Cyclist: Gearing Up a Level* collects all of the information needed to maximize your cycling potential. While the book specifically addresses issues and concerns for the female cyclist, it also provides invaluable information on numerous subjects including nutrition, altitude training, weight training, stretching and goal setting. Bernhardt summarizes all of the relevant studies on these subjects in a concise and informative manner, enabling you to make the decisions required to optimize your training program.

This book is a must-read for all aspiring cyclists, male or

female. Whether trying to improve your "personal best," or becoming a world-class cyclist, this book provides the necessary tools to help attain your dreams.

—Linda Jackson

VeloNews, North American Female Cyclist of the Year, 1998, 1997.

1998 Hewlett-Packard International Women's Challenge champion.

1998 Canadian road race champion.

1997 Tour de l'Aude champion.

1996 Atlanta Olympics time trial, 9th.

ACKNOWLEDGMENTS

I want to thank my husband, Delbert, for being my number one fan and supporter. He provided encouragement throughout my work on this book, as well as during a risky career change. He continues to support my athletic endeavors and says attending races is still exciting after eighteen years.

In 1987, my interest in racing moved from satisfaction with participation to wanting to increase speed and endurance. Thankfully, Joe Friel agreed to be my coach. Since that time he has become a mentor, a friend, and a business partner. He agreed to preread this book and provide valuable feedback. Cathy Sloan also read each chapter and contributed business support while the book was under construction. A good friend, she is featured in several photographs in Chapter 8.

Also featured in Chapter 8 photos, pumping iron and stretching is Fran Bell. The strength-training chapter was improved with Fran's suggestions, and she's been helpful for my personal strength training technique.

Award-winning photographer, Norman Rehme, took most of the photographs throughout the book. He is a man of many talents and a great neighbor.

What I thought would be an easy chapter to write, Chapter 3, ended up being one of the most difficult. When I began a data search to illustrate well-known information, I found the data didn't support information considered "standard" about female dimensions and bicycle fit. I'm grateful to Dr. Andy Pruitt, Lennard Zinn and Dr. Patrick Allen for taking time out of their busy schedules to answer questions and further increase my confidence in the data. Kyle Radford gave expert mechanical advice on Chapter 3, and his professional skills kept my bicycles in top condition for several years. He is featured in the bicycle-fit photographs and has been a reliable riding partner for the past two years.

Dr. Betsy Cairo proofread the chapters concerning the female body, the reproductive system, and menopause. Typically sharing her knowledge in a classroom or with clients in a private business, she made time to further educate me about the female body and how it is supposed to function when healthy. She is a champion at celebrating women and their gifts.

Chris Book, a registered dietitian, was a tremendous help in the transformation of my own diet and furnished a good deal of information for the nutrition chapter. Athletes and nonathletes alike value her expertise. Dr. Deborah Shulman — registered dietitian, exercise physiologist and elite-distance runner — reviewed Chapter 11 and supplied useful information based on first-hand experience and her work with endurance athletes.

Dennis McGrath, owner of Orchards Athletic Club, generously let us use the club to shoot photographs of strong and flexible women in action.

Certainly, this project wouldn't have been possible without encouragement and support from publisher, Amy Sorrells, editor Lori Hobkirk, and designer Daisy Bauer.

Finally I want to thank my father George and all of my family and close friends for understanding the huge amount of effort it takes to write a book. They patiently listened during the tough times, understood when I was staring at the computer instead of having fun with them, and told me, "You can do it," as they always have.

PREFACE

My love affair with cycling began when I received a cherry-red tricycle for Christmas at age two-and-a-half. My parents tell me I spent hours on that tricycle, riding up and down the same flagstone sidewalk, in and out of driveways. Surely the tricycle offered freedom, adventure, and transportation that was faster than walking and easier than running.

Cycling became more exciting when my parents moved to a new section of town. There were new roads to explore and a blue Schwinn replaced the red tricycle. The Schwinn was a trusty steed; it was sometimes a bicycle and sometimes an imaginary horse. And although it was not designed for dirt trails, the Schwinn was often an off-road vehicle.

The next trusty bike had to be earned. At age nine or ten, I saved my allowance and with my parents' help, bought a lime-green three-speed Stingray with a banana seat and big, slick back tire. It had the nifty stick shift, like a car's, on the top tube. That bike was cool.

The Stingray spent hot summer days at the cyclo-cross course — before the kids on my block knew anything about cyclo-cross — made specifically for 10-year-olds, and known as the infamous "Rumper-Bumper." Mounds of fill-dirt dumped in an empty lot by construction workers made a perfect place to play. Neighborhood kids wore several trails around and over the mounds of dirt. One route was particularly difficult because of "Deadman's Curve." An instant of misjudgment would send bicycle, pigtails, bare arms and legs airborne before the final landing into a patch of Canadian thistle. It always made for an exciting racecourse, where the rewards were simply bragging rights.

Through my early teen and college years, the bicycle remained a viable mode of transportation, even though a car was also an option. The bicycle was refreshing to ride in the cool morning air; it was easy to find parking, and it was cheap transportation.

A few years after college graduation, my interest in cycling longer distances increased. My first long-distance goal was to ride home from my job: 18 miles. The second major long-distance accomplishment was to ride to and from work in the same day. I can recall being tired, yet exhilarated, for a week after completing that ride.

In those years, I cycled for fitness, riding only in perfect weather. This meant riding in the summer, two to three days per week, and doing other sports during the winter. Riding with other people and occasional reinforcement from brief moments of speed gave me a desire to go faster for longer periods of time. In my late twenties, I sought to improve both speed and endurance.

As I gained knowledge about cycling-specific training and endurance athletics, more people began to ask for my advice. Seeking opportunities to teach or coach sports, since the age of 16, I channeled my energy into coaching endurance athletes, including cyclists.

As a coach and author, I occasionally receive requests to write a magazine column on coaching women athletes. Each time that I've been asked to write about the differences between coaching men and women, I've given the same response: "I can see no blanket differences between training all women versus all men. The people I coach all have different goals, strengths, performance limitors and personal life challenges, and each one has a different personality. These differences are enough that I've never written two plans exactly alike — even if I have two athletes, of the same gender, with similar racing schedules."

With that said, why would there need to be a book on cycling that specifically addresses women? Although women and men can use the training schedules within this book, there are anatomical and physiological differences between women and men that influence the peripheral aspects of athletic training. These are the primary reasons for this book.

The detailed training schedules are another reason the book was written. Some people are not able to hire a coach, but they want a plan to help them get faster or go farther. I've designed five such plans to fill that need. The plans bridge the gap between cycling for recreation and cycling for more distance or speed.

Finally, my hope is that the information between the covers of this book will encourage more women to ride. It is possible to increase speed and become a part of the weekend group ride or race.

INTRODUCTION

Health and cycling are interrelated. It takes a healthy cyclist to optimize her genetic gifts. The process to ensure good health has historically been filled with misconceptions. Perhaps one day readers will reflect on this book and comment about how little science knew about optimizing health and cycling, as I did with other books when researching Chapter 1.

Chapter 1 reviews a bit of women's sports history and some of the past beliefs about the limits of women in sports. Although in the late 1990s I thought we were well past old belief systems, an article in Runner's World magazine, August 1998, reminded me we are not as far as I thought. Danelle Ballengee, a world-class endurance athlete, was not allowed to run the 1996 Ixta eighteen-mile mountain run because officials claimed it was too difficult for women. Ballengee said, "I guess they were afraid my ovaries would fall out or something." We are making progress at eliminating barriers to women's opportunities, but the job is not complete.

Chapter 2 is an overview of some of the current research being conducted with women test subjects and women athletes. As research continues, perhaps more paradigms about women's performance and limitations will change.

Women and men have some obvious anatomical differences, but it is the not-so-obvious differences that make bike-fit a hair-pulling experience. Chapter 3 gives tips for proper bike-fit, which is critical to cycling comfort and success. It also dispels common misconceptions about all women having shorter torsos than men do.

One item common to women is the reproductive system and the hormones associated with good health. Although the physical components of the system can be surgically altered, the hormones associated with being a woman are critical to good health. Chapter 4 covers hormones and the menstrual cycle, and how they affect athletic performance. The text also addresses some of the important issues allied with good health. For example, hormonal balance is essential to preventing osteoporosis.

Many women who become pregnant wonder if they can remain active throughout the full nine months. Women who have already made the journey and current medical recommendations are covered in Chapter 5.

As we age, should we trade in our bicycle wheels for a recliner? Or should we forge ahead as if we were sweet sixteen? There are changes that occur to our bodies as we age. Those changes are discussed in Chapter 6, along with recommendations to minimize some of the inconveniences associated with aging.

Chapter 7 begins the discussion about athletic training. It contains information on the concept of periodization to improve athletic performance, how to determine intensity of exercise, tests to determine target heart rate exercise zones, and tests to evaluate progress. Much of Chapter 7 covers cardiovascular conditioning.

Although cardiovascular conditioning is important, strength training and stretching are also significant components of fitness. Strength training can help prevent and repair damage from osteoporosis. Stretching can improve strength, range of motion, and aid in the prevention of injury. Strength training and stretching recommendations are included in Chapter 8.

Dreaming about improved fitness is the beginning of change. The actual changes to fitness and health can be undermined by unreasonable goals. If goals are unreasonable, too high, athletes become discouraged and often progress halts. Chapter 10 gives tips on goal setting to help athletes avoid common mistakes.

With goals in mind, Chapter 10 gets down to detail and provides plans for six different cycling objectives. There is a twelve-week plan to prepare a cyclist to ride fifty miles; a twelve-week plan for a one hundred-mile ride; a thirteen-week plan for an athlete preparing for a three-day tour; a twenty-five-week plan for an athlete preparing to race a forty-kilometer time trial or someone just wanting to improve their group riding speed; and a twenty-five-week plan to improve hill-climbing.

Physical training isn't enough to optimize athletic performance and certainly not health. Proper nutrition is crucial. Chapter 11 covers macro and micronutrients, phytochemicals, caloric intake, and nutrition elements important to athletic training and recovery. Always a hot topic, this chapter does not recommend a single "diet," but rather suggests that dietary needs be customized daily in order to meet the needs of the athlete. It also gives industry formulas to estimate several food-intake parameters.

Two athletes can begin an event with equal genetic gifts, equal physical strength and conditioning and equal nutritional status. The race will go to the athlete with the strongest mental skills. Mental skills are so valuable; an athlete with prime physical skills can lose a race to an athlete with highly developed mental skills. The mind is a powerful ally. Chapter 12 offers mental tools that can be used in daily life and athletics.

Finally, Chapter 13 is a collection of ideas that can help make cycling more comfortable and safer. There are tips on saddle sores, travel, and hot- and cold-weather riding. This information is included because it answers some of the questions frequently asked by athletes.

This book represents only a small portion of the body of useful knowledge available to today's athletes—especially women. But this book is also intended to be male-friendly. Not only is some of the information "gender-blind," but, hopefully, the female-specific wisdom will help some men understand what is going on with the women in their lives.

Enjoy!

Gale Bernhardt
February 1999

CHAPTER ONE

Past, present *and fut**ure***

"It was in this same time frame (1869) that Johanne Joergenson and Susanne Lindberg—two Danish women—were breaking numerous cycling records set by their humiliated countrymen."

MYTHOLOGY AND EARLY WOMEN ATHLETES

Women have been involved in athletic pursuits for a long time, a very long time. Some of the earliest recorded athletes were the Greek goddesses. Artemis, the goddess of the moon, was also a huntress. Atalanta, a virgin huntress of Greek mythology, was abandoned when she was only an infant and raised by a she-bear. Her physical abilities included huntress, wrestler and runner. Atalanta was so strong and fast that she often competed against men. Her confidence in her running speed and reluctance to marry, found her betting for her virginity and freedom. So, she agreed to marry the first suitor who could outrun her. Legend had it that she would follow her suitor and spear him, if she could catch him. And after defeating several challengers, she lost to Melanion.

1

Each time Atalanta began to outrun Melanion, he would toss out one of three golden apples given to him by Aphrodite, the Greek goddess of love, beauty and fertility. This maneuver distracted Atalanta, tempting her to pause, which eventually cost her the race—a race she should have won.

As with the goddesses, some of the early sports contests for mortal women were related to securing a husband. The Spartan women—of the fourth and fifth century B.C.—sang, danced and exercised naked, intending to entice young men into marriage. Their sports contests were used to demonstrate fitness and their ability to bear healthy sons. Women were admired for their fitness ages ago.

In addition to luring a husband, scholars speculate that some of the early sports contests for Spartan women were rights of passage into womanhood, or prenuptial rights. In particular, there was participation in annual athletic games, called the Heraia. The Heraia were foot races held in the spring, approximately one month before the men's qua-drennial Olympic games. The distances ran by women were one-sixth less than those ran by men, possibly because the geometrically oriented Greeks determined race distance from their speculations that women were one-sixth less the size and stature of men.

Contests for entry into womanhood as well as husbands was also documented in some of the Diola and Gambia African tribes. Prepubescent girls wrestled as part of their ritual initiation into womanhood. Among some of these tribes, girls wrestled other girls and boys wrestled boys. The champions of each competition often entered into marriage.

These Greek and African cultures were independent of each other in time and place. But even cultures that are very close geographically and of the same era will vary a great deal. For example, while the Spartans encouraged physical fitness, other Greek cultures of the same era were more restrictive. Athenian women, for example, admired themselves as sophisticated and above physical displays of power. Physical fitness, as it related to competition, was intended for those women who were not yet married. Mature or married women stayed at home and cared for the family.

Culture and religion continued to have an influence on sports into Roman times; economic status was beginning to be felt as an influence as well. At one end of the economic and social spectrum, daughters of the affluent were thought to participate in running races. Evidence of athletics was found in the famed "Bikini" mosaic, found on the Piazza Armerina, a south central Sicilian hilltown. It depicts ten young women clad in bikinis. Three of them carry palm branches that are thought to depict victory, while others represent a javelin thrower, a jumper, a discus thrower, two runners and two ball players.

While some affluent women participated in these Olympic-type sports, there were daughters of peasants and slaves who found themselves in running races or fighting as gladiators in the Roman arena. Gladiators, chariot races and sporting events had close associations to pagan gods, as far as the early Christians were concerned. For women in Christian society, sports, and training for sport as well as battle was not encouraged by the church. It is hard to imagine that the church, for which the role model for women is the Virgin Mary, would encourage women to train for competition or battle. As part of a Christian society, women were expected to behave in a certain manner, as interpreted by scholars of the Bible.

Other doctrines of particular societies continued to dictate what women were able to do. And in a hierarchical society, social status determined who had what privileges. In a society of agriculture, seasons determined activities. As a result, women's participation in sports were heavily influenced by several demands of their lifestyles.

At the end of the Middle Ages—the late fourteenth century—some women on the lower end of the economic spectrum played "folk football," which eventually evolved into modern soccer. They were able to push, shove and run with the men because they worked beside the men as part of the agrarian economy. The aristocratic women, on the other hand, had nothing to do with folk football; rather they played more "civilized" sports, such as court tennis, hunting, horseback riding, chess and backgammon.

THE NINETEENTH CENTURY

In the early nineteenth century, inventors in several countries began working on the beginnings of what we call the bicycle. History has the bicycle born out of a hobby horse with wheels. The rider would sit upon the saddle and propel the horse with his or her feet. In time, the horse disappeared and was replaced with a frame. One inventor applied for a patent and said the machine was capable of traveling uphill as fast as a man could walk; on the flats it would go 6 to 7 miles per hour in poor road conditions— even after a heavy rain; when roads were flat, dry and firm it would run at a rate of eight to nine miles per hour, equal to a horse's gallop; and on a descent, it would equal a horse at full speed.

Some of these prebicycle versions were called "hobby-horses," "dandy horses," "swift-walkers," and other creative titles. As with previous history, the social elites were the people investing in these new machines, which was becoming a new sport. Around 1890, a fellow in the London suburb of Soho opened a riding school and offered rental swift-walkers for those unable to afford to purchase one of their own. As part of the rental fleet, he offered "women's" swift-walkers with side-saddles and some with three wheels.

By the late nineteenth century, the bicycle had a variety of styles and mechanical drives. Cycling was becoming more popular than imagined possible. Historians believed the bicycle gave women the first "acceptable" form of physical exercise. This sport wasn't limited to just unmarried women; most women were enjoying cycling. Women were gaining new freedoms: Their awkward skirts gave way to bloomers, which were more accommodating to cycling.

MEDICINE AND ATHLETICS

As cycling became more popular in the late 1800s, sporting competition also grew. Arena sports have always had an appeal, due to their spectator-friendly atmosphere, and cycling races around a track seemed a perfect fit. While men were racing around the track, British track owners lost their licenses if they allowed women to race. The French, however, were more willing to risk ridicule and bend the rules. In 1868, the French actually promoted women's racing, and cheering crowds were pleased.

In 1869, the Olivier brothers promoted a 50-mile dash from Paris to Rouen, and four spunky French women joined the men. James Moore won the race averaging 7.5 miles per hour. Unfortunately, the women, who were part of the peloton, weren't recorded by name.

Early names in women's road racing included Hélène Dutrieu, Amélie Legall (racing as Lisette), Clara Grace, Johanne Joergenson and Susanne Lindberg. Dutrieu became a world champion and she set the hour record in 1895, going 39.19 kilometers in the 60-minute time trial. Lisette was known for her speed in a series of six-day and eight-day races. The high point of her career was when she beat Grace in a 100-kilometer race, in a winning time of 2:41:12. Lisette was handily beating the women she challenged, so she began to challenge men. With a 4-kilometer head start, she was able to defeat Albert Champion in a 25-kilometer race. It was at this same time that Johanne Joergenson and Susanne Lindberg, two Danish women, were breaking numerous cycling records set by their humiliated countrymen.

In the midst of new technology and new knowledge, women were also in the middle of medical controversies. In 1893, Tessie Reynolds, at sweet sixteen, caused an uproar by riding a cross-barred men's bicycle to London and back to Brighton for a distance of one hundred-twenty miles. She accomplished her feat in eight-and-a-half hours. People asked, "Should women really be encouraged to do this sort of thing?" "How will it affect their ability to bear children?" "Isn't this entirely too much for the frail, weaker sex?" In addition to the possible physical atrocities, Tessie's hair was disheveled, she was disgustingly sweaty, red as a lobster, and her hairpins were strewn along the course—wasn't that unwomanly?

While some women were busy cycling, others were laboring in the fields (even while pregnant), others were becoming socialites and the medical community was still busy trying to figure out how the human body worked. Although some of their ideas may seem ridiculous now, it was the best knowledge of the time. Remember that; it will ring true more than once.

In 1869, one doctor concluded that while women were being treated for diseases of the stomach, liver, kidneys and other organs, upon investigation, most of these were really symptoms of just one disease, that of the womb. American and European doctors were handing out similar advice.

By 1871, although women were encouraged to exercise, doctors recommended women cease exercise during the "sexual storms" of one's menstrual period. Stern warnings to avoid dancing, shopping, riding and partying came from doctors who were more than likely providing medical care to the upper class—those who could afford such a luxury.

For these frail women, exercise during pregnancy was also not recommended by the medical professionals. A woman should rest during and after pregnancy in order to cope with the demands of pregnancy and recovery from the delivery. These serious urgings were probably never heard by the working-class woman. Employers had no sympathy, nor did they give time off for carrying a child and recovering from delivery.

Women working in the agrarian economy of the time were needed to do chores such as working in the field, cooking, cleaning and caring for children. They did not have access to prenatal care and they probably had limited time to read the information being published by the so-called experts.

These working women were a great asset to our perceptions of what a woman could and couldn't do before, during and after pregnancy. They probably listened to their bodies, rested when they needed to, and worked harder when they were able. Some doctors—European and American—took note of these exceptions to the "rules" and encouraged women to be physically active. Some said active women were more immune to "uterine disease." Maybe this meant they suffered fewer problems with their menstrual cycles and the delivery of children.

THE TWENTIETH CENTURY

The twentieth century brought more changes for women. In the U.S., World War I put droves of men into war, and women were running the factories to support the war effort. They began taking roles and responsibilities only a few of them had possessed in the past. In the United States, the medical community encouraged women to exercise as an antidote to long hours and typically poor working conditions. Some employers even organized sports teams for their workers.

Into the 1920s women enjoyed more autonomy in the United States. They had won the right to vote and represented at least one-third of the workforce. These women soon had money and leisure time, and many turned to sports, which wasn't limited to the upperclass any longer. Although working-class women weren't kept from certain sports, they were still restricted to those sports that they could afford.

When the Great Depression hit in the 1930s, fewer women occupied jobs. Women who took men's jobs were considered unpatriotic. When the nation as a whole became more financially conservative, oddly, there were conservative recommendations for optimal health. One idea was that a woman who was muscularly developed would have problems with motherhood.

Track and field athlete, Mildred "Babe" Didrickson, was one of the more famous athletes of that time to endure accusations about her lack of femininity, and probably of possible lesbianism as well, which, at that time, was a horrible thing. Not even her marriage to professional wrestler George Zaharias was enough to end the rumors. Even though she is considered to be one of the greatest female athletes of all times, clearly not even the best athletes are immune to psychological scare tactics and misleading information that may discourage them.

Why did it take another war to change these attitudes? World War II again took U.S. men to Europe, while women ran the factories. A unique consequence of the men being in

Europe was the formation of an all-woman's professional base-ball league in 1943. People filled the stadiums; the league was popular and successful. The league lasted for twelve years before it lost out to the return of the men's league and undoubt-edly, social pressures.

While there were individual examples of women excelling in sports, a good deal of credit for women's current status in sports can be given to federal mandate Title IX. It was legisla-tion that prohibited discrimination, on the basis of gender in federally funded higher-education programs. This ruling affect-ed most academic institutions in the U.S., and put athletic pro-grams under inspection. In 1978, Title IX took affect for secondary and post-secondary schools. Schools could not deny women the right to facilities, coaches, uniforms and budgets. And the programs did not have to be equal to that of the men's, nor did the ruling benefit only women. Programs that had dif-ficulty existing—men's volleyball and field hockey—could also take advantage of the new rules.

As we approach the twenty-first century, an assessment of women's sports shows that we are heading in the right direc-tion. There has been more documentation about female ath-letes of the 1970s, '80s and '90s than any other eras. As we entered the 1990s, there was an impressive and visible differ-ence in the documentation of women in sports, while there was also a substantial increase female sports reporters.

THE LATE TWENTIETH CENTURY

In one way, it's an injustice to begin writing about the women athletes of the 1970s through the '90s. A small portion of a chapter cannot describe a story that could easily occupy an entire book. In the effort to keep this single chapter from becoming a book, the focus will be only on women cyclists. Again, there is a great amount of information and a number of impressive women cyclists, and this chapter will tell about a few of them. The story is far from complete, but maybe someone can tell the entire history of women cyclists at a later date.

The first time road racing for women was included in the Olympic Games was in 1984. The gold medal went to Connie Carpenter from the U.S.; Rebecca Twigg, also from the U.S., won the silver medal; and Sandra Schumacher from West Germany won the bronze. Carpenter was a tremendous cyclist, having won the U.S. women's national cycling championships thirteen times prior to competing in the 1984 Olympics.

The U.S. has never been the only country with great cyclists. Italy is the home of three-time Giro d'Italia Femminile winner and three-time Tour Cycliste Féminin winner, Fabiana Luperini. She began cycling at the age of seven. In 1997, Luperini won the grueling, twelve-stage Tour Cycliste Féminin by cycling 1184 kilometers—725 miles—in just more than 34 hours, averaging 34.234 kilometers per hour—21.273 miles per hour. She was, of course, working with her team, Sanson, but still managed an impressive average speed on her own through the variety of terrain.

Also from Italy comes Paola Pezzo, winner of the inaugural 1996 Olympic mountain-bike race. Alison Sydor of Canada won the silver medal, and Susan DeMattei from the U.S. took home the bronze. In 1997, Pezzo went on to win the world cross-country mountain-bike championship as well as an impressive eight of ten World Cup mountain-bike races. And not only was she racing mountain bikes, but she was also studying law—a testiment that athletes are often committed scholars.

Several road racers have been lured to the dirt trails. In 1989, Juli Furtado was the U.S. national road racing champion, and in 1990, she won the national collegiate road championship and the world cross-country mountain-bike championship. She managed to race bicycles and receive honors in biology as well.

No list of influential female cyclists would be complete without mentioning French rider Jeannie Longo, who has won about every title there is to win in women's road and track cycling. She has been the French national cycling champion eighteen times. She won four consecutive world road racing championships between 1985 and '88. In '89, she broke her own world hour record, traveling 46.352 kilometers—28.803 miles—in sixty minutes. She has won the Tour Cycliste Féminin three times and has won the world track individual pursuit title three times. She broke her hour record again in 1996. And that same year, she won the gold medal in the Olympic road race, and a silver medal in the individual time trial. Also in 1996, she was third in the Tour Cycliste Féminin and first in the world time trial championship, which gave her an eleventh career world title. She is a truly remarkable cyclist.

Endurance cycling can be a team or an individual event. Seana Hogan won her fourth individual Race Across America title in 1997. In the '97 race, Seana traveled from Irvine, California to Savannah, Georgia in ten days, one hour and thirty-five minutes. In 1998, she was the only woman to compete at all, though the heat and humidity zapped her, and she was unable to turn in her usual winning performance.

You might be reading this and thinking, "Yes, but those are young people, people who get paid to race. I could never!" That thought won't hold a drop of energy-replacement fluid with Margaret Nolan or Martha Hanson. They both competed in the 1997 U.S. Masters National Cycling Championships and won their age groups in the individual 20-kilometer time trials. Nolan won the 65-69 category in 35:29 and Hanson won the 70-plus age category in 46:12. These women are role models in action.

Racing aside, nearing the end of the twentieth century, there are several sports magazines dedicated to women: *Sports Illustrated for Women, Conde Naste's Sports For Women*, and *Women Outside* to name a few.

Women in the cycling world are gracing the covers of *VeloNews* and *Bicycling* magazine—two of the most popular cycling periodicals in America.

FUTURE

What about the future? Which direction will women's sports go? Where will women's cycling go? It depends on us: you and me. It doesn't matter if you are male or female, we need to get out there and be active role models, and encourage others to be active. We need to mentor young women who are hungry for help. We need to encourage manufacturers to provide women with clothing and equipment to meet their needs and wants. We need to influence corporate advertising dollars to support women's sports, including cycling, and we need to support those events ourselves. Remember the women's professional baseball league back in 1943? It was successful because thousands of spectators encouraged the idea. Go out and watch a women's bike race; give it your personal support. Encourage your mother and father, daughter and son, sister and brother, aunt and uncle, friends … everyone you know, to cycle.

You will find your way as a bicycle racer, one way or the other, and this book can help you avoid some common mistakes. It will help you shorten the learning curve by giving you some of the information that has helped many people become better cyclists. The information is not all-inclusive; however, it will help you move from being a purely recreational cyclist to being a faster cyclist, whether you are racing or riding with your buddies. Anyone can ride hard, but not everyone can ride fast.

BRIEF THOUGHTS

Thoughout history, there were several major themes affecting women and sports. These themes continue to influence sport today:

- Social culture
- Religion
- Economic status—national, local and personal
- Science and technology
- Personal education
- Personal beliefs
- Personal support system

Be aware of how these items influence your thoughts about women athletes and their capabilities.

REFERENCES

Cycling USA, Volume XIX, Number 4, 1997 Masters Championships, pg. 14 .

Guttman, Allen, Women's Sports, A History, Columbia University Press, 1991, pp. 7-52, 101-102.

Jew, Bryan, Fast Learner, VeloNews, Volume 26, Number 15, pg. 50.

Lutter, Judy Mahle and Lynn Jaffee, The Bodywise Woman, Second Edition, Human Kinetics, 1996, pp. 1-20.

Perry, David B., Bike Cult, Four Walls Eight Windows, 1995, pp. 12-15.

St. Claire, Murraine, "Oh Danny boy," VeloNews, Volume 26, Number 14.

Stephen, Marti, "Longo at long last," VeloNews, Volume 25, Number 13, pp. 106-108.

Stephen, Marti, "Dunlap still climbing," VeloNews, Volume 26, Number 17, pg. 34.

Stephen, Marti, "The way of the wolf," VeloNews, Volume 26, Number 19, pg. 11.

The Olympic Century XXII Olympiad, Volume 21, World Sport Research and Publications Inc. 1996, pp. 54, 90-92, 164.

Triathlete magazine, September 1997, "Female Market Huge but Ignored," pg.13.

The Oxford Classical Dictionary, Oxford University Press, 1970, pp. 80, 136.

VeloNews, Volume 25, Number 20, 9th Annual VeloNews Awards.

VeloNews, Volume 26, Number 4, "Twenty-five momentous years," pg. 40.

Wilcockson, John, "Olympic mountain biking," VeloNews, Volume 25, Number 14, pp. 16-20.

Zeitvogel, Karine, "A hat-trick for Luperini," VeloNews, Volume 26, Number 16, pg. 32.

Zeitvogel, Karine, "In a class of her own," VeloNews, Volume 26, Number 17, pg. 32.

Zinn, Lennard, "Pezzo glitters again," *VeloNews*, Volume 26, Number 17, pg. 12.

CHAPTER TWO

Physiology,
Research and
Recommendations

"My opinions may have changed, but not the fact that I am right."
— Ashleigh Brilliant

U ndoubtedly, female athletes of the past raised questions about the capabilities of the female body. Women became inspired to pursue an athletic endeavor, and it was after they were able to accomplish the feat that science wondered how women could have been capable of such activity? Often, athletes are the ones who raise issues and questions for science. Science prepares a set of paradigms based on experiments, results and logical deductions. It is when someone performs outside the current set of paradigms that science questions current thinking.

In the past, it was difficult to get female test subjects to participate in scientific studies because there weren't as many female athletes as there were male. Male subjects who were active in sports were easier to find. And scientists once thought it didn't really matter if males or females were studied at exercise—a human is a human and they're all physiologically the same, right?

Scientific research and so-called "experts" generally attempt to give us, the general public, information that is sound and reliable. As much as scientific knowledge has advanced, there is still much to be learned. Our knowledge of human performance can, and has in the past, been limited by technology—the type of technology we use to measure and examine attributes of the human body. Sometimes, current paradigms can block our vision to new information. Technology and our current perceptions can inhibit new information from being discovered and so can the availability of the "right" subjects for testing. Hence, "average Americans" are often used as test subjects for athletic studies. Although the average American test subject can give us valuable information about the workings of the human body, they hardly represent an athlete's body.

Perhaps the same social influences that have drawn more women to athletics, have drawn more women to business, industry, science and management roles; and these women are asking, "Does the female body really react the same as the male body to exercise?" "Does the female body have the same nutritional needs?" "Should women train differently than men?" There are husbands and fathers who are interested in helping their wives and daughters optimize performance, and they too are influencing further research into women's physiology. Certainly, there are scientists who simply ask, "Why, why not and how?" purely for scientific knowledge. The sources for questions, which drive new research, are diverse.

We may have asked the questions before, but as previously mentioned, we may not have had the technology to perform experiments to give meaningful results. Perhaps there was data that went totally undetected. The constant development of technology and communication tools have improved our ability to discover and disperse information. In the communication area, for example, an October 1997 search for scientific studies on "Exercise and females, adults 19 to 44 years of age, reports written between 1993 and '97," on the Internet's Web site for Medline, yielded 229,746 items. When the search was opened to "Exercise and females, all ages, reports written between 1993 and 1997," the number of published journal articles grew to 494,208. The research and information available to any author, at the time of this writing, is overwhelming.

While it was not possible to review the results of all the studies, and their possible usefulness to women's cycling, several items stand out and have received attention in recent literature. They include genetic influences on athletic ability, altitude effects, outstanding female performance in ultra-endurance events, the importance of retaining bone mass, the influences of the menstrual cycle on injuries, gastric emptying rates, and the use of testosterone as test flag for anabolic steroid use. Let's examine each.

I PICKED THE WRONG PARENTS

Several scientific studies have been conducted to determine if genetics are responsible for great athletic performances. One group, Claude Bouchard, Ph.D., and a team of researchers at Laval University in Québec, Canada, looked at monozygotic (identical) twins and put a group of twenty— ten pairs—on a twenty-week training program. The twins trained four to five times per week for forty-five minutes per session at an average intensity of approximately 80 percent of maximal heart rate. The result? Identical twins did, in fact, respond nearly identically to the training program. One pair gained 10 and 11 percent on their VO_2 max while a second pair gained 22 and 25 percent. Most of the variation in performance gains was between sets, rather than within sets, of twins.

Although the study on twins revealed 82 percent of the variation in VO_2 max was due to genetics, it also showed that only 33 percent of the differences found in ventilatory threshold (another benchmark of improvement) was attributed to genetics. This is important, since ventilatory threshold and the closely related lactate threshold, which are covered in Chapter 9, are frequently found to be the best predictors of actual performance. In other words, lactate threshold speeds tend to be more "trainable" than VO_2 max, which is good news for all of us.

The researchers at Laval conducted other studies, in addition to the one already mentioned here, and, in short, they concluded that genetic factors account for only 20 percent of the variation in performances of endurance athletes. Non-genetic factors—including nutrition, lifestyle, past exercise patterns, age, socioeconomic status and mental skills—influence twice as much, or 40 percent of the variation. Gender differences accounted for 10 percent. The final 30 percent was in how a particular set of genes reacts to a particular training program (some people will respond to one training program, but not another.)

What's the bottom line? Roughly 70 percent of your performance is under your control, and what works for you won't necessarily work as well for the cyclist next to you.

What about the differences between athletes on the same program? The researchers at Laval conducted another study to determine how much variation there would be in fitness gains if people followed the same training program. In this study, twenty-four similar subjects, who were initially sedentary, followed the same training program for twenty weeks. After that time, there were some big changes. The average gain in VO_2 max was 33 percent and one person in the group gained a whopping 88 percent. Unfortunately, another individual, sweating on the same plan, increased VO_2 max only 5 percent.

Within the same study, scientists measured power output on a bicycle ergometer. Subjects pedaled away for ninety minutes and their mean power output was measured before the training program began and again at the completion of the twenty weeks. The average power improvement was a nice 51 percent. One happy person gained a gigantic 97 percent, while another gained only 16 percent.

Why do some people seem to make big gains and others make minimal gains? Are their gains at equal rates? The studies at Laval led researchers to believe there are "responders" and "non-responders." Those who are considered to be responders make big improvements in aerobic capacity and power as a result of their training, while non-responders barely show a gain, even after twenty weeks of hard work. The scientists estimate around 5 percent of us are high responders who can make improvements of more than 60 percent, while about the same number are low responders and may only expect a 5 percent improvement.

In addition to responders and non-responders, the studies revealed a difference in response rates—a scale of responsiveness. Some people made nice gains after just four to six weeks of training, but seemed to plateau and made minimal gains in weeks seven to twenty. Others were late bloomers and were at a stand-still for six to ten weeks, but then blossomed, improving their aerobic capacities by 20 to 25 percent after ten weeks of additional training.

An important point is, given any single training program, not all individuals will react exactly the same. Some people will make big gains, while others may make marginal gains. You will need to learn how your body responds to training, and then make adjustments. Chapter 10 outlines training programs to help you on your path to new levels of fitness. You may need to modify the programs, based on your personal needs. Tips on how to modify the programs are included.

WHERE VO$_2$ MAX ORIGINATES

While on the subject of genetics, some speculate that it is your mother who is responsible for providing you with a large VO$_2$ max. When you were being formed, your mother's egg (ovum) contained a large amount of mitochondria—which provides most of the energy required for endurance performance—and your father's mitochondria were limited to the tail portion of the sperm.

By viewing the fertilization process through electronmicroscopy, it can be seen that sometimes a portion of the sperm's tail, and hence paternal mitochondria, make it into the egg, but not always. If mitochondria from the sperm do make it into the egg, they are not believed to influence the mitochondrial DNA of the new being.

So, it is mom who gave us our aerobic capacity? Well, not necessarily. Although individual mitochondrial DNA appear to be maternally determined, the total number of mitochondria may be influenced by both the father and mother. We also know that mitochondria can be influenced by training, which can increase their number and size, and there could be a potential doubling of aerobic system enzymes. How much this training effect is governed maternally or paternally is not known.

Mitochondria is just one parameter contributing to the complex issue of aerobic capacity. Examples of other parameters that influence aerobic capacity and can improve with training are heart rate, stroke volume and blood volume; muscle size and metabolic activity; respiratory exchange rates; and exercise economy.

Certainly, there is much we don't know about genetic influences on athletic performance. At this time, we don't even know which genes are critical in predicting or improving athletic performance. Will there be a day when we can take a DNA sample and determine how to optimize each individual's performance? Who knows?

HIGH-ALTITUDE TRAINING

If you are a lowlander and have traveled to the mountains to bike, hike, ski, race or sightsee, you may have experienced uncomfortable symptoms of high altitude. You may have gotten a rip-roaring headache, nausea, or just felt lousy all over. Still, you have heard that high-altitude training is good for you. Is altitude training really worthwhile?

ALTITUDE STRESS

The barometric pressure at sea level averages 760 millimeters of mercury (mm Hg), whereas the barometer reads 510mm Hg at 10,000 feet. The density of oxygen in the air decreases in direct proportion to increasing altitude. In other words, when you take a normal breath of air at altitude, you will have less oxygen in your lungs, than you would if you were to take the same size breath at sea level. Being an aerobic animal, you know your muscles want and need lots of oxygen to operate a bicycle.

To compensate for less oxygen and reduced pressure, the body tries to adjust, occasionally rebelling. The most important compensations include an increase in respiratory drive, which means you breathe faster and, as a result, may hyperventilate; and secondly, an increase in blood flow at rest and during submaximal exercise. Additional responses to altitude can include increased resting heart rate, lightheadedness, headache, insomnia, nausea and loss of appetite. As altitude increases above 15,000 feet, people may experience vomiting, intestinal disturbances, dyspnea (labored breathing), lethargy, general weakness and an inability to make rational decisions.

In the first few days of altitude adaptation, cardiac output and submaximal heart rate may increase 50 percent above sea level values. No wonder people feel like their hearts are going to leap from their bodies! Because your body requires the same amount of oxygen to work at altitude as it does at sea level, the increase in submaximal blood flow partially compensates for reduced oxygen levels. In terms of total oxygen circulated in the body, at rest, and moderate levels of exercise, a 10-percent increase in cardiac output can offset a 10-percent reduction in arterial oxygen saturation. In other words, your heart can pump 10-percent faster to compensate for 10-percent less oxygen in your blood stream.

It is beyond the 10-percent range where things get tough. The greatest effects of altitude on aerobic metabolism seem to be during maximal exercise. At top intensities, the ventilatory and circulatory adjustments to altitude cannot compensate for the lower oxygen content of arterial blood. What this means is the athlete has to slow down to reduce the demand for oxygen.

ADAPTATIONS TO ALTITUDE STRESS

With all the seemingly negative effects, why would someone want to train at altitude? The biggest reason to train at altitude is the body's long-term adaptation, which is an increase in the blood's oxygen carrying capacity.

Two major factors affect the adaptation. During the first few days at altitude, there is a decrease in plasma volume. Because of this decrease, red blood cells become more concentrated. For example, after about at week at 7400 feet, the plasma volume is decreased by 8 percent, while the concentrations of red blood cells and hemoglobin are increased by 4 and 10 percent, respectively. The changes observed after a week cause the oxygen content of arterial blood to increase significantly above values observed immediately upon arrival at altitude.

Following this adaptation of decreasing plasma volume is an increase in red cell mass. Through responses initiated by the body, reduced arterial oxygen pressure stimulates an increase in the total number of red blood cells. For example, a healthy high-altitude native may have a red blood cell count that is 50-percent greater than a native sea-level dweller. These two adaptations to altitude have an effect that translates into a large increase in the blood's capacity to transport oxygen.

Just how high is "altitude"?

Elevations between 10,000 and 18,000 feet are generally considered high altitude. Scientists refer to moderate altitudes being between 4000 and 10,000 feet. Generally, there is minimal scientific discussion about altitudes between sea level and 4000 feet, although some believe altitude effects may show up as low as 2000 feet.

What about speed and power at altitude?

Lots of red blood cells that flood the body with oxygen carrying capability sounds like a good deal. People ought to be aerobic animals after they adapt to altitude. But now it's time for the "bad news." When exposed to higher altitudes, it's nearly impossible for athletes to train at the same intensity as they were able to train while at sea level. In other words, if you are a lowlander capable of averaging twenty miles per hour for a 40km time trial, at a heart rate of 175 beats per minute, and a perceived exertion of 17 on the Borg Scale (breathing hard), your average speed (assuming a duplicate course profile) could be decreased by 5 to 10 percent for the same heart rate and perceived exertion when exposed to even moderate altitudes. This means your speed will decrease by two miles per hour, which is quite a reduction.

What if people who already live at high altitude travel to sea level? Is there an automatic gain in speed? That's a good question, and one that is not easily answered. Since people living at a higher altitude are not able to train at the same intensity levels relative to the maximum they are capable of, as low-landers, they have not trained their bodies to perform at higher speeds. Unproven by science, perhaps the highlanders don't have the neuromuscular programming, in addition to the metabolic speeds, necessary to cycle fast at sea level.

How long is it before the benefits of high altitude disappear when that athlete travels to race at sea level? Estimates for an athlete to lose their native, high-altitude-adaptations, are in the six- to eight-week range.

What about the live-high, train-low theory?

One training theory is to live at a moderately high altitude and train at a lower one. This means living in the mountains to gain more oxygen-carrying capacity, and driving to sea level to do your speed work to achieve maximum power—or do what the Finns have done. In northern Finland, a researcher named Heikki Rusko constructed a house that simulated an altitude of 8200 feet. Outside the house, everything was at sea level. The athletes living in the high-altitude house were runners who did their workouts on roads, tracks and trails at maximum intensity levels. They spent at least 16-18 hours per day inside the house, while all of their workouts were outside, in the oxygen-rich environment. Did it work?

The athletes showed the physiological improvements typical of living at altitude and they had performance breakthroughs as well. Other athletes living at the same sports institute and presumably using the same training program, but not residing inside the "altitude house," did not see performance breakthroughs. As expected, they also did not see the physiological changes associated with altitude. Two of those physiological measures included an increase in erythropoietin (EPO), the key chemical which stimulates increased red-blood-cell production, and an increase in 2.3 DPG, the chemical that makes oxygen more available to the muscles.

Does training at high altitude always work?

The studies that examine training at high altitude for one to six weeks, then returning to sea level or moderate altitudes to race, are conflicting. Since most of us do not have access to a special high-altitude house with sea-level training out the front door, our best opportunity to take advantage of high-altitudes adaptation is to go the mountains and train for awhile.

Some studies have shown that performance will increase

after training for a period of time at high altitude, while others have claimed that training at sea level will yield faster race times.

Dave Morris, exercise physiologist with USA Cycling—the governing body for competitive cycling in the U.S.—thought that many of the conflicting results found in high-altitude research were due to poor design of the studies. Many of the studies tested athletes within one to two days of returning from high-altitude exposure. Morris would not recommend being tested or racing for at least fifteen to twenty-one days following exposure to high altitude. For the first fourteen days after exposure to high altitude, expect decreased performance as the body tries to repair from the stress.

As far as the science of high altitude training goes, 100 percent proof is lacking that training at a higher altitude for some specific period of time is beneficial. As for anecdotal evidence, many athletes feel it helps. There are two schools of thought on the anecdotal evidence: Altitude training really does improve performance; and athletes feel so terrible and stressed while training at high altitude that when they return to sea level, they feel great.

"We do know a few things for certain," Morris said. "We know that when people are exposed to altitude and adapt, their red-blood-cell count increases, and along with it so does the oxygen-carrying content of the blood. We know that myoglobin increase, which are inside of muscle and give the muscle an affinity for oxygen. At the same time, altitude decreases the buffering capacity of the body, which decreases it's ability to work at lactate threshold and translates to slower speeds."

WHAT ABOUT INDIVIDUAL
AND GENDER DIFFERENCES?

One study on the effects of high altitutde on women was conducted on Colorado's Pike's Peak at 14,111 feet above sea level. As with many other areas of medical and physical research, many studies assumed that women's bodies reacted the same way to high altitude stress as men's. This may no longer be a good assumption.

For example, previous studies have shown that men's metabolism at high altitude increases around 17 percent, and their bodies burn more carbohydrates. Traditional high-altitude information has recommended people increase their consumption of carbohydrates upon arrival at a higher altitude. The Pike's Peak study revealed that women's metabolism increases between 17 and 29 percent. In addition, a woman's body burns more fat at a higher altitude. Does this mean women require a different nutritional strategy at high altitude? We simply don't know, yet.

In this study, as with others, there was that nagging "individual thing." One of the women who was part of the study, tested abnormal. Her results in the medical and performance tests nearly equaled her marks in the same tests at sea level near her home in San Francicso, California.

JUST TELL ME WHAT TO DO!

If all the information seems confusing, it is. Advice that was supported by several studies is compiled in two sidebars. One sidebar gives tips for training at high altitude,

High-altitude training
WHAT YOU SHOULD KNOW

If you come from sea level, training at altitudes between 4000 and 9000 feet seems to produce the best results. Training at altitudes higher than 10,000 feet, seems to have as many negative effects on racing as there are positive effects.

• Train at high altitude for approximately three weeks to get the full benefits of altitude acclimatization.

• Plan so that your target race at sea level is fifteen to twenty-one days after returning to sea level from higher altitude.

• While at high altitude, maintain your sea-level pace by doing shorter work intervals, and lengthening active rest period.

• Drink plenty of fluids. The air at high altitude is very dry, so you will breathe more and loose more water vapor.

• Appetite will more than likely decrease at high altitude. Be certain to consume enough calories.

• Get plenty of rest. The stress of high altitude, along with the stress of training may put you over the edge. Pay extra attention to your stress indicators and take days off if necessary.

• People who already live at 8000 feet may benefit by driving to 4000 feet to do speed work. For this group, an added benefit may be to train or live one or two days per week at altitudes at or high than 10,000 feet.

and the second gives tips for racing or riding aggressively at high altitude.

High-altitude training is an area of research where we will continue to see more studies and information published. Hopefully, some of the studies can tell us why high altitude effects individuals differently. Since we know there are individual differences, it would be great to deter-

High-altitude racing

HOW TO PREPARE

If you have the means to do so, prepare to race at altitudes up to about 6500 feet by spending around two weeks living and training at that altitude. Don't forget to keep the pace of your workouts the same as you would at sea level. For races between 6500 and 8000 feet, you'll need three weeks to train, and for competitions higher than 8000 feet, you'll need four weeks.

You don't have unlimited time or cash? Arrive between one and three days prior to your event. You will reduce the adverse effects to power and speed. If you are a person who suffers from high altitude with illness or nausea, you may be better served arriving three days before your competition. This will allow your body enough time to recover from the immediate symptoms of high altitude, and it is enough time for your body to recover the acid/base balance.

When racing or training at higher altitudes, take more time to warm up. Begin race or speed work at a slower pace, 75-85 percent of normal, and slowly pick up the pace during the latter stages of the competition or speed session. And, since post-race recovery may be prolonged at higher altitudes, spend plenty of time cooling down.

mine what it is about some people's body chemistry that makes them indifferent to high altitude. Then, maybe we can begin to influence the effects of high altitude for others. In the meantime, since high altitude seems to effect individuals differently, you may be able to race or ride faster at moderate altitudes with minimal, if any, effects on your pace.

THE LONG HAUL

Our skeletal muscle is made of different types of fibers with different metabolic and functional properties. Classified by contractile and metabolic characteristics are type I fibers, commonly called slow-twitch fibers, and type II fibers, commonly called fast-twitch fibers. Slow-twitch fibers generate energy primarily by means of long-term aerobic (with oxygen) energy transfer. They are fatigue resistant and well suited for endurance events—prolonged exercise at moderate intensity.

The fast-twitch fibers are activated in sprint-type activities and those activities requiring forceful, muscular contractions such as short hill climbing. These type II fibers are divided into three categories:

• *Type IIa fibers* are considered intermediate in that they have a capacity to transfer energy by aerobic and anaerobic means.

• *Type IIb fibers* are the real anaerobic engines and are considered the true fast-twitch fibers.

• *Type IIc fibers* are rare and won't be covered here.

Sedentary men, women and young children exhibit 45 to 55 percent slow-twitch fibers. The remaining fast-twitch fibers are usually equally distributed between type IIa and type IIb. Among competitive athletes, those in sports requiring a large amount of endurance will have a higher percentage of slow-twitch fibers. Distance runners and cross-country skiers will have slow-twitch fibers occupying as much as 90 percent of their total. Weight lifters and sprinters tend to have more fast-twitch fibers and lower relative VO_2 max numbers.

With training, can we change the percentage of slow-twitch fibers we have? The studies on this question yield con-flicting results. In one study, six men participated in a five-month program of aerobic cycling. Although their capacity for work and aerobic power improved considerably, their muscle fiber composition remained unchanged. Another study had subjects doing sprint training, instead of aerobic training. In the sprint training study there was a 23-percent increase in fast-twitch fibers and an equal decrease in slow-twitch fibers. Although more research needs to be done in this area, it appears that some transformation in fiber type, through training, is possible.

Interestingly, another study followed the muscle transfor-mation of fifty-five men and twenty-eight women between the ages of sixteen and twenty-six. The aim of the study was to investigate muscle fiber changes from adolescence to adulthood. Scientists took muscle biopsies from the vastus lateralis muscle, which is one of the quadriceps muscles, and did an analysis for fiber type. Although the fiber areas didn't change, the percentage of fiber types in the two populations did change. The slow-twitch fibers tended to increase in women and decrease in men. Could this be one of the rea-sons why women excel in ultraendurance events?

When it comes to long events, women do very well, con-sistently performing at the top of overall finishers at ultraen-durance races. In 1993, women ran their way to victory and won twelve ultra-races held in the U.S. Granted, it was twelve of two hundred twenty-three, yet women were placing first—overall—in some prestigious races.

Research conducted at South Africa's Comrades

Marathon, found women out-perform men at the 90km distance. In a specific study conducted by the Department of Physiology at the University of the Witwatersrand Medical School in Parktown Johannesburg, scientists matched men and women for performance in the marathon (42.2km). These performance-matched runners, ten men and ten women, were then examined at running distances of 10km, 21.1km, 42.2km and 90km.

The women's group weighed less than the men's, but the women had significantly higher body fat at 22 percent, compared to 16 percent for the men. The women had lower VO_2 max than the men when the measure was expressed relative to body mass, and when corrected for altitude. There were no significant differences in running economies nor lactate threshold between the men and women. The two groups were also similar in training volume and intensity.

The scientists measured VO_2 max, running economy, lactate accumulation, and running speeds at 10km, 21.1km and 42.2km, and the matched men and women performed about the same. At the 90km distance, however, the women's performance was significantly better than the men, as were their average run times. The men's performance declines at 90km was attributed to a decline in their fraction of VO_2 max work load.

Critics of the Parktown study point out that all the world records for men are faster than those for women at the same distance and event. This may be influenced by women having a relatively smaller heart than men. Also, on average, women have up to 10 percent less hemoglobin than men, meaning less oxygen-carrying capacity. Further criticism for the study is concern that the men used in the study were not built for longer distances; they were much larger than the women.

The Parktown study, admittedly, is not suggesting that elite women will soon outperform elite men. There are, however, some exceptional elite women athletes, as well as exceptions to the last statement. As mentioned previously, women are winning ultra-distance running races. One notable example is Ann Trason, who finished more than 4 miles ahead of the nearest male competitor when she won the USA 24-hour running championships.

The men's performance declines at the 90km distance in Parktown was attributed to a decline in their VO_2 max work load. It appears women are able to exercise at higher percentages of their VO_2 max, for longer amounts of time, allowing them to maintain a higher work rate over longer distances. Women are able to better utilize fats while using less carbohydrates than men who are equally trained and nourished. Women make better use of their fat stores, a real advantage in moderate-intensity, long-duration exercise.

Another fascinating contributor to a woman's endurance ability is estrogen. The female hormone acts as a natural antioxidant and may help women deal with central fatigue. Additional research suggests estrogen may be a defense against muscular injury caused by overuse. Better fat utilization and estrogen may help women be well-suited endurance athletes.

INCREASED INJURY RATES DURING OVULATION

While some researchers have found estrogen to be helpful to endurance exercise, researchers at the University of Michigan Medical Center have linked high levels of estrogen and relaxin, found in a woman's body during ovulation, to increase ligament injury. The researchers studied forty young women with acute anterior cruciate ligament injuries and found the injury rate to be nearly doubled when the women were ovulating. The speculation is that higher levels of estrogen and relaxin affect soft tissues like tendons and ligaments as well as the neuromuscular system. More research is needed to determine the exact role of estrogen, relaxin and other hormonal changes present during the menstrual cycle and their relationship to athletic training in endurance sports, power sports such as basketball, and strength training.

BONE MASS

One of the major health concerns for women is osteoporosis. Osteoporosis occurs if bone isn't replaced as quickly as it is lost. When bone loss occurs, bones can become thin and brittle, and susceptible to fracture. A gradual loss of bone mass—beginning at about age thirty—occurs in both men and women. The concern for women is that they may lose up to 30 to 50 percent of their bone density. Men may only lose 20 to 30 percent.

The exact cause of osteoporosis is not known. However, a number of factors increase risk. The risk factors include a calcium-poor diet, high sodium intakes, physical inactivity, reduced levels of estrogen, heredity, excessive cortisone or thyroid hormone, being underweight, smoking and excessive alcohol use.

A major preventive measure against bone loss is regular

weight-bearing exercise. The exercise should be one that combines movement with stress on the limbs. Cycling is thought to be one of the exercises that maintain bone strength.

It was once thought that women over thirty were unable to add calcium to their bones. But some good news came from a study at Tufts University at the Human Nutrition Research Center. Their research indicated that strength training, at any age, can actually increase bone mass. Their research looked at a group of thirty-nine women between the ages of fifty and seventy. Nineteen of the women served as a control group and did no strength training. Twenty of the women did a strength-training workout twice a week. After one year, bone density measurements in the spine and hip of the strength-training group revealed an increase of 1 percent. The control group, who was sedentary, lost 2.9 percent of their bone mass. A healthy balance of cycling and strength training can significantly influence a woman's bone mass.

Maintaining a healthy lifestyle by eliminating smoking and excessive alcohol use will also contribute to keeping healthy bones. Some individuals may require the help of a physician to determine if calcium and vitamin D supplements are necessary. A physician may also prescribe hormone replacement therapy for postmenopausal women to aid with reduced estrogen levels.

DIFFERENT DIGESTION RATES

When athletes embark on a training ride or a race, some athletes are ravenous throughout the event, while others can't make themselves eat because they always feel full. One study looked at the differences in gastric emptying rates of solid meals between men and women. Sixteen men and fourteen women were studied to determine if there were any gender differences.

In the study, men had faster emptying rates than women. The men's half-empty time averaged forty-seven minutes faster than the women's. The differences were enough to be statistically significant and, now, separate reference values are recommended for young men and women.

These differences may influence how athletes consume foods prior to, during and after events. Although current recommendations for fueling are general in nature, this study indicates there may be gender-related strategies.

ANABOLIC STEROID TESTING

One of the methods to test athletes for anabolic steroid use is the "T/E" test. The test evaluates the ratio of testosterone to epitestosterone. The normal ratio is 1:1 and the allowable level is 6:1—a margin of error for testing. Any ratio higher than 6:1 is viewed as a positive test, indicating anabolic steroid use. Testing of women athletes during menstruation when estrogen levels are low may cause false positive results—a physiological disadvantage. Dr. Mauro Di Pasquale, author of "Anabolic Research Review," says that testing women athletes for the use of testosterone can easily produce false positive results. "If urine samples are taken and improperly stored," he says, "bacteria may produce testosterone by acting on naturally occurring chemicals such as cholesterol and bile acids."

For those athletes aspiring to highly competitive levels, intimate knowledge about testing standards, protocols and potential testing flaws is critical. In 1996, U.S. runner

Evaluating research claims

How do you know when to believe the results of a scientific study? It's helpful to ask the following questions:

• Was the study published in a reputable scientific journal?

• Who were the researchers and did they have financial incentives to gain by the results of the experiment?

• What are the limitations of the study? Were the studies done on animals and not humans? Were the studies done on populations that are significantly different than those being questioned by the hypothesis? For example, if we want to determine the effects of 60-second interval training on masters level women cyclists, we don't want the study group to be twenty-year-old sedentary men. At best, the experiment may lend suggested relationships between the question and the results from the study group.

• Is the study "an amazing discovery"? Are there studies that directly contradict the amazing find? Or does the study, in some way, support research that is already known? This particular point will need to be reviewed, simply due to the lack of past research on women and women athletes.

• What was the size of the study group? A study on hundreds of people will carry more weight than a study of ten people.

Mary Slaney tested positive for excessive epitestosterone in her urine during. She appealed the charge and was eventually cleared of the allegation at a great financial and emotional cost.

BRIEF THOUGHTS

In the past, there were different standards for training men and women athletes. These differences were generally based on the areas in which females weren't as "good" as males, such as strength and power. Although much more research is needed, perhaps we have missed some opportunities to capitalize on the differences between men and women. Yes, there are differences and the differences could be advantageous.

Between the time this book was written and the time you read it, most certainly there will have been additional research. The sidebar gives tips on how to evaluate the validity of research. Understand that knowledge is always increasing. You will need to keep abreast of current research by reading books, listening to news and reading magazines that have a reputation for keeping readers informed of current information. Not all information will work for you. You will have to determine what actions are best for you. You will become your own scientific experiment.

REFERENCES

Anderson, O., "Are women better than men in the long run?" *Running Research News*, November-December, 1994, Volume 10, Number 6.

Anderson, O., "Question and Answer Section," *Running Research News*, May 1995, Volume 11, Number 4.

Anderson, O., "Getting High: Part Seven," *Running Research News*, July 1995, Volume 11, Number 5.

Anderson, O., "The best place in the world to train is in ... Finland!," *Running Research News*, August 1995, Volume 11, Number 6.

Anderson, O., "Dad, Mom, and you: Do your genes determine your performances?" *Running Research News*, October 1995, Volume 11, Number 8.

Bernhardt, G., "The Hi-Life," *Triathlete*, February 1997.

Downing, S., "The Body Shop, The latest wisdom about sports medicine from the best minds in the business," *Women's Sports and Fitness*, October 1997.

Hermansson G., Sivertsson R., "Gender-related differences in gastric emptying rate of solid meals," Department of Clinical Physiology, Ostra Hospital Goetborg University, Sweden. Dig Dis Sci, 41(10) 1994-8, 1996 Oct.

Idea Personal Trainer, "Knee Injuries in Female Athletes," October 1997, pp. 12.

Idea Personal Trainer, "Evaluating Research," January 1998, pp. 13.

Levine, B.D., "Living high-training low: effect of moderate-altitude acclimatization with low-altitude training on performance," *Journal of Applied Physiology*, 83(1):102-12, July 1997.

McArdle, William D.; Katch, Frank I.; Katch, Victor L.: Exercise Physiology, Energy, Nutrition, and Human Performance, Third Edition, Lea & Febiger, 1991.

Reider, M. Ph.D., Dept. of Molecular Biotechnology, University of Washington, Personal correspondence with author via e-mail note, May 1998.

"Research Matters," U.S. Council on Exercise, May 1995, Volume 1, Number 1.

Seiler, S., "Gender Differences in Endurance Performance Training," Exercise Physiology Web site for MAPP, March 1998.

Speechly DP, et. al, "Differences in ultra-endurance exercise in performance-matched male and female runners," Medicine and Science in Sports and Exercise, 28(3):359-65, March 1996.

The U.S. Medical Women's Association, The Women's Complete Handbook, Delacorte Press, Bantam Doubleday Dell Publishing Group, Inc., 1995, pp. 557.

Verrengia, Joseph B., "Peak Condition," *Rocky Mountain News*, Sunday November 10, 1996.

CHAPTER THREE

Female anatomy
and bike fit

> *"In forensic pathology, we do not determine the sex of skeletons, based on ratios of leg lengths to torsos. That type of data (ratios of leg lengths to torsos) varies with the particular population sampled, including nationality."*
> — Dr. Patrick Allen, Larimer County, Colorado, coroner and forensic pathologist

'For years I've felt like 'ostrich-woman,'" claimed a frustrated woman. "My legs are too long for my height, and my waist is, well, nonexistent. When I purchase a woman's suit, if the pant fits correctly, the jacket shoulder-width is usually too narrow and the arms on the jacket are too short. When I shop for a fitted dress, if it fits in the shoulders and arms, it is typically too long, the waist of the dress is at my crotch. Okay, I'm an ostrich-woman with wide shoulders and wingspan. When I shop for jeans, I often shop in the men's department or purchase 'boy-cut' jeans. Do I have male dimensions?

"And purchasing clothing is just the beginning. Sports equipment is equally challenging, particularly bicycles. Many shops don't even carry high-end bicycles for shorter people. . . ."

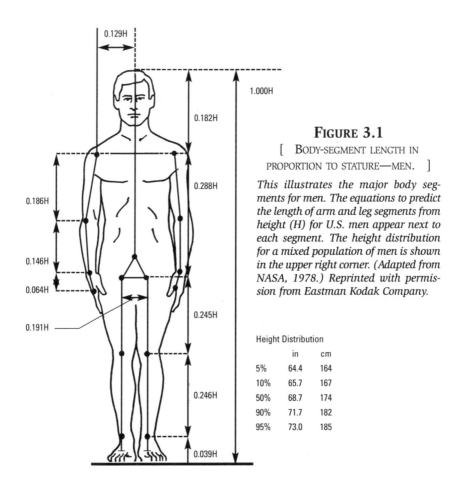

0.129H

1.000H

0.182H

0.288H

0.186H

0.146H

0.064H

0.191H

0.245H

0.246H

0.039H

FIGURE 3.1

[BODY-SEGMENT LENGTH IN
PROPORTION TO STATURE—MEN.]

*This illustrates the major body seg-
ments for men. The equations to predict
the length of arm and leg segments from
height (H) for U.S. men appear next to
each segment. The height distribution
for a mixed population of men is shown
in the upper right corner. (Adapted from
NASA, 1978.) Reprinted with permission from Eastman Kodak Company.*

Height Distribution

	in	cm
5%	64.4	164
10%	65.7	167
50%	68.7	174
90%	71.7	182
95%	73.0	185

The woman who made the comments in the two previous paragraphs has been frustrated in the past when attempting to buy clothing and bicycles. Her first hunt for a performance bicycle was in 1990. At the time, her selection of high-performance bicycles in a size that would fit her 5-foot 4-inch body was limited. Fortunately for the smaller cyclist, women or men, the market is changing.

A Bicycling magazine statistic claimed that in 1997 women made up 48 percent of the cycling market in the U.S. It also noted two out of five of those women sought more per-

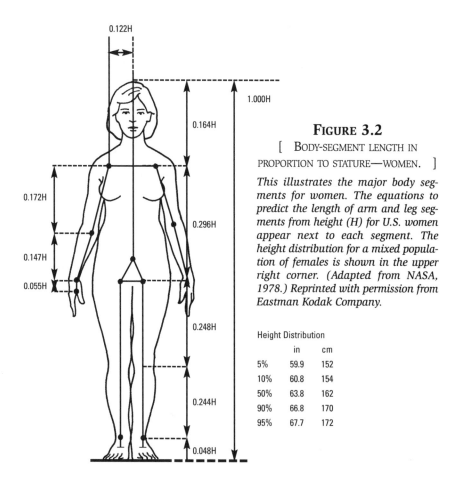

0.122H

1.000H

0.164H

0.172H

0.296H

0.147H

0.055H

0.248H

0.244H

0.048H

FIGURE 3.2

[BODY-SEGMENT LENGTH IN PROPORTION TO STATURE—WOMEN.]

This illustrates the major body segments for women. The equations to predict the length of arm and leg segments from height (H) for U.S. women appear next to each segment. The height distribution for a mixed population of females is shown in the upper right corner. (Adapted from NASA, 1978.) Reprinted with permission from Eastman Kodak Company.

Height Distribution

	in	cm
5%	59.9	152
10%	60.8	154
50%	63.8	162
90%	66.8	170
95%	67.7	172

formance, and intended to upgrade their bicycle within the next five years. With that in mind, do women really need bicycles specifically manufactured for women?

Figure 3.1 shows anthropometric data for men, and figure 3.2 shows the same data for women. The average woman is 63.8 inches tall—5-feet 3.8-inches—and the average man is 68.7 inches tall—5-feet 8.7-inches. Roughly only 5 percent of the male population is 64.4 inches tall—5-feet 4.4-inches. In past years, if a manufacturer were building performance bicycles to serve the majority of the market, the majority of the

TABLE 3.1			
COMPARATIVE BODY MEASUREMENTS FOR A MALE AND FEMALE OF EQUAL HEIGHT.			
	Male	**Female**	**Diff***
H= *Height in decimal inches*	64 in	64 in	
Femur length	.245H 15.68 in	.248H 15.87 in	0.19 in
Tibia length	.246H 15.74 in	.244H 15.62 in	-0.13 in
Leg length	.53H 33.92 in	.54H 34.56 in	0.64 in
Torso length	.288H 18.43 in	.296H 18.94 in	0.51 in
Hand to Shoulder length	.396H 25.34 in	.374H 23.94 in	-1.41 in

*Difference between female and male data, in inches. Positive numbers indicate the female dimension was greater than the male dimension. Negative numbers indicate the female dimension is less than the male dimension.

market would not have been people who measured in at 64 inches. It was simply not cost effective to mass-market high-end bicycles for shorter people.

Since the market is changing and the demand for smaller performance bicycles is increasing, should a 64-inch woman or man seek gender-specific bicycles? Table 3.1 shows estimated dimensions for a theoretical female and male, 64 inches tall, based on the anthropometric data in figures 3.1 and 3.2. For the same height, a woman's torso is longer by about a half-inch and her legs are slightly longer than a man's by about 0.6 inches. Her arm reach is less than the male's by approximately 1.4 inches.

This data allows a look at two people of equal height. Since bicycles are typically not sized to a person's height, rather their leg length, what does the data show for two people, a man and a woman, who have equal leg lengths? The data for these two people are shown on Table 3.2.

For the two subjects having equal leg length, their torsos are

TABLE 3.2

COMPARATIVE BODY MEASUREMENTS FOR A MALE AND FEMALE HAVING EQUAL LEG LENGTHS OF 35 INCHES.

	Male	Female	Diff.*
H= Height in inches	66.04	64.81	
Femur Length	.245H 16.18 in	.248H 16.01 in	-0.11 in
Tibia Length	.246H 16.25 in	.244H 15.81 in	-0.43 in
Leg Lenghth	.53H 35.00 in	.54H 35.00 in	0.00in
Torso Lenghth	.288H 19.02 in	.296H 19.19 in	0.17 in
Hand to Shoulder Length	.396H 26.15 in	.374H 24.24 in	-1.91 in
Hand Length	.064H 4.23 in	.055H 3.56 in	-0.66 in

*Difference between female and male data, in inches. Positive numbers indicate the female dimension was greater than the male dimension. Negative numbers indicate the female dimension is less than the male dimension.

within a tenth-of-an-inch of each other, which is very close. Of major concern, if the two subjects were to purchase the same bike, the woman would have a shortened reach to the brake levers by nearly 2 inches. Additionally, her smaller hand length would make squeezing the brake levers more difficult. From this example, the woman would need to be concerned about stem length, the distance from the center of the transverse tube of the handlebars to the brakes, and brake-lever set up. Stem length and the distance from the transverse tube of the handlebars to the brakes are shown on figure 3.3.

The data represented so far was based on data taken by the National Aeronautics and Space Administration (NASA) from a mixed population of men and women in the U.S. military. Because there are certain physical selection criteria that must be met in order to be accepted into the military, anthropometric extremes are not well represented in the data. For example, obese and very small people are more likely found in a sample of a people on the street, than they are in the military. Also, anthropometric data can vary between countries, and this data was collected from a U.S. population. For instance, on average, people from Mexico differ in stature by approximately 5cm (2 inches) when compared to U.S. data.

And although a person may be in the fiftieth percentile for one dimension, they may be in the twentieth percentile for a second dimension, and the eighth percentile for a third dimension. It is very difficult to define an entire population by averages.

In a 1971 study, the physiques of sixty-six college-aged women track-and-field athletes were compared to data from a study on the physiques of men track-and-field competitors from the 1960 Olympics. The study found women and men to have similar proportions. The bottom line was the size and body proportions of the athletes were consistent for both sexes, including hip and shoulder widths.

Dr. Patrick Allen, coroner and forensic pathologist for Larimer County, Colorado, agrees that people are proportioned differently. Part of his job is to determine gender from skeletal remains. In determining gender from skeletal remains, the highest accuracy of is if the entire skeleton is available. If the skull alone is available, there is about a 90 percent accuracy rate. If only the pelvic bone is available, the accuracy is about 95 percent.

"In forensic pathology," Allen said, "we do not determine the sex of skeletons, based on ratios of leg lengths to torsos. That type of data (ratios of leg lengths to torsos) varies with the particular population sampled, including nationality."

Therefore, it is difficult, if not impossible to support the blanket statement that "a woman has a shorter torso if she is the same height as a man". It is also difficult to support the idea that a woman has a shorter torso than a male, given equal leg lengths. When populations of athletic women and men are compared, anthropometric proportions are very similar.

FINDING A BIKE THAT FITS

Finding a bike that fits and is comfortable is as challenging for men as it is women. In either case, finding the right bike and a good fit is more than just standing over the top tube and looking for clearance. Let's look at the important considerations for determining if a bike fits you.

Figure 3.3 shows the anatomy and geometry of a road bicycle. Learning the proper terms is helpful in purchasing a bicycle. And the remainder of this chapter is focused on selecting a road bike and not a mountain bike.

One rule of thumb for selecting a road bike frame is to begin the selection by standing over the bicycle in stocking feet and lift the bicycle until the top tube is snug in your crotch. There should be 1 or 2 inches of clearance between the tires and the floor. Riding a frame that is either too large or too small compromises performance and handling, and can put you at risk for injury.

Bicycle size is typically given in centimeters and refers to the length of the seat tube. A 54cm bike will have a 54cm seat tube.

Frames are measured in two ways, center-to-top and center-to-center. Center-to-top measures the distance from the center of the bottom bracket to the top of the top tube or seat lug. Center-to-center measures from the center of the bottom bracket to

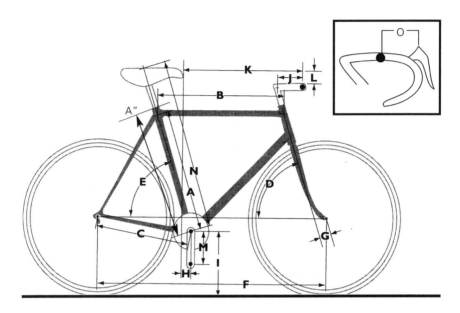

FIGURE 3.3
[ROAD BIKE MEASUREMENTS.]

A'—Seat tube length, measured center-to-center

A"—Seat tube length, measured center-to-top

B—Top tube length

C—Chainstay length

D—Head tube angle

E—Seat tube angle

F—Wheel base

G—Fork offset

H—Seat setback

I—Bottom bracket height

J—Stem length

K—Saddle to transverse centerline of handlebar

L—Seat to handlebar drop

M—Crank

N'—Seat height, measured from bottom bracket centerline (also shown in figure 3.5a)

N"—Seat height, measured from pedal spindle (not shown here, shown in figure 3.5b)

O—Transverse centerline of handlebar to brake hood

the center of the top tube at the seat lug. The center-to-center measurement is 1.0-1.5cm smaller than the center-to-top measure. Be aware of this when you compare frames.

Some time trial bikes have curved seat tubes. In this case, the "functional" length of the seat tube is used, which is the straight-line distance measured center-to-center or center-to-top as discussed in the previous paragraph.

Frame sizes in the 49-60cm range are fairly easy to find. Some manufacturers make 48cm, 47cm and even smaller frames to 43cm. Small frames will often have 650cc wheels, which keep your foot and the front tire from interfering with each other on turns, and shortens the overall length for better handling.

Different frames may have different seat-tube angles, the most common being in the range of 73 to 75 degrees, which allows the "average" cyclist to position their knee over the pedal axle with minor adjustments in the fore and aft position of the saddle. A cyclist with a proportionately short femur wants a steeper seat-tube angle to position their knee correctly over the pedal. A cyclist with a long femur wants a shallower seat-tube angle. A cyclist who is planning to purchase a time-trial-only bike may choose a seat angle greater than 75 degrees. A steeper seat angle shortens the wheelbase, putting the rider in a more powerful and aerodynamic position. The ride of the bike, however, can be uncomfortable and not as responsive as a regular frame.

The next consideration when selecting a frame size is the length of top tube. Top tubes are typically within 2cm of the seat tube length. A guideline to use is to divide your height by your inseam length, as measured in figure 3.4. If that value is between 2.0 and 2.2, you are considered average and a frame that has a top tube equal to the seat tube will fit you. If your value is greater than 2.2, you have a long torso and a longer top tube may be what you need. Less than 2.0 indicates your torso is short, in comparison to your legs, and you will be better off with a top tube that is shorter than the seat tube.

For example, if a person's inseam is 32.5 inches and height is 64.5 inches, their ratio is 64.5 divided by 32.5, equaling 1.99. This person is just under the 2.0 guideline. They may be able to ride an average frame, depending on the length of their arms. If their arms are not considered to be long, they may be more comfortable on a frame in which the top tube is shorter than the seat tube.

Top tube and seat tube lengths will vary between manufacturers and within the product line of a single manufacturer. Catalogue sales will typically list frame dimensions and bike shops will have brochures that list the frame dimensions of each bike they sell.

SEAT HEIGHT

There are several ways to estimate seat height. If you already have a bike and know the seat height is correct, take the measurement with you to the bike shop (as shown in figure 3.5b. If you aren't sure what your correct seat height is, you can estimate it by taking an inseam measurement from figure 3.4 and multiplying by 0.883. The product of those two numbers is the distance from the center of the bottom bracket to the top of the saddle, as in figure 3.5a.

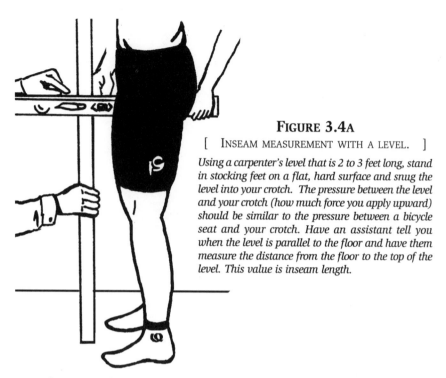

FIGURE 3.4A

[INSEAM MEASUREMENT WITH A LEVEL.]

Using a carpenter's level that is 2 to 3 feet long, stand in stocking feet on a flat, hard surface and snug the level into your crotch. The pressure between the level and your crotch (how much force you apply upward) should be similar to the pressure between a bicycle seat and your crotch. Have an assistant tell you when the level is parallel to the floor and have them measure the distance from the floor to the top of the level. This value is inseam length.

The type of pedal and shoe used influences seat height. If you use toe clips, the seat-height method mentioned in the previous paragraph will be close to what you need. If you use clipless pedals, you may have to adjust the seat height measurement around 3mm. How much you adjust the value will depend on your shoe, cleat and pedal combination, and how far that combination puts your foot farther from the pedal axle. Seat height is also affected by muscle flexibility. If you decide to change your current seat height, make changes slowly, about one-quarter-inch per week.

Another easy way to estimate seat height is to sit on the bike while it is mounted in a stationary trainer. A quality bicycle shop puts the bicycle in a trainer to help you get the bicycle set-up correctly. On the trainer, pedal the bike at a seat-height that seems comfortable. Unclip your cleats from the pedal system, put your

NORMAN REHME

FIGURE 3.5A

[SEAT HEIGHT MEASURED FROM THE CENTER OF THE BOTTOM BRACKET.]

The distance from the center of the bottom bracket to the top of the saddle, measured along a line which would connect the bottom bracket to the point where the rider's crotch would rest on the bicycle saddle is one way to measure seat height.

heels on the top of the pedals and pedal backward. The height of the seat should be at a location that allows you to keep your heels on the pedals while pedaling backward, and doesn't allow your hips to rock from side to side. When you are clipped into the pedals and begin to pedal forward again, you should have a slight bend in your knee, about 25 to 30 degrees.

Some visual cues to indicate the correct height are "quiet hips" and knees that align with your feet and hips. With the bicycle in the trainer, pedal for a few moments until you are somewhat settled and comfortable with your riding position. Then, continue to pedal and have someone look at your hips from the

FIGURE 3.5B

[SEAT HEIGHT MEASURED FROM THE TOP OF THE PEDAL SPINDLE.   ]

The distance from the top of the pedal spindle to the top of the saddle, measured along a line that would connect the spindle to the point where the rider's crotch would rest on the bicycle saddle is a second way to measure seat height. This particular method is helpful when changing crank lengths or saddles. The distance from the saddle rails to the top of the saddle varies from saddle to saddle. When changing saddles or cranks, be certain the saddle height remains the same, otherwise discomfort or injury may result.

rear. Your hips should have a slight rocking motion, but it should not be excessive. Excessive rocking, as if you are straining to reach the bottom of every pedal stroke, indicates your seat is too high.

While still pedaling, a view from the front should reveal your knees tracking in a straight line from your hips to the pedal. There is minimal side-to-side motion of your knees. This is normal. Knees that travel far outside a straight line from the hip to the pedal may indicate the seat is too low. Some people are bowlegged and this should be taken into consideration when watching knee tracking.

Some people have an anatomy that may need special adjustments. People with very wide hips may need spacers added to the pedal spindles in order to move their feet more in line with their hips. Others may have a pedaling motion that, when viewed from the rear, seems uneven. It may appear as though they are "limping" on the bike. This may indicate a leg-length discrepancy. Modifications can be made to the bike to accommodate leg-length discrepancies that include spacers in the shoe or on the cleat, and fore-aft positioning of the cleat on the pedals.

If you suspect you have some anatomy issues that cause you problems on the bike, it is best to seek the help of a qualified professional. A good start is a sports medicine physician. They can take X-rays, physical measurements and make physical examinations to determine if you have anatomical abnormalities. One of the most reputable resources is the Boulder Center for Sports Medicine run by Andy Pruitt, at 303/544-5700.

PEDALS

Clipless pedals are the pedals of choice for most competitive road cyclists. Pedals that allow some rotation may prevent injury by allowing your foot to "float" instead of being "fixed." It is commonly thought that a pedal, which allows for some knee and foot travel, minimizes the risk of injury.

No matter which type of pedal you choose, a guideline

FIGURE 3.6A
[KNEE IN RELATION TO THE CRANK ARM.   ]

Measured with a common yardstick, the yardstick should touch the knee and align with the end of the crank arm. The assistant can make certain the yardstick is perpendicular to the ground.

is to position the ball of your foot over the pedal axle. When the ball of your foot is ahead of the pedal axle, the lever arm from your ankle to the pedal axle is shortened and puts less stress on your Achilles tendon and calf muscles. If you have tight Achilles or problems with calf tightness, you can consider moving the ball of your foot ahead of the axle. This position also requires less force to stabi-

NORMAN REHME

FIGURE 3.6B

[KNEE IN RELATION TO THE CRANK ARM]

When a plumb line is looped around the leg and dropped from the front of the knee, the line should touch the end of the crank arm. A plumb line can be constructed with light-weight nylon string and a nut, available at most hardware stores.

lize your foot. Time-trialists use this position because it allows the cyclist to produce more force while using larger gears.

If the ball of your foot is behind the pedal axle, it lengthens the ankle to pedal-axle lever arm. Some track cyclists prefer this position because it allows a higher cadence during fixed-gear events.

SADDLE POSITION

While on the stationary trainer, pedal the bicycle until you feel settled. Once settled, stop pedaling and put the crank arms horizontal to the ground, in the 3 and 9 o'clock positions as shown in figures 3.6a and 3.6b. Your feet should be horizontal, or as close to horizontal as your flexibility allows. A neutral foot position will have your knee in line with the front of the crank arm. The position can be measured with a common yardstick, a plumbline, a wooden dowel, a sturdy piece of 1-by-1-inch lumber, or a carpenter's level. Whatever you use, be certain the measuring tool remains perpendicular to the ground and doesn't bend beneath the measuring pressure.

Some time-trial specialists prefer to have their knee slightly forward of the neutral position. Remember that if you slide the seat forward on its rails, you are, in effect, lowering seat height. So, if you adjust the seat forward, you may have to fine tune your seat-height, or increase the measure shown in figure 3.5. A rule of thumb is for every centimeter forward you move your seat, you need to raise the seat post a half-centimeter.

Tom Petrie, U.S. representative for Italian-made San Marco saddles, recommends the saddle be level or parallel to the ground for general riding purposes. If the saddle nose is pointed downward, you will tend to put more pressure on your upper body because you are trying to keep from sliding forward. He proposes those who need their saddle pointed down, probably have their seat too high or perhaps their handlebars too low. If you decide to tilt your

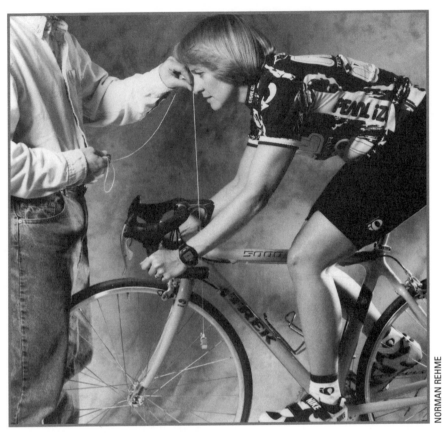

NORMAN REHME

FIGURE 3.7

[STEM LENGTH MEASUREMENT]

To determine if the stem length is correct, position the hands in the drops, in a comfortable riding position, with bent elbows. With the proper stem length, a plumb line dropped from the nose, while looking down at approximately 45 degrees, will bisect the stem.

seat downward a degree to two, be certain you aren't constantly pushing yourself back on the seat. Some people prefer to tilt the nose of the seat up a bit, be certain it doesn't put pressure on your genital area and cause pain or numbing.

You can use a carpenter's level to get your seat level. Have someone hold your bike, while you check seat tilt. If

FIGURE 3.8

[STEM HEIGHT   ]

Using one straight edge, like a yardstick, touch the saddle and hold the yardstick parallel to the ground, to the handlebars. Using a second straightedge, measure the distance from the bottom of the first straightedge to the stem.

you check seat-tilt while your bike is on a stationary trainer, be certain it is level and both tires are equally raised off the ground.

STEM

The position of your knee over the pedal is important. Do not compromise this position in an attempt to reach the handlebars. John Bradley, product manager for Trek's road bike division and former mechanic, says a common mistake is to move the seat forward to accommodate a short-arm reach. If your arm-reach is short, the stem on the bicycle can be changed. Some shops hesitate to make the change because it may require unwrapping the handlebars and rerouting the brake cables after the new stem is positioned. Some manufacturers, such as Trek, use stems that can easily be changed and do not require cable rerouting. If the bike shop has to change stems to make the bike fit you, they may charge you extra, but it is well worth the cost to be comfortable.

Along the same line, do not use a longer stem to compensate for a frame size that is too small. If you need a stem length beyond about 14cm or shorter than 6cm, it is an indication your top tube length is incorrect. The sizes most often used are 11-13cm.

One method to determine if the stem length is correct is to pedal the bicycle while it is in a stationary trainer. Again, pedal until you feel settled. With your hands on the drop bars, in your comfortable cycling position, your stem length is correct if the front wheel axle is blocked from view by the top, transverse part of the handlebars. This method will be affected by fork rake, so may not always be reliable. A second way to measure the correct position is to have a friend drop a plumb line from your nose toward the ground while you are looking forward, settled in your comfortable riding position. The plumb line should intersect the center of your stem, as shown in figure 3.7.

The amount of stem post visible affects the height of your handlebars. Stem height can be measured by using the same tool you used to measure your knee position over the crank arm.

Lay the straight edge across the saddle and have someone measure the distance from the straight edge to the top of the handlebars, as shown in figure 3.8. Typically, handlebars are about 1 to 2 inches below the top of the saddle. Some tall people or those with long arms will go as much as 4 inches below the top of the saddle.

A lower stem puts your body in a more aerodynamic position. To be comfortable in a lower position, you need flexible hamstrings and an ability to rotate your pelvis. Signs that the stem may be too low include pain or numbness in the genital area; if your quadriceps hit your torso on each pedal stroke; neck, shoulder or arm pain; or hand numbness.

Raising the stem puts you in a more upright riding position and can take some of the pressure off of the areas mentioned in the previous paragraph, which are painful or numb. There is a mark on the stem post that warns you not to raise the stem beyond that line. Raising the stem beyond the line risks damage to the head tube or breaking the stem post off in the head tube. There are adjustable stems on the market, such as the Look Ergostem that allow quick length and height adjustment, allowing you to make changes as your fitness or cycling needs change.

HANDLEBARS AND BRAKE LEVERS

The width of the handlebars is roughly the same width as your shoulders. Handlebar widths are different and can be changed to suit your anatomy. Typically, handlebars are either level with the road, as seen in figure 3.3, or rotated slightly up, so the handlebar ends point toward the rear hub.

If you happen to have small hands, you might consider shorter brake levers. Shimano and Dia-Compe manufacture some that may suit your needs.

CRANK LENGTH

Crank length is a much-debated topic when it comes to optimizing performance. In general, crank length should be proportional to leg length, which is the dimension that originally determined frame size. Generally speaking, new bicycles come with crank arms that are proportional to frame size. If you are building a custom frame, consider the following data as a starting point for crank length:

CRANK LENGTH BEGINNING MEASURE ESTIMATES

Frame size	Crank length
45 to 48cm	160-165mm
47 to 52cm	167.5mm
50 to 58cm	170mm
55 to 61cm	172.5mm
59 to 65cm	175mm
62 to 67cm	177.5mm
64 to 70cm	180mm

For those with disproportionately long legs, or those who will focus on time trialing, consider using longer cranks. Longer cranks have a mechanical advantage and are good for pushing larger gears, such as in time trialing. Keep in mind, however, the crank arm length influences cadence, can cause extra stress on the knees and may affect saddle height. A switch to longer cranks may mean you need to lower your seat in order to keep your hips from rocking at the bottom of the pedal stroke. Once the seat height is properly adjusted, these new, longer cranks may cause interference between the quadriceps and your torso, which is not good. If there is interference, you may need to return to the shorter cranks.

SADDLES

Saddle style is probably the most intimate and frustrating part of bike fit. No saddle is going to make up for an ill-fitting bicycle and no one wants to ride any distance if their private parts are in pain or have gone numb. Saddles come in various styles, lengths and widths. As we've already learned, individual anatomy varies. Whether your anatomy prefers a wide or narrow seat; minimal padding or a gel insert; solid seat or a seat with a cutout depends on your riding style, the length of time you will spend in the saddle, and personal preferences. The saddles touted as "women's models" tend to be wider. And due to the recent publicity around male impotence, many men find that these wider saddles suit their anatomy just fine and eliminate genital numbness.

Some saddle discomfort is due to fitness and riding style. Novice cyclists do not have the leg and glute muscles of an experienced cyclist. Strong leg muscles will help support a cyclist, so the saddle doesn't become a chair. Novice cyclists who haven't developed strong leg muscles tend to "sit" on the saddle and move their legs, while experienced cyclists are somewhat suspended by their legs. The message for the novice is to slowly build cycling miles, so you can build leg strength and saddle time. Even experienced cyclists need to build saddle time after being off of the bike for awhile.

It is important that a saddle is padded for comfort; however, too much padding can cause numbness, too. If the saddle has too much padding, it can conform to the perineum, which is the area between your sit bones. That area has arteries and nerves running through it that, when compressed, can cause pain.

Unfortunately, there is no easy sizing system for saddles. It would be great if they were like shoe sizes, having length and width designations, "I'll need a size 5 in a C width." Until that happens, test some saddles until one feels comfortable. Some shops will change a saddle and let you try it out while riding the stationary trainer. If you ask around, you're likely to find saddle choice is a bit like ice cream flavors, everyone has a favorite for different reasons.

CUSTOM FRAMES

Unfortunately, there is no easy way to determine if you need a custom frame or not. That formula, yet undeveloped, is a function of overall height in addition to the ratio of leg length, torso length and arm length to height. Custom framemaker Lennard Zinn says people who are on the low and high ends of the spectrum might consider a custom frame. Generally speaking those under 5-feet 3-inches or over 6-feet 4-inches with an inseam more than 36 inches are good candidates for a custom frame. Also, people who have trouble getting a normal frame to fit due to abnormally short or long torsos.

TIME TRIAL POSITIONS

If you decide to do a time trial, aerodynamics is a big concern. To reduce the effect of wind drag, you want to be as compact as possible. Being compact means getting a lower body position with clip-on aero' handlebars, getting your arms as close together as possible, riding with a flat back, lowering your chin to fill the open space between your arms and keeping your knees in while cycling. All this needs to be done without sacrificing safety or comfort.

Riding in an aerodynamic position may take some time to accomplish. With your arms close together, resting on your forearms will effect steering responsiveness and balance. Riding with a flat back requires flexible back and hamstring muscles and will require a rotation of the pelvis forward. This forward rotation and new position may put added pressure on genitals. A seat that has a portion of the nose relieved or gel padding on the nose may help.

When lowering your head, to become more slipstream and fill the cavity between your arms, be certain it's possible to comfortably see where you are going. Eye or sunglasses with thick frames may cause forward-vision problems. If seeing the road ahead is an issue, you may have to sacrifice some aerodynamics for safety. Also, craning your neck to see the road may be a prescription for a stiff neck, again adjust your position to get comfortable.

Finally, while keeping your knees in will make you more aerodynamic, it can be uncomfortable and cause sore knees. Again, sore knees are not a good sacrifice for aerodynamics, so make a position adjustment.

BRIEF THOUGHTS

We are all individuals and have individual dimensions. Just because you might be "average height" does not mean your legs are of average proportion. Finding the right bicycle fit is as challenging for men as it is for women. In either case, a bicycle should be reasonably comfortable to ride, given a gentle build-up of mileage.

When you shop for a new bicycle, be informed. Know bicycle geometry and the rules of thumb for bike set-up so you can be an informed shopper.

Go to a reputable bicycle shop where the personnel are willing to help you and spend time answering questions. A shop with good mechanics that are willing to teach you about a bicycle is a place worth doing business with.

Out of courtesy, do not request component changes from a bike shop, unless you are serious about purchasing the bike. Do not expect friendly service on your purchase if you use a bike shop to find your perfect fit, then order the bike by mail.

REFERENCES

Allen , P., MD., interview with author February 24, 1998.

Bradley, J., product manager for Trek road bike division, telephone interview, February 19, 1998.

Burke, Edmund R., Ph.D., High-Tech Cycling, Human Kinetics, 1996, pp. 94-96, 159-185.

Burke, Edmund R., Ph.D., Serious Cycling, Human Kinetics, 1996, pp. 79-99.

Colorado Cyclist, Bike Fit, hyperlink http://www.coloradocyclist.com/, March, 1997.

Eastman Kodak Company, Ergonomic Design for People at Work, Volume 1, Van Nostrand Reinhold Company Inc., 1983, pp. 284-297.

Eastman Kodak Company, Ergonomic Design for People at Work, Volume 2, Van Nostrand Reinhold Company Inc., 1986, pp. 448-453.

Henry, S. J., "Do you need a women's bike?" *Bicycling*, April 1997, pp. 46-48.

Krogman, W.M., Ph.D., LL.D., (h.c.), The Human Skeleton in Forensic Medicine, Charles C. Thomas Publisher, Third Printing, 1978, pp. 149-150, 188.

Petrie, T., Velimpex Marketing, telephone interview with author, March 19, 1998.

Pruitt, A., facsimile communication with author, March 3, 1998.

Puhl, J., et. al, Sport Science Perspectives for Women, Human Kinetics, 1988, pp. 6.

Radford, K., Professional Bicycle Mechanic, personal interview, May 1998.

USA Cycling elite coaching clinic manual, February 17-19, 1997.

USA Cycling International Coaching Symposium, The Integration of Science, Technology, and Coaching in the Sport of Cycling, 1997, personal notes.

Zinn, L., Custom framebuilder, e-mail interview with author, March 16, 1998.

Zinn, L., Custom framebuilder, Chapter Review, January 1999.

Zinn, L., Custom framebuilder, "Crank length for Women's bikes," *VeloNews*, March 1, 1999.

CHAPTER FOUR

Menstrual *cycles*

Some take "gearing-up" seriously, as women have won medals and set world records at every phase of their menstrual cycles.

S ome women view the menstrual cycle as a curse, while others view it as a blessing. How a woman views her cycle may depend on what her mother told her, what peers say about it, whether or not her period begins in the middle of a long bicycle tour, or if she is trying to become pregnant. The menstrual cycle is included in this book because it is important—critical—to the short term and long term health of any woman.

This chapter will explain how a "normal" cycle is supposed to work, what hormonal changes affect the cycle, how hormonal changes may affect athletic performance, why there should be concern if menstrual cycles cease, tools for tracking a cycle, and tips for making things as comfortable as possible.

HOW IT ALL WORKS

The average menstrual cycle is typically twenty-eight days, plus or minus eight days. What is "normal" for one woman is abnormal for the next. If you are a woman reading this book, it is in your best interest to know what normal is for you. The way to do that is to keep records. Track the length of your cycle, your physical and psychological symptoms and anything that seems unordinary. A tracking tool is discussed later in the chapter.

The menstrual cycle can be divided into four functional phases on the basis of structural, physical and hormonal changes:

• *Menstruation* is marked by the first day the uterine lining begins to shed as menstrual blood. This "bleeding" is actually sloughing tissue, which is expendable and needs to be cycled out of the body. The tissue sloughing helps prevent endometrial cancer. Menstruation is also the transition from the luteal phase to the follicular phase.

• *The follicular phase* is the period of time when the ovarian follicle is preparing to ovulate. A key ovarian hormone, estrogen, is on the rise. The endometrium or uterine lining is building in preparation for a fertilized egg.

• *Ovulation* is marked by high peaks of lutenizing hormone (LH) and follicle stimulating hormone (FSH). Lutenizing hormone levels increase rapidly, doubling within two hours, with the mean duration of this surge being 48 hours. The exact timing of ovulation is still unknown; however, it is thought to occur between 35 and 44 hours after the onset of the LH surge.

• *The luteal phase* gets its name from the corpus luteum—is Latin for "yellow body"—which is formed by cells left behind in the ovary after the ovum (egg) is released. In this phase, the cycle shifts from an estrogen dominance to progesterone dominance. Progesterone "ripens" the endometrium.

Figure 4.1 shows a twenty-eight-day cycle and various changes occurring within the body. The figure has been greatly simplified. As seen on Figure 4.1c, estrogen and progesterone—ovarian hormones—are at their lowest levels just prior to and during the first few days of menstruation. The low levels of these hormones just prior to the beginning of menstruation are a signal to the body that an egg has not been fertilized. The time of bleeding—menses—typically lasts three to seven days.

Menses, when the uterine lining is shed, takes place during the first few days of the follicular phase. During this time, estrogen levels are on the rise. Ovulation occurs shortly after estrogen levels are at the highest, somewhere around thirteen to fifteen days in a twenty-eight-day cycle.

After ovulation, in the luteal phase, estrogen levels decrease, increase slightly, then decrease again to their lowest level just prior to menstruation. Meanwhile, progesterone levels rise during the luteal phase to thicken the lining of the uterus in preparation for a fertilized egg. Progesterone then decreases, and if no fertilization has occurred, bleeding will begin marking the beginning of a new cycle.

Let's look at each phase in a bit more detail.

FIGURE 4.1 [DAYS OF THE MENSTRUAL CYCLE]

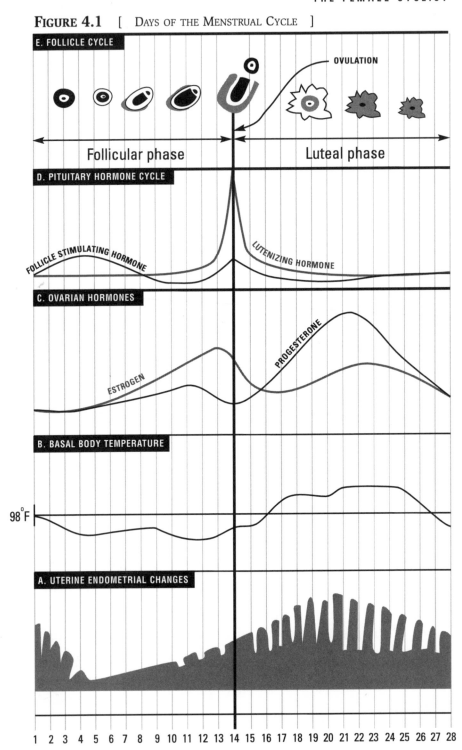

MENSTRUATION

Menstruation, "Menses," "having a period," and countless slang expressions are all terms for the time of the month when postpubic women experience uterine bleeding. The few days prior to and the first day or two of menstruation can be uncomfortable for some women. Common complaints include lower abdominal cramps, headache, backache, fatigue, breast soreness or tenderness, weight gain, gastro-intestinal problems, diarrhea and unpredictable bowel movements. The degree of discomfort and the number of symptoms experienced varies from woman to woman. Extremely painful menstruation is called dysmenorrhea. Other terms relating to the menstrual cycle are listed on Table 4.1.

Many women cyclists agree that beginning their period right before a race or during a multiday tour can be depressing. Others, however, say, "If I allow my period to bother me, it will. If the race is important to me and I've put a season of training into this event, I gear-up, focus on the matter at hand, and give my all to the race. I can't let it bother me." Some take "gearing-up" seriously, as women have won medals and set world records at every phase of their menstrual cycles.

Perhaps great performances come at any phase of the cycle, but being as comfortable as possible can make the performance more enjoyable. To help alleviate premenstrual and early menstrual symptoms, some health care providers recommend a balanced diet, eliminating binging behaviors, cutting down on caffeine, reducing salt intake, exercising and using relaxation techniques. While these recommendations work for some, others may need additional help.

TABLE 4.1	

MENSTRUAL CYCLE DEFINITIONS

MENARCHE	the first occurrence of menses
LATE MENARCHE	delayed age at the onset of first menses
EUMENORRHEA	regularly occurring menstrual periods
DYSMENORRHEA	difficult or painful menses
OLIGOAMENORRHEA	irregularly occuring menstruation
MENHORRHAGIA	profuse flow
METRORRHAGIA	spotting or bleeding between menses
AMENORRHEA	the abscense of menses; primary amenorrhea (menses have never occurred; secondary amenorrhea (cessation of menses after menarche has occurred)

For example, women with extreme cramping may need prescriptions drugs. Others might be able to use over-the-counter, nonsteriodal anti-inflammatory drugs (NSAIDS) and find relief. NSAIDS, such as ibuprofen and naproxen sodium (trade names such as Advil and Aleve, respectively), work to inhibit prostaglandins, which are substances released by your body to cause your uterus, intestines and other smooth muscles to contract. NSAIDS seem to work best if taken the day before, or as soon as, flow begins, before prostaglandin levels are high enough to produce cramping. NSAIDS may also help reduce those emergency trips into the bushes for a bowel movement. Do not take NSAIDS on an empty stomach as they may irritate the stomach lining or cause gastrointestinal distress.

Some remedies to relieve menstrual cramping may include diuretics to reduce water retention. This type of medication is not recommended for women riding and racing multihour events in which hydration is critical.

As for exercise helping to relieve menstrual aches and pains, the studies yield conflicting results. Currently, exercise doesn't seem to make a difference one way or the other. But for relieving premenstrual symptoms (PMS), such as depression and mood swings, exercise does seem to have a positive effect.

It is peculiar, at the time of the month when a woman feels as personable as a saber-tooth cat, as fast as a snail, and sleek as an elephant, may be the time when she could turn in a personal best performance. Just prior to and during menstruation, when estrogen levels are at their lowest, aerobic capacity is at its peak. It is believed that, more than likely, this increase will not make a difference in recreational athletes. In elite athletes, where every advantage matters, the change may be enough to mean the difference between first and second place. The difference, the increase in aerobic capacity, is also enough to make scientists control menstrual cycles when they do experiments to test physical performance in females.

FOLLICULAR PHASE

The follicular phase is typically seven to twenty-one days long, with the average being fourteen. As the follicular phase progresses, estrogen levels continue to rise and aerobic capacity decreases. The other function that decreases is spatial visualization, or the ability to judge distances. While these two functions are on the decline, carbohydrate metabolism, mental capacity, mental focus, problem solving capabilities, and fine motor function all increase. There is also an increase in perceptual speed—how quickly women notice things. If you happen to be a female road racer, and problem solving and quick decision making become critical, any increases in estrogen may be helpful.

OVULATION

Women are born with approximately 2 million underdeveloped eggs. For women with normal cycles, an egg is released about once per month. It is possible to have a menstrual cycle in which no egg is released. This type of cycle is anovulatory. Oddly, anovulatory cycles are usually those cycles free from cramping during menstruation and in which PMS symptoms are less noticeable.

Estrogen levels peak just prior to ovulation, then drop off significantly. Two other hormones released by the anterior pituitary gland rise to peak levels that cause a mature ovarian follicle to release an egg. These additional hormones are the follicle stimulating hormone (FSH) and the lutenizing hormone (LH). Fluid-filled chambers—follicles—in the ovary are prompted by FSH to begin growing. Within each follicle, a single ovum is growing as well. An LH surge triggers a follicle to rupture, releasing its egg.

During ovulation, while mental focus and fine motor function remain high, aerobic capacity and spatial visualization are decreased.

LUTEAL PHASE

The luteal phase follows ovulation and is usually twelve to fourteen days long. During the luteal phase, estrogen declines, increases slightly, and then proceeds to its lowest level near the end of the phase. While estrogen is declining, progesterone rises to its peak around mid-luteal phase and declines to low levels at the end of the phase.

Declining estrogen levels mean aerobic capacity is improving, the ability to conceptualize is improving, and glycogen storage rises a bit. But memory, perceptual speed, and fine motor ability are not at their best during this phase.

Studies on runners have shown ventilation during the luteal phase can increase by around 8 percent, which makes any given pace feel harder. Running economy—which is the percent of VO_2 max the runner is able to work at—dips by about 3 percent; mental vigor or toughness declines and near the end of the phase, depression and fatigue increase.

With all these seemingly "bad" conditions, studies on runners have shown the luteal phase to be good for fat burning. Studies on normally menstruating runners has shown fat furnished 70 percent of the energy at 35 percent VO_2 max, 58 percent of the energy at 60 percent VO_2 max, and 46 percent of the energy at 75 percent VO_2 max. Compare those values to the midfollicular phase, in which 52 percent of the energy is provided by fat at 35 percent VO_2 max, 43 percent of the energy at 60 percent VO_2 max, and 39 percent of the energy at 75 percent VO_2 max.

The last few days of the luteal phase are premenstrual—the few days prior to menstruation and the start of a new cycle. Some women have multiple premenstrual problems, while others have minimal difficulties. For roughly 10 percent of women, premenstrual symptoms are enough to disturb their life.

There remains controversy about what PMS is, what causes it, and whether or not it is actually a "condition." For women with PMS problems, it is best to keep a log of physical and psychological problems and when they occur within the cycle. If the symptoms become problematic, a record of the problems and when they occur will be helpful to the physician.

AMENORRHEA

There is a tendency to mix the terms amenorrhea and oligoamenorrhea. Oligoamenorrhea is few periods, but periods still occur. Amenorrhea is classified into two categories, primary and secondary. Primary amenorrhea means menses have never occurred. Young girls who have been under a heavy exercise program may experience primary amenorrhea. Secondary amenorrhea is the cessation of menses after menarche has occurred.

Some of the studies conducted consider three or less periods per year to be amenorrhea, although amenorrhea literally means periods have stopped. Using either term, if a woman hasn't had a period for ninety days, it's time to seek help.

There are conflicting studies and opinions regarding the exact cause of secondary amenorrhea. Some believe it is a combination of factors, including:

- Low body weight
- Low body fat
- Obesity
- Sudden increases in training volume or intensity
- Low calorie, low fat, low protein or low nutrient diets
- Psychological stress
- Hormonal imbalances
- Physical disorders
- Perimenopause or premenopause

When a woman experiences amenorrhea, it is not time to celebrate nor use period cessation as a means of birth control. Due to the nature of amenorrhea being unpredictable, a woman is likely to ovulate when she least expects it, possibly resulting in an unwanted pregnancy. It is also possible to ovulate and not have menstrual bleeding. Perhaps you have heard of a woman who became unexpectedly pregnant? She may have said, "We had a moment of passion, just one time." Perhaps the moment of passion was tied to increased estrogen levels, which also increase libido. Studies have shown women have increased libido around ovulation and near menses.

How does a woman know when she's ovulating or when her luteal phase is shortened? The overall length of her cycle is not a good measure because it may remain constant, but she may not be ovulating, or her luteal phase may be decreasing in length. One of the common ways to track ovulation, the length of the follicular phase and the length of the luteal phase is with body temperature. Taking a basal body temperature measurement is simply taking one's temperature before getting out of bed in the morning. A chart of basal body temperatures for a normally menstruating woman will generally reveal temperatures less than 98 degrees Farenheight during the follicular phase. Just prior to ovulation, body temperature will decrease, then increase the next day or two. During the luteal phase, body temperature tends to climb above 98 degrees.

The best way to determine what is normal for any particular woman, is to chart body temperature for a few months. If body temperature fluctuates widely or does not vary much at all, the cycle was probably anovulatory. Women who are trying to conceive are certainly concerned with anovulatory cycles and may also experience fertility problems with cycles having a short luteal phase.

For women not trying to conceive, the biggest concern with anovulation and shortened luteal phase is long-term health. Some types of anovulation and short luteal phase are related to low estrogen levels. Low estrogen is a contributing factor to bone loss and osteoporosis because the body does not as readily absorb calcium when estrogen levels are low. Even women who had amenorrhea and resumed normal menstrual cycles have lower bone mass than those who have always had normal menstrual cycles. Osteoporosis is a serious condition, whose symptoms and effects don't show up until well in the future. Keeping a normal menstrual cycle is one way to prevent the risk of bone loss.

Whether or not anovulation or low estrogen levels adversely affect athletic performance is not known. If low estrogen levels create an out-of-balance situation for all hormones, does it affect a woman's ability to recover from exercise? Does hormonal imbalance affect mental as well as physical aspects of training? Although some athletes consider amenorrhea to be a good thing, perhaps they don't understand all the ramifications. More research needs to be done to determine the effects of anovulation, and its associated low estrogen levels, on athletic performance.

CERVICAL MUCUS

The cervical mucus changes during the course of the menstrual cycle. These changes, if tracked, can help a woman determine where she is in the menstrual cycle. During menses, it is difficult to determine the consistency of cervical mucus. In the follicular phase, the mucus tends to have a yellow color and be tacky in texture. In the days surrounding ovulation, mucus is clear, stringy and stretchy, and very fluid. During the luteal phase, the mucus returns to a yellow color and more of a tacky texture. Prior to menstruation, there will be a yellow tinted mass of mucus excreted, this is called the cervical plug. Infections, contraceptive creams, and douching cut down on mucus, possibly changing its color and texture.

GETTING BACK TO NORMAL

Some of the possible causes for amenorrhea, mentioned in the previous section include low body weight and low body fat. They are not one in the same. A woman can have low body weight and not have low body fat. The studies on both of these issues are conflicting as to whether or not they are directly linked to amenorrhea.

Studies on training volume and intensity, as related to amenorrhea, are also conflicting. While some studies have found that women will adapt to new levels of training and resume a normal menstrual cycle, after some irregularities, other studies found a reduction in training and/or intensity to be necessary to solve abnormal cycles.

Training mileage was found to be the only difference between fourteen amenorrheic athletes, compared to fourteen regularly menstruating controls. The study sought to find if there were any significant differences in their nutritional status—and none were found. In a separate study, dietary habits and nutrition did affect the menstrual cycle. This study found regularly menstruating athletes ate five times more meat than amenorrheic athletes. For these athletes, 82 percent of the amenorrheic athletes were vegetarian—defined as consuming less than 200 grams per week of meat, white or red.

Stress has also been thought to affect the balance of hormones and may affect the menstrual cycle. Stress can stem from the rigors of training and competition, family and support system or the lack thereof, interpersonal relationships with a significant other, and self image. Although a certain amount of stress can spur good performance, too much stress is thought to be detrimental to overall health, as well as affecting a normal menstrual cycle.

When a woman is concerned about her menstrual cycle, or the lack of a cycle, consultation with a doctor who is savvy to sports is helpful. A visit to the doctor is more informative if the woman has information regarding past menstrual cycles:

• Typical length of the cycle, before any changes
• Basal body temperatures, if available
• Typical menstrual flow patterns and any changes
• Bodily changes such as insomnia, hair loss, skin changes or night sweating
• Changes in training, diet or body weight
• Family history

This information, in addition to an exam, can rule out concerns that the irregularity is caused by something more serious, such as an unwanted growth in the uterus or a pituitary tumor. Knowing the cause of menstrual dysfunction will alleviate stress, further enhancing health.

After physical disorders and disease are ruled out, the athlete can work with her doctor to make changes that may include:

• Reducing exercise

• Increasing food intake

• Changing the macronutrient profile, the amount of carbohydrate, fat and protein of foods eaten

• Changing the nutrient profile to include more whole foods and less processed foods

• Hormonal supplements

TRACKING THE MENSTRUAL CYCLE

Tracking, charting or otherwise keeping track of a woman's cycle is important to her for several reasons. The reasons include:

• It is easier for a physician to help solve problems with a menstrual cycle if the woman keeps historical records.

• Tracking the cycle can help separate bodily changes associated with the menstrual cycle from the aches and pains associated with athletic training.

• Personal knowledge of how her body is working can alleviate stress for a woman.

• Tracking the cycle can predict PMS and menstrual problems, which allows a woman to take measures to eliminate or significantly reduce symptoms.

• Being able to predict the beginning of menstruation allows a woman to be prepared. For instance, taking tampons along on a bike tour.

Figure 4.2 is an example of charting a menstrual cycle. The woman who filled out the sample recorded the number of days since her last period, her menstrual flow pattern, her cervical mucus pattern, PMS symptoms, menstrual symptoms, treatments applied, and a few notes.

Her period began on March 20, and it had been twenty-six days since the beginning of her last period. Her period began with one light day, two heavy flow days, and so on. Her PMS symptoms included tender breasts and generally feeling blue. She noticed back pain and cramping on the second day of her period, and began taking ibuprofen to relieve the discomfort. Two days of ibuprofen was all that was necessary for her. She made a note to herself to begin the ibuprofen one day earlier, in hopes of completely eliminating menstrual cramping.

Other notes on her chart include cervical mucus and race day comments. She raced on March 22, and had a great race. She is beginning to chart her cervical mucus changes because she believes she can use it as a tool to predict the beginning of her period.

Although there is space on this chart to track body temperature, this woman is not taking her basal temperature at this time. Daily temperature measurements may cause this particular chart to be too busy for some women. Women who already know what their temperature typically does in a month's time, can take occasional temperature samples and record them on a chart similar to 4.2.

For those wishing to track basal temperature each day, a different chart is recommended. A sample basal body tem-

FIGURE 4.2   [SAMPLE MENSTRUAL RECORDING   ]

Month _March_

Date	1	2	3	4	5	6	7	8	9	10	11	12	13	14	15	16	17	18	19	20	21	22	23	24	25	26	27	28	29	30	31
Days since last period	8	9	10	11	12	13	14	15	16	17	18	19	20	21	22	23	24	25	26	1	2	3	4	5	6	7	8	9	10	11	12
Basal Body Temperature																															
Menstruation																															
Cervical Mucus					C/H	C/H	C/H		Y/H		Y/H		Y/L	Y/L																	
PMS Symptoms:																															
Tender Breasts																	M														
Feeling Blue																S	S														
Menstrual Symptoms:																															
Backache																				M											
Cramps																				M											
Treatments:																															
Advil																					X	X									

Menses: **S**-Spotting **L**-Light flow **M**-Medium flow **H**-Heavy flow

PMS or menstrual symptoms: **S**-Slight, hardly noticable **L**-Light, but noticable **M**-Moderate, aware of problem **H**-Problem, high aggravation, affecting activities, lifestyle

Cervical Mucus: **C**-Clear, stringy **Y**-Yellow, tacky **L**-Limited mucus **M**-Moderate mucus **H**-Heavy flow, copius mucus

87

perature chart is shown in Figure 4.3. Due to its graphical nature, it is easier to "see" what is happening to body temperature as the menstrual cycle progresses. The format is the same as Figure 4.2, so the two can be aligned by the day of the month. Changes in temperature may correlate well to other changes occurring during the month.

Blank copies like those shown in Figures 4.2 and 4.3 are included in Appendix A and B. PMS and menstrual symptoms are left blank so each woman can fill in her own symptoms. A list of typical symptoms are listed in Appendix C. The list is not all inclusive, rather it is intended to help verbalize typical symptoms.

ORAL CONTRACEPTIVES

Birth control pills come in two forms: combination pills containing estrogen and progestin, and "mini-pills" containing progestin only. Progestin is the synthetic version of progesterone. The amount of estrogen in birth control pills suppresses ovulation. The progestin blocks the release of an egg during ovulation and creates an environment in the uterus that makes pregnancy unlikely.

There are benefits and risks associated with taking birth control pills. The benefits include:

- They produce regular menstrual cycles.
- They decrease dysmenorrhea.
- Oral contraceptives reduce bleeding and help with anemia.
- They have shown to offer protection against ovarian cysts, uterine fibroids, cancer, endometrial cancer and ectopic pregnancy. An ectopic pregnancy is one in which a fertilized

FIGURE 4.3   [BASAL TEMPERATURE CHART   ]

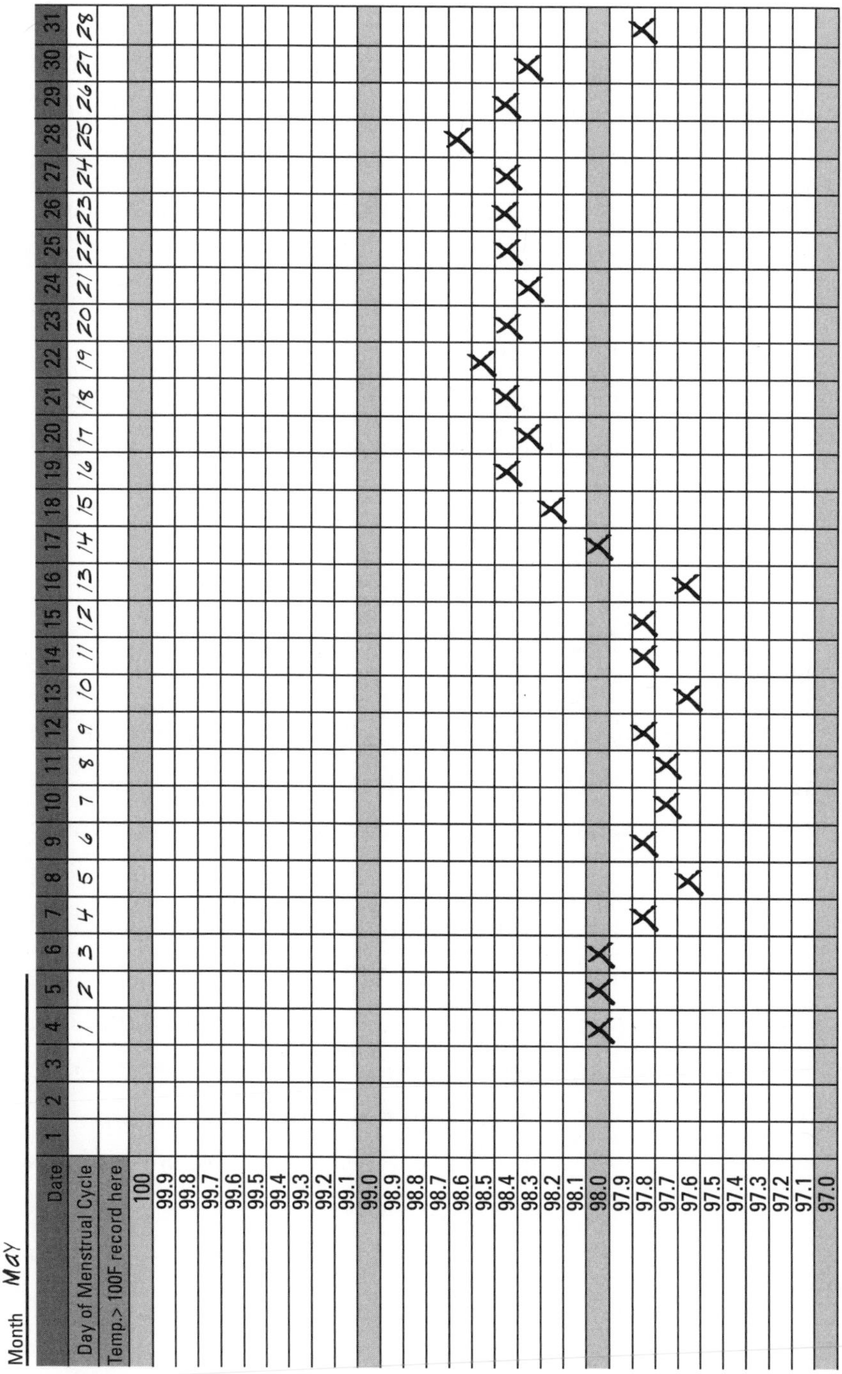

Month MAY

Date: 1 2 3 4 5 6 7 8 9 10 11 12 13 14 15 16 17 18 19 20 21 22 23 24 25 26 27 28 29 30 31

Day of Menstrual Cycle: 1 2 3 4 5 6 7 8 9 10 11 12 13 14 15 16 17 18 19 20 21 22 23 24 25 26 27 28

Temp.> 100F record here

100
99.9
99.8
99.7
99.6
99.5
99.4
99.3
99.2
99.1
99.0
98.9
98.8
98.7
98.6
98.5
98.4
98.3
98.2
98.1
98.0
97.9
97.8
97.7
97.6
97.5
97.4
97.3
97.2
97.1
97.0

egg implants somewhere other than the uterus. This mis-placed, fertile egg can begin to grow within the fallopian tube, on the surface of the ovary, within the abdominal cavity, or within the pelvic cavity.

- Estrogens significantly reduce osteoporosis and cardiovascular disease, which are some of the reasons why post-menopausal women are prescribed estrogen replacement therapy.
- Estrogens may reduce the risk of Alzheimer's disease.
- Oral contraceptives are a convenient means for birth control.
- They can reduce acne.
- Because birth control pills reduce menstrual problems, they allow athletes to train more predictably.

With all of the reported benefits associated with oral contraceptives, there remain concerns:

- They have been linked to certain types of cardiovascular disease.
- The risk for blood clots is increased.
- Risk for stroke is increased.
- One study has shown a link between the use of oral contraceptives and certain types of breast cancer. Other studies have not been able to confirm this finding.
- Estrogens may slightly lower aerobic capacity and promote fluid retention, which may affect athletic performance.

The decision whether or not to take birth control pills depends on each individual situation. The current, lower dose formulations may decrease many of the undesirable side affects. A woman's family history and current health status, including alcohol consumption and smoking, are all factors to consider when making the decision to take oral contraceptives. Generally speaking, women should not take oral contraceptives if they are: are over age 35 and smoke, have a history of stroke or blood clotting, have uncontrolled high blood pressure, have diabetes with vascular disease, high cholesterol, active liver disease, cancer of the endometrium or breast cancer.

BRIEF THOUGHTS

A normally functioning menstrual cycle is essential to the health of women. Low levels of estrogen associated with amenorrhea and ogliomenorrhea decrease bone mass, and contribute significantly to osteoporosis, even in active athletic women.

Each phase of the menstrual cycle appears to have physical and emotional advantages and disadvantages. Women are taking steps to reduce or eliminate the disadvantages at any phase and have gone so far as to break world records at various phases of the menstrual cycle.

Women should not consider uncomfortable menstrual cycles somehow Puritan; "All this pain is part of being a woman, I'll just suffer through it." There are things women can do to make their monthly cycles less imposing. Some of the measures may call for the cooperation of her health care provider in the form of prescription drugs. At the same time, each woman can do a great deal to recognize and reduce some of her own difficulties by tracking her cycle, noting what makes her feel better, what makes her feel worse, and taking action on future cycles.

Estrogen is a powerful hormone and should be celebrated.

R E F E R E N C E S

Anderson, O., "Female athletes fire up fat burning after ovulation, but does it make a difference for weight loss and competitive performances?" *Running Research News*, October 1995, Volume 10, Number 5.

Baker, A., M.D., Bicycling Medicine, Argo Publishing, 1995, pp. 209.

Barr, S., PhD., "Women, nutrition, and exercise: a review of athletes' intakes and a discussion of energy balance in active women," Progress in Food and Nutrition Science, 1997, Volume 11, pp. 307-361.

Dueck C. A, et. al, "Treatment of athletic amenorrhea with a diet and training intervention program," *International Journal of Sport Nutrition*, March; 6 (1), 1996, pp. 24-40.

Drinkwater, B.L., et. al, "Bone mineral content of amenorrheic and eumenorrheic athletes," *New England Journal of Medicine*, August 2; 311 (5), 1984, pp. 277-281.

Fruth, S.J., Worrell, T. W., "Factors associated with menstrual irregularities and decreased bone mineral density in female athletes," Journal of Orthopedic Sports Physical Therapy, July; 22 (1), 1995, pp. 26-38.

Ganong, W.F., "Medical Physiology," Lange Medical Publications, 1979, pp. 174-175, 184-185, 344-350.

Lutter, J. M. , Jaffee L., The Bodywise Woman, Second Edition, Human Kinetics, 1996, pp. 139-179.

Myerson, M, et. al, "Resting metabolic rate and energy balance in amenorrheic and eumenorrheic runners," *Medical Science and Sports Exercise*, January, 23 (1) 1991, pp. 15-22.

Puhl, J., et. al, Sport Science Perspectives for Women, Human Kinetics, 1988, pp. 111-126.

Scialli, A. R., Zinaman, M. J., Reproductive Toxicology and Infertility, McGraw Hill, 1993, pp. 133-186.

The U.S. Medical Women's Association, The Women's Complete Handbook, Delacorte Press, Bantam Doubleday Dell Publishing Group, Inc., 1995, pp. 210-213.

Yen, Jaffee, Reproductive Endocrinology, Third Edition, W. B. Saunders Company, 1991, pp. 275-279.

CHAPTER FIVE

Pregnant cycling

The "right" answer is the one that's right for you—it may not be the same answer as the one for the world-class athlete next door, nor the woman down the street having complications with her pregnancy.

When active women become pregnant, a whole host of questions dominate a good portion of their thoughts. They wonder if they can continue their current exercise or training program. How much is too much exercise? Should there be a limit to the intensity of exercise? Can the baby suffer harm with exercise? While questions are multiplying like rabbits, well wishers add more questions— "Perhaps you should just rest and concentrate on growing a baby. All that exercise can't be good for a developing fetus, can it? You exercise too much anyway, this is a good time to take a break from all that; after all, you don't want to be responsible for harming your own baby—do you?"

Those questions haunt the expectant mother's every pedal stroke. Of course, she doesn't want to harm the baby. Motherhood is revered. Everyone wants the best for the expectant mother and the unborn child. The question is, what is best?

This is a difficult question to answer in a single statement. If you recall from Chapter 2, science often looks at the accomplishments of a female athlete and says, "How did she do that? We didn't think women were capable of that." Scientific studies are often born of past performances, an examination into the anatomy of feats already accomplished. To ask pregnant women to be part of a laboratory study group for nine months, in which they are asked to exercise to exhaustion to see if the affects are harmful to the unborn fetus, is unethical. For this reason, much of the information regarding exercise and pregnancy is collected from women who have already made the journey. This data, in combination with studies done at, typically, low exercise intensities, yields some guidelines and useful information.

WOMEN WHO HAVE MADE THE JOURNEY

There are numerous examples of women who have remained active, highly active, right up to the day of delivery. Mary Jane Reoch, who was a world-class road-racer, remained active. At age 35 she became pregnant. She pedaled from conception to delivery and raced a criterium during her fifth month. Although she was criticized for "hurting the baby," her doctors were supportive of her exercise program. She was active right up to the end, literally, by pedaling herself to the delivery room, 10 miles away, and giving birth to a healthy 7-pound 12-ounce baby girl.

Blaine Bradley Limberg completed four triathlons, a

Peggy Shockley prepares to swim during her sixth pregnancy. She finds the pool relaxing, and she's able to swim right up to delivery day. She typically resumes swimming around two weeks after delivery.

biathlon and a cross-country ski race before he was born. Blaine's mom, Barb, found out she was pregnant in the months just prior to the Hawaii Ironman World Championships, a race including a 2.4-mile swim, 112 miles of cycling, and 26.2 miles of running. After consulting her team of health care providers, midwives, her obstetrician-gynecologist, and others having information about exercise and pregnancy, she decided to go ahead with training and the race. She completed the event when she was three-and-a-half months pregnant. In training and racing, she decided there were three critical areas. First, she kept her core body temperature below 101 degrees Farenheight. Second, she was sure to stay hydrated. And third, she took actions to reduce fatigue by cutting her training in half. Although she wasn't able to achieve her original time goal of 12 hours, she completed the event and did not drive herself into a deep state of fatigue. At a respectable 14 hours 30 minutes, Barb completed the event long before the cut-off time of 17 hours.

What about after a woman delivers? Will she be able to compete at high levels? Numerous women have come back, after delivering a child, to higher levels of performance. One example is the Race Across America champion Susan Notorangelo. In this transcontinental bicycle race, the clock never stops. In 1989, two years after delivering her daughter, she was the only female finisher in the Race Across America. In that year, she covered the distance in nine days, nine hours and nine minutes, coming closer to the first place male—at one day, twenty-four minutes behind—than any woman had in the five previous races. Overall, she finished seventh amid thirteen male finishers.

In a study of elite athletes from Finland, 53 percent did not notice any change in their exercise performance during pregnancy, 10 percent subjectively felt they were in better condition, and 23 percent felt they were in worse condition. After the births of their children, eighteen of the thirty athletes surveyed continued to compete. Of those who continued to compete, 11 percent achieved better performances, 61 percent reached the same level as before pregnancy, and 28 percent did not achieve the same performance level. Researchers found the endurance training had no harmful side effects on the pregnancies or the deliveries and concluded the effect of pregnancy on exercise performance is individual.

These women are examples of how exercise can remain a part of a woman's pregnancy. They are not meant, however, to suggest all women need to complete an ultraendurance event before their pregnancy can be complete. Many women can remain quite active throughout their entire pregnancy, but the body does change.

EMOTIONAL AND SEXUAL CHANGES

Not only are there physical changes occurring during pregnancy, there are emotional changes as well. The emotions vary with the individual woman and the number of children to which she has already given birth. Some common emotions for the mother-to-be include reminiscing about her own childhood, becoming more focused on the baby's father and homelife, feeling overweight and fat, and feeling less desirable.

In contrast, some women embrace pregnancy and its positive changes to their skin, hair and sexual desire. For some women, the increased levels of hormones accompanying pregnancy increase their desire for sex. Although some parents-to-be are concerned about sex during pregnancy, in most cases there is no harm to the fetus that is cushioned by the sac of amniotic fluid.

Exercise can help some women keep a positive attitude about their changing body. In studies conducted by the Melpomene Institute, women said, "Being physically active was definitely an emotional plus."

It's worth mentioning the Melpomene Institute is a non-profit agency with the mission of linking physical activity to women's health. The institute is named in honor of the Greek woman Melpomene (pronounced Mel-POM-uh-nee) who defied officials by running the marathon in the 1896 Olympics. She was told that women could not enter the race. For more information on the organization call 612/642-1951 or e-mail Melpomene@Webspan.com.

THOSE FIRST THREE MONTHS CAN BE ROUGH

Early pregnancy may bring restless nights, fatigue, vivid dreams, morning sickness—nausea and vomiting—and breathing difficulties. All of these maladies can make "this should be easy" exercise require greater effort. Many women who were already active before pregnancy find some relief by cutting back on pre-pregnancy exercise volume and intensity, and finding more time to rest. The morning sickness and gaggy feelings can be reduced by not riding on an empty stomach and eating several smaller meals throughout the day.

As for breathing difficulties, the pressure of the uterus on the bottom of the diaphragm can cause a feeling of shortness of breath. This can be helped by a more upright riding position, which may mean raising the stem on the road bike or perhaps switching to a mountain or cyclo-cross bike—one that can be used on roads and trails. Later in the pregnancy, the fetus drops and relieves this feeling. Some of the feeling of breathlessness is also due to an increase of progesterone during pregnancy, which makes the body more sensitive to carbon dioxide.

Although breathing may be difficult, on the upside, aerobic capacity increases thoughout pregnancy until it is roughly 30-percent greater than nonpregnant levels. Blood volume increases by 35 to 50 percent, and more blood is pumped through the new mother's body as a result of an increased heart rate. Some women view this as an added bonus of being pregnant.

AS TIME ROLLS ON

As the pregnancy continues past the third month, the mother continues to gain weight, which affects her center of gravity and balance. Larger breasts and abdomen move her weight forward, which can mean lower back pain. Again, a higher handlebar and more upright riding position may help. Reducing time in the saddle may also relieve some of the discomfort. Although overall riding time may have to be reduced at some point, some women find breaking their ride up into smaller segments helps. For example, going for two forty-five-minute rides instead of a single ride that is one-and-a-half hours long.

Pregnant women secrete the hormone relaxin, which causes the body's connective tissues to soften and stretch. While this is a great help during delivery, it also affects joints like the ankle and knee. Usually this is not as much of a concern in cycling as it is in a sport like running. Pregnant cyclists should still be aware of the changes.

Pregnancy may cause a once-comfortable bike seat to be too narrow and generally ill-fitting. As mentioned in Chapter 3, the selection of the most comfortable bike seat is highly personal. During pregnancy a woman may be more comfortable with a seat that is wider in the back than her regular saddle.

As the need to urinate more often accompanies pregnancy, more time out of the saddle may be necessary. It is also critical for the mother-with-child to stay well hydrated, as dehydration has been associated with premature labor. Staying well hydrated will allow the exercising mom to perspire easily and stay cool.

Just as overheating is a concern, so is cold temperature. For example, the Underseas Medical Society discourages pregnant women from scuba diving. It appears that pressure, cold environment, and other factors contribute to a high number of birth defects among women who continue to dive while pregnant.

Likewise, the affects of exercising at altitude may be synergistic. A female cyclist may not necessarily be diving while she's pregnant, but she may be traveling to higher altitudes. For a general guideline, an altitude of 8250 feet—2500 meters—should not be exceeded in the first four to five days of short-term exposure from sea level. And similar to nonpregnant athletes, the woman may find she needs to decrease her volume and intensity of exercise upon arriving at altitude to give the body time to adjust.

Some changes occur during pregnancy that have minimal affect on a cycling program and may be eliminated or reduced by exercise. They include:

- varicose veins
- swelling in the hands, legs and face
- muscle and leg cramps
- hand numbness or tingling in toes and fingers.

Promoting circulation helps alleviate some of these problems, but other changes occur that are probably not influenced by exercise. They include:

- skin changes
- gums that bleed more easily
- and thicker hair growth.

These changes generally return to prepregnancy condition after the child is born.

SPECIAL CASES

Women who have never had diabetes or high blood pressure can develop them during pregnancy. Diabetes, which occasionally develops during pregnancy, is called gestational diabetes. The typical sequence of treatment has been through diet, close monitoring of glucose levels, then a prescription of insulin when diet alone fails. It appears that exercise may be an alternative to insulin prescription. If exercise doesn't eliminate the need for insulin, it may reduce the amount needed.

High blood pressure during pregnancy, when accompanied by protein in the urine and swelling, is called pre-eclampsia. If either diabetes or high blood pressure show up during pregnancy, they require the attention of a doctor.

IN GENERAL

Studies have shown women who exercise during pregnancy gain less weight and deposit less subcutaneous fat. This is fat just below the skin's surface.

BENEFITS TO THE BABY

There are several benefits to the mother if she maintains an exercise program while she's pregnant. But what about the unborn baby? Numerous studies have followed offspring of exercising mothers and have found the babies to be healthy and have normal growth and development.

In an interesting study conducted at Case Western Reserve University, head researcher James Clapp, M.D., matched two groups of pregnant families for socioeconomic status, education, marital stability and body size. The fathers were also included in the body size data. The two groups were matched for pre- and post-pregnancy exercise habits; both groups of mothers breast fed, both groups had similar child care, and both groups had comparable parental weight change over time.

The only difference between the two groups was exercise during pregnancy. One group exercised "vigorously" by running, doing aerobics, cross-country skiing, or some combination of all three. They exercised at least thirty minutes, three times per week, throughout their pregnancies. The second group ceased all exercise except walking.

What the research found was that by age five, the children of the vigorous exercisers had less body fat than the children born to the walking group. The children born to the second group were called "a bit on the fat side." In addition, the vigorous exercisers' children scored significantly higher on the Wechsler test of general intelligence and coordination as well as on tests of oral language skills.

GENERAL GUIDELINES

While some women will be able to keep a vigorous exercise program during pregnancy, others will not. Some exercise, however, is better than none. The U.S. College of Obstetricians and Gynecologists (ACOG) revised its guidelines for pregnant women in 1994, which had recommended restricting the exercising mother's heart rate to one hundred-forty beats per minute. Chapter 9 gives more information on exercising heart rates, and it will be more obvious why one hundred-forty beats-per-minute may be appropriate for one woman and not the next. The new ACOG guidelines are less restrictive.

With the ACOG changes in mind, the following is a collection of general guidelines for women who want to exercise during and after pregnancy:

• Pregnant women should consult their health care provider about an exercise program, particularly if they are beginning an exercise program after becoming pregnant.

• Mild to moderate exercise routines produce health benefits. Regular exercise at least three to five times per week is preferable to intermittent activity.

• Exercise in the supine position—lying on the back, face up—should be avoided after the fourth month of pregnancy to prevent restricting blood flow to the fetus.

• Pregnant women should avoid standing motionless for

prolonged periods of time.

• Exercisers should use good judgment and reduce intensity, or stop, when they become fatigued.

• Selecting low-impact activities, such as cycling and swimming, decrease the injury risk to mother and fetus—as long as women avoid situations that put them at risk for falling. If women experience difficulties with balance, particularly during the third trimester of pregnancy, they would probably be better off cycling on a stationary trainer, indoors.

• Women who are pregnant need to consume adequate calories. The developing fetus reduces the amount of glycogen and energy expectant mothers will have available for cycling. Pregnant women require roughly three hundred calories per day, in addition to their normal intake. "Normal" includes calories necessary for exercise.

• Exercising women need to consume adequate fluids, and avoid overheating and dehydration. Light-colored urine is one indication of proper hydration. Dark yellow or foul-smelling urine are indicators of dehydration.

• Wearing proper clothing and exercising in a cool environment help avoid overheating. This may mean exercising in cool morning conditions, cool evening conditions, indoors in air conditioning, or indoors in front of a fan.

• Many of the physical changes associated with pregnancy last for four to six weeks postpartum. For this reason, women are encouraged to resume their prepregnancy routines gradually.

• Tears and episiotomies—the incisions made to ease delivery—need to be healed before sitting on a regular bicycle seat.

• Women who have had Cesarean sections should avoid vigorous exercise for six to eight weeks after delivery.

WHEN THERE ARE PROBLEMS

A pregnant woman should seek the advice of a physician if she experiences any of the following warning signs:

• Vaginal bleeding can mean a problem with the placenta, or can be a sign of miscarriage.

• If vaginal discharge changes in amount or appearance, it may be a signal of preterm labor or infection. Vaginal fluid discharge is also a signal that the amniotic sac has ruptured and labor may begin soon.

• Back pain and cramps, which increase in intensity or duration, could be signs of miscarriage or preterm birth.

• Headache, blurred vision and unusual swelling occurring with high blood pressure.

• Sharp abdominal pain should be examined if it doesn't improve with changes in physical position.

• Fever or chills are signals of infection.

• The doctor should be contacted if there is a decrease in fetal movement for around twelve hours after week twenty-eight.

MAKING IT EASIER TO BE PHYSICALLY ACTIVE

• Do not set goal times for races or events. Be flexible about exercise goals and be willing to turn around and go home when you're not feeling well.

• Listen to your body and exercise at an intensity that is comfortable for you.

- Talk to family and friends to get their support for an active pregnancy. Their moral support can be important.

- Seek other women who have exercised or who are exercising during their pregnancy. Get information about their experience.

- Studies show positive physical and emotional benefits to women who begin an exercise program after becoming pregnant. If you decide to start a program, talk with your health care provider.

- In the end, you are the only one who can decide how much exercise is too much, too long, or too hard. The "right" answer is the one that's right for you—it may not be the same answer as the one for the world-class athlete next door, nor the woman down the street having complications with her pregnancy.

STRENGTHENING PELVIC MUSCLES

An issue for pregnant, postpartum and menopausal women is urinary incontinence, or the involuntary loss of urine. Two major causes are unstable bladder and stress incontinence. With an unstable bladder, there may be an urgent need to urinate accompanied by a fear of leakage and a high frequency of urination. Stress incontinence is the leakage of small amounts of urine after a cough, sneeze, or any maneuver that increases the abdominal pressure exerted on the bladder. There are other causes for incontinence, which include medications, surgery and infections.

Dr. Arnold Kegel developed exercises to strengthen the pelvic floor or the muscles surrounding the urethra, vagina and anus to help women with stress incontinence. Kegal Exercises, as they have been named, strengthen the pubococcygeus muscle. Doing these exercises during and after pregnancy have shown to reduce problems with urinary incontinence. This is a welcome relief for many pregnant and postpartum women.

In order for women to locate the pubococcygeus muscle, sit on the toilet with your legs apart. When the flow of urine begins, try to stop it. That feeling and that muscle is what you will be doing "dry land" work on. Do not continue to try to stop urine as part of your normal exercise program.

Just like weight-room strength training, you will contract this muscle and hold the contraction for about three seconds, then release it for about three seconds. Repeat the exercise twelve to fifteen times in a row, three to six times per day. To achieve optimal benefits, at least forty contractions per day are necessary. Do this exercise while you perform other daily routines such as brushing your teeth, driving to work, during the rest portion of regular weight training sessions, while watching the news, or during other regular activities. With regular training, results can be seen a few weeks.

BRIEF THOUGHTS

For healthy women, continuing or beginning an exercise program during pregnancy appears to benefit both the mother and the unborn baby. Women continue to comment that exercise makes their pregnancy more enjoyable by helping them maintain a positive attitude, good self esteem, and a sense of control. Exercise can help with the management of gestational diabetes, depression and other problems that occasionally accompany pregnancy.

Many women who are competitive athletes and become pregnant have found they are able to return to competitive levels after having the baby, if competition is a priority for them. Some comment on a newfound strength and mental toughness, which appears in their training and competition after they've given birth. Others have found a new balance that allows them to put athletic training in perspective with other priorities in their lives.

When exercising during pregnancy, the health of the unborn baby is always the number-one priority. Each woman will need to determine what level of exercise is appropriate for her and her unborn child. A well-informed health care provider can furnish information to assist a woman in the fitness-during-pregnancy journey. And a supportive network of family and friends make the journey easier.

REFERENCES

Baker, A., M.D., Bicycling Medicine, Argo Publishing, 1995, pp. 209.

Bean, A., "Running Mom = Smart Kid," *Runner's World*, June 1997, pp. 28.

Clapp, J. F. III, Effect of recreational exercise on pregnancy weight gain and subcutaneous fat deposition, *Medicine and Science in Sports and Exercise*, February; 27 (2), 1995, pp. 170-177.

Clapp, J. F. III, Morphometric and neurodevelopmental outcome at age five years of the offspring of women who continued to exercise regularly throughout pregnancy, *Journal of Pediatrics*, December 129 (6), 1996, pp. 856-63.

Clapp, J. F. III , The one-year morphometric and neurodevelopmental outcome of the offspring of women who continued to exercise regularly throughout pregnancy, *American Journal of Obstetrics and Gynecology*, March; 178 (3), 1998, pp. 594-599.

Dumas, G. A., Reid, J. G., Laxity of knee cruciate ligaments during pregnancy, *Journal of Orthopedic Sports Physical Therapy*, July, 26 (1), 1997, pp. 2-6.

Dye, T. D., et. al, Physical activity, obesity, and diabetes in pregnancy, *American Journal of Epidemiology*, December 1; 146 (11), 1997, pp. 961-965.

Foley, N., "The Mommy Track," *Women's Sports and Fitness*, April, 1998, pp. 48-51.

Huch, R., Physical activity at altitude in pregnancy, Semin Perinatol, August; 20 (4), 1996, pp. 303-314.

IDEA Today, Highlights from the 1996 World Research Forum, October, 1996, pp. 31.

Kardel, K. R., Kase, T., Training in pregnant women: effects on fetal development and birth, *American Journal of Obstetrics and Gynecology*, February, 178 (2), 1998, pp. 280-286.

Koltyn, K.F., Schultes, S. S., Psychological effects of an aerobic exercise session and a rest session following pregnancy, *Journal of Sports Medicine and Physical Fitness*, December; 37 (4), 1997, pp. 287-291.

Lutter, J. M. and Jaffee, L., The Bodywise Woman, Second Edition, Human Kinetics, 1996, pp. 181-217.

Norton, C., Pre/Postnatal Water Exercise, IDEA Health and Fitness Source, April 1998, pp. 55-59.

Ohtake, P. J., Wolfe, L. A., Physical conditioning attenuates respiratory responses to steady-state exercise in late gestation, *Medicine and Science in Sports and Exercise*, January; 30 (1), 1998, pp. 17-27.

Penttinen J., Erkkola, R., Pregnancy in endurance athletes, *Scandinavian Journal of Medicine in Science and Sports*, Aug; 7 (4), 1997, pp. 226-228.

Puhl, J., et. al, Sport Science Perspectives for Women, Human Kinetics, 1988, pp. 151-160.

Sampselle, C. M., et. al, Effect of pelvic muscle exercise on transient incontinence during pregnancy and after birth, Obstetrics and Gynecology, March, 91 (3), 1998, pp. 406-412.

Schramm, W. F, et. al, Exercise, employment, other daily activities and adverse pregnancy outcomes, *American Journal of Epidemilogy*, February 1; 143, 1996, pp. 211-218.

The U.S. Medical Women's Association, The Women's Complete Handbook, Delacorte Press, Bantam Doubleday Dell Publishing Group, Inc., 1995, pp. 210-213.

Weaver, S., A Woman's Guide To Cycling, Ten Speed Press, 1991.

CHAPTER SIX

The silver fox,
master cyclist

I don't remember her name, but she made a lasting impression on me. I vividly recall her looks because she resembled my great grandmother. She was a short woman, had broad shoulders and a sturdy body—much like the German farmers in my family. Heavy brows and a strong nose accentuated her friendly eyes. She proudly told me she was seventy-four years old, her German accent spicing each word. "They only let me enter five events," she said. "I can do more, you know."

She began her first event, diving off of the starting blocks in a masters swimming meet. When she finished, I told her the time on my clock. She smiled as though she knew a secret. Raising one eyebrow she asked, "Good, eh?" Good? No ... great!

As a child, my concept of an old person was someone who was at least thirty years old. I'm finding, as do many people, that the older I get, the older "old" becomes. One of the things that so impressed me about the seventy-four-year-old German woman was her commitment to exercise and it seemed she was having great fun. During the time she was growing up, exercise was the manual labor associated with earning a living. Now, she was diving into a swimming pool and racing as fast as she could, apparently for the sheer fun of it. I want to do the same thing.

As we age, what can we expect? Was this German dynamo an exception? Or can we all be just as active as we age? While it is possible to remain highly active and fit as we age, our bodies do change. The rate of change appears to be individual, but changes are inevitable. Women tend to live longer than men, and the average life expectancy for both genders has been increasing. People born in the U.S. in 1900 could expect to live to be around forty-seven years old, with women living about four to ten years longer than men. For people born in the U.S. in 1946, women could expect to live seventy-eight-and-a-half years and men seventy-one-and-a-half years. There is disagreement among experts concerning predictions of average life expectancy for those born in the 1980s or '90s. There are also different theories as to why women and men have dissimilar life expectancies; those won't be covered in this chapter.

The average life span, differing from average life expectancy, is defined as the age by which all but a very few members are deceased. Although average life expectancy has been increasing, the average life span has remained stable at eighty-five years of age.

This chapter covers the general aging of humans and within that topic, the process of menopause. We begin our look at what women can expect with menopause. General information follows on what to expect as we age.

MENOPAUSE

There was a time when some women would commit suicide or submit to alcoholism to escape the physical and mental hell they were experiencing during midlife. Their bodies and minds seemed to turn against them. Husbands didn't understand. At the time, science didn't understand menopause and doctors weren't able to help patients comprehend what was happening as their bodies changed. Furthermore, some doctors believed the symptoms were in the women's heads.

Thankfully, science continues to discover more about menopause and can offer advice to women so they may continue to lead healthy lives during and after "the change of life." The knowledge supplied by science, coupled with simply discussing menopause with women who have experienced it can help younger women be more prepared.

Young women begin producing estrogen in the ovaries somewhere between the ages of ten and fourteen. Most women reach their peak reproductive capability in their late twenties. As they age, diminishing levels of estrogen result in the beginning of menopause. Technically, menopause is considered to have occurred when one year has passed without menstruation and can be confirmed by a doctor testing for elevated levels of FHS. Although the "U.S. Heritage Dictionary" defines menopause as "the cessation of menstruation that occurs between the ages of forty-five and fifty" because the symptoms can last for several years, menopause is actually a process rather than a single event. This is important to remember.

For about half of all women menopause occurs between the ages of forty-five and fifty. One-fourth of all women will reach menopause when they are younger than forty-five, and one-fourth will reach menopause when they are older than fifty. The decreasing level of estrogen production can last for five to seven years.

The signs and symptoms of menopause vary, with the most common being hot flashes. Hot flashes can be described as a warm, tingly feeling that floods the body. Flashes can begin with a sensation of pressure in the head, similar to a headache. The intensity of the headache can increase, then be accompanied by a sudden feeling of heat flushing through the body. Skin temperature actually increases and there can be an outbreak of sweat from the head, neck, upper chest or back. Hot flashes can be short, only lasting a few minutes; others can last more than thirty minutes.

Several studies have looked at hormonal changes occurring during hot flashes. Although the levels of circulating estrogen have not been found to fluctuate before or after hot flashes, there does appear to be a correlation between a pulse in lutenizing hormone and the occurrence of hot flashes. One study found a pulse in the follicle stimulating hormone as well, while a second study did not. Although estrogen does not seem to fluctuate during hot flashes, it may be the low levels of estrogen that create a hormonal imbalance, causing hot flashes.

Unfortunately, many hot-flash episodes occur during the night, waking the woman, and causing a loss of sleep. It has been found that nocturnal hot flashes are significant contributors to sleep deprivation and fatigue.

Insomnia and fatigue are thought to be major contributors to mood swings, irritability and depression. These three symptoms can occur in menopausal women, but are not necessarily present in all women. Other symptoms of menopause include irregular, unpredictable and sometimes heavy bleeding. Being able to look at past history of menstrual cycles is particularly helpful in tracking gradual changes, and is a good reason to keep records of menstrual cycles from year to year.

During menopause, vaginal tissues become dryer, thinner and less flexible, which can cause intercourse to become painful. Products that can be used to lubricate the vagina include aloe vera gel, vitamin E capsules—puncture the capsule and use the gel—and commercial products including Replens, Gynmoistrin, K-Y Jelly and Astroglyde.

Because tissues begin to lose some elasticity, there can be sagging of the pelvic organs. This can contribute to incontinence. Fortunately, the Kegal exercises covered in Chapter 5 can strengthen the muscles of the pelvic floor and eliminate some, if not all symptoms of incontinence.

Dropping estrogen levels can also cause new—and unwanted—hair growth. Reduced estrogen levels upset the balance between estrogen and testosterone in the female body, and the result can be dark, course hairs growing from the upper lip or chin areas.

As estrogen levels drop, so do women's natural protection from heart disease. Lower estrogen levels are associated with increased levels of LDL, lower levels of HDL, increased triglycerides and blood pressure begins to rise. With these changes, a woman's risk factors for heart disease become similar to men's.

In women and men, bones continually undergo a process of remodeling—a process in which old bone is replaced by new bone. When we are young, old bone is lost, but because new bone is formed at a faster rate, total bone mass increases. The process of building new bone is called "formation," and in young adulthood, formation equals the pace of bone loss. Somewhere in our mid- to late-thirties, bone loss exceeds formation and we can begin to lose bone mass at a rate of approximately 1 percent per year. Fully developed osteoporosis is considered to be when bone loss is 2 to 3 percent per year. Table 6.1 summarizes the risk factors for osteoporosis.

Because estrogen helps with the absorption of calcium, decreasing levels of estrogen are associated with increased risk of osteoporosis. Supplemental estrogen can help alleviate some of the risk.

Other ways of decreasing the risk for osteoporosis are decreasing sodium intake, insuring adequate calcium in the diet, participating in weight-bearing exercise and stopping smoking. Ingesting calcium levels of 1000 to 1500 milligrams per day—a recommendation to keep osteoporosis at bay—is now being extended to premenopausal women as well. Calcium supplementation and estrogen treatment work only to slow calcium loss, or slow bone loss. Exercise is critically important because it has the ability to increase bone formation, even in older adults.

Exercises that work best to increase bone formation are those that are weight bearing. Walking, running, indoor aerobic classes, tennis and weight lifting are examples of weight-bearing exercises. Gravity and muscular contraction apply force to bones, which influences the structure and integrity of the bone. The mechanical force of exercise is converted to electrical energy—a process that activates the

TABLE 6.1

RISK FACTORS FOR OSTEOPOROSIS

• Low levels of physical exercise increase bone loss.

• Low levels of calcium intake—less than 1000 milligrams per day—are not adequate to maintain and build bone mass.

• Smoking increases bone loss.

• Caffeine use increases the excretion of calcium.

• Alcohol use increases the excretion of calcium.

• High sodium intake increases calcium loss.

• Being confined indoors can affect bone loss because sunlight provides vitamin D, which increases calcium absorption from the intestines and reabsorption from the kidneys. Likewise, sunlight, in moderation, helps calcium absorption.

• Intake of some drugs such as anticonvulsants, corticosteroids, antacids containing aluminum, which inhibits the absorption of calcium, and diuretics, which increase the excretion of calcium, will affect bone loss.

• Excess consumption of protein can increase the excretion of calcium. This does not mean that you should eliminate protein from the diet.

• Consuming too many products high in phosphorous is a risk because phosphorous inhibits calcium absorption. Red meat is high in phosphorous and some soft drinks are high in phosphorous. While soft drinks are not necessary to the maintenance of good health, red meat consumed in moderation does provide essential vitamins and minerals.

• Foods containing phyates such as oatmeal and bran, and oxalates such as spinach, rhubarb and beet greens can interfere with calcium absorption.

• Foods rich in fiber combine with calcium in the intestine and increase the rate at which foods are passed through the intestinal tract.

Note: There are no "good" foods and "bad" foods. A diet high in variety and whole foods is recommended.

bone-forming cells in the area of the stress and increases calcium levels.

Controversy exists as to whether cycling is an exercise that helps prevent osteoporosis or not. It is not clear why some scientists find cycling helpful while others do not, but it may have to do with how the cycling is done. If a woman simply sits on the bicycle and spins her legs, there is minimal stress to muscles and bones. If, however, she climbs hills, does intervals, or cycles out of the saddle, it would better fit the bill of "weight bearing." In hill climbing, while seated, a woman can use forces that are similar to weight lifting by powering each pedal stroke to climb up a hill. Certainly, if she is out of the saddle climbing a hill, she supports her body weight with each push of the pedal. She may also apply great force to the pedals while doing interval work. Until more is known about cycling's ability to increase bone mass, it is probably best to augment cycling with a weight-training program or other weight-bearing exercises.

Some women have found relief for menopausal symptoms by exercising and watching their diet. A diet, which has plenty of fruits, vegetables and lean meats may be helpful. Exercise not only helps prevent osteoporosis, but it can boost self esteem, help maintain proper weight, tone muscles, and improve circulation, digestion and elimination.

Another relief for menopausal symptoms is estrogen replacement therapy. Since one of the markers for menopause is diminishing estrogen, doctors in the 1960s began to experiment with estrogen supplementation. The results were very promising, and estrogen began being touted as a key to the fountain of youth. There were promises for the elimination of hot flashes, depression, vaginal drying, vaginal thinning and suggestion of wrinkle prevention. Women taking supplemental estrogen had high hopes of retaining their youthful appearance and sexual vigor.

In the late 1970s, the picture for estrogen changed. Researchers were finding that women who took estrogen alone—without progesterone—were six to fourteen times more likely to

TABLE 6.2	
BENEFITS AND RISKS OF HORMONE REPLACEMENT THERAPY	
Benefits	**Risks**
Reduces or eliminates hot flashes	Menstrual periods and/or cramping may begin again
Reduces the risks of osteoporosis	May increase the risk of breast cancer
Reduces the risk of developing heart disease	May increase the risk of uterine cancer
Reduces vaginal dryness	May increase the risk of gallbladder disease
May help with insomnia, depression and memory problems	Can experience nausea, vomiting, swelling of the extremities, and breast tenderness

develop uterine cancer than non-estrogen users, due to uterine lining overgrowth. As more research was conducted and more women began using supplemental estrogen, doctors found they were able to lower the doses of estrogen to achieve positive effects and minimize the negative side effects. In addition, progestin—a synthetic version of progesterone—can be given with estrogen to keep the uterine lining overgrowth problem in check.

Estrogen therapy is not necessarily for everyone, though. Women who should not use supplemental estrogen during and after menopause are those who have severe liver disease; thrombotic disorders—blood clots; malignant melanoma; and estrogen-dependant tumors of the breast, uterus or the kidney. Other reasons for not utilizing estrogen therapy include a family history of uterine or breast cancer. A family history of uterine and breast cancer—risks increase with estrogen supplemention—has to be weighed against a family history of heart disease and osteoporosis—risks increase without estro-

Herbal remedies for menopause

All women will, at some point, have to deal with menopause. While some women have few symptoms or problems, the majority of women will suffer at least some of the problems covered in this chapter. For the lucky ones, menopausal symptoms are mild and tolerable. A percentage of the others will chose synthetic estrogen replacement to minimize discomfort and prevent problems such as osteoporosis. Another percentage of women may spend years of their life in misery because they wanted to avoid synthetic estrogen replacement therapy. For them, the loss of quality of life can be costly.

For women wanting to relieve the symptoms of menopause, yet not take synthetic estrogen, there may be another choice. In plants, are naturally occurring estrogens. Licorice, sage, saw palmetto, black cohosh, soybeans, tofu, miso, flaxseeds, pomegranates and dates contain phytoestrogens—all estrogen-like compounds, which when ingested, mimic the chemistry of estrogen. Their chemical activity is slower and weaker than that of synthetic estrogens, however, they appear to be free of the side effects associated with those synthetics. Some of these substances are being combined in tonics, such as black cohosh-licorice compound—a liquid-drop form, available at some vitamin and supplement stores.

While some plants contain estrogen, others like chaste tree berries are thought to restore a normal estrogen-progesterone balance by inhibiting the release of FSH, and increasing LSH. A tonic named Pulsatilla-Vitex Compound contains chaste tree berry, pulsatilla, motherwort, black cohosh, and licorice and some women use it for menopausal relief.

Certain natural remedies, such as those mentioned above, are thought to influence estrogen, progesterone, FSH and LSH; other remedies are thought to relieve symptoms. Those thought to help relieve hot flash symptoms include lecithin, an emulsifier for Vitamin E; primrose oil or black current seed oil; Vitamin E and Vitamin C.

Although called "all-natural-herbal," when used for pharmaceutical purposes, these herbal options for relieving menopausal symptoms are still considered drugs. Herbal remedies are not without problems. Some herbs can cause heart palpitations, interfere with the absorption of iron, and other vitamins and minerals. If you choose to self-medicate, it is important to learn as much as possible on this topic and the specific doses of herbs that may be necessary to relieve symptoms.

gen supplementation. Unexplained vaginal bleeding, a history of high blood pressure, or gallbladder disease are also reasons for caution. A summary of risks and benefits for hormone replacement therapy are shown on Table 6.2.

In the late 1990s new estrogen therapies have been introduced. New, synthetic versions are promising because they appear to provide all of the benefits and none of the risks. Additionally, some women are finding relief from herbal remedies (see sidebar), and others find relief from antidepressants. Women need to discuss all the options with their doctors.

AGING

As years pass, the process of aging affects everyone. How much aging affects each person and at what rate, how-

TABLE 6.3	
EVENTS OF AGING **Effect**	**Actions to Minimize Efffects**
Skin becomes thinner, dryer, less able to produce sweat.	Keep skin moisturized and, when exposed to the sun, protected with sunscreen. Wear light-colored clothing when in the sun and be cautious when exercising in extreme heat.
Basal metabolism decreases	Exercise can increase metabolism.
Strength and flexibility decrease.	A strength-training program, including a stretching plan will help.
Aerobic capacity and anaerobic capacity decrease.	An aerobic cycling program, including some anaerobic work will reduce the losses.
The body does not repair itself as quickly as it once did.	Older athletes may need to decrease the number of high-intensity or high-volume workouts per week. Another option is to increase the frequency of rest weeks thoughout the training cycle.
Bone density decreases.	Participate in weight-bearing exercise and get an adequate intake of calcium, reduce factors that increase calcium loss (Table 6.1), and perhaps get hormone replacement therapy for women.
Decreased sight and hearing loss.	Keep vision prescriptions current and use a hearing aid if necessary.
Decreased sense of smell, taste and thirst sensation.	Thirst is particularly important. Be adequately hydrated drinking at least eight to ten glasses of water each day. When participating in athletic events, employ a hydration plan—do not wait to be thirsty in order to rehydrate.
Decreased ability to absorb and use vitamins, minerals and essential nutrients in foods.	Prepare foods that are nutrient-dense. Nutrient dense foods tend to be the ones that are minimally processed: fruits, vegetables, lean meats, nuts, and dairy products are some of the top contenders.
Digestion rate slows.	Increase the time between vigorous athletic events and heavy meals. Use easily digestible foods or liquid meals prior to athletic events.
Reaction time slows.	Adjust bicycle speed to accommodate corners and steep downhills.
Sleep patterns change.	Go to bed at a regular time each night. Avoid caffeine for at least two hours before bedtime. Exercise at least two hours before bedtime. Possibly eat a small snack.
Bladder capacity decreases.	Plan more frequent pit stops.

ever, is individual. Why is it that some people are frail, inactive, and highly dependent on others, while other folks are virile, athletic and self-sufficient? The rate of aging, or the change in function of organs and body systems per unit of time, is different for men and women. For example, women age at a slower rate between the ages of forty-five to sixty, than they do between seventy to eighty years of age. Men's aging rate, on the other hand, slows at a pace unvarying in time. In other words, the rate at which men age slows down as they age and doesn't vary in particular years as does women's aging rate.

What can we expect as we age? Well, that depends. How our bodies change as we age depends on genetics, sex, living environment, exposure to harmful chemicals, exercise history, and overall health maintenance, to name a few. When asked their "secrets" to longevity and health, eighty-five-year-old participants in one study listed hard work, exercise, and keeping active both physically and mentally. Other secrets included inheriting good genes; lifelong good health—including use of health care resources; strong religious beliefs; good nutrition; abstinence from alcohol, smoking and drugs; adequate rest and sleep; a positive attitude toward themselves and others; and a good support system—parents, friends, spouses or children.

There are changes we will all face as we age. The rate at which we each experience these changes is individual. Table 6.3 lists some of the changes that occur as we age and how we, as athletes, can compensate or reduce the effects of these changes. Most studies on aging, however, have been conducted on nonathletes. Only recently have there been enough older athletes to study and evaluate established paradigms about the aging process.

Here's the beginning of lots of good news about aging. A study at the University of Florida had ten sedentary senior men and women—average age sixty-seven—begin a training plan at the same time as eleven sedentary, thirty-year-old men and women. Both groups worked out three times per week for sixteen weeks. Over the course of sixteen weeks, they all increased their exercise duration from twenty to forty minutes, and increased intensity from 60 to 80 percent of maximal heart rate. At the end of sixteen weeks, the youngsters increased their aerobic capacity by 12 percent, and the seniors increased their aerobic capacity by 14 percent. The difference between the two groups was not statistically significant. The finding was the older bodies responded to training similar to the way the younger bodies did, when the training stimulus was similar.

San Diego State University conducted a study on masters women cyclists. Researchers recruited thirteen women who were highly competitive members of the United States Cycling Federation (USCF) and whose average age was forty-seven-and-a-half years. The women were field-tested in 13.5km and 20km time trials—testing aerobic capacity and lactate threshold. The USCF women's aerobic capacity tested approximately 10 percent higher than those reported for other age-matched women athletes. Researchers found their maximal heart rate was unrelated to age. The women's laboratory lactate threshold heart rates tested to be 88 percent of their maximal heart rates. During the time trials, the women were able to average between 92 and 94 percent of their maximal heart rates. Some of the conclusions drawn from the study were that traditional methods of estimating maximal

PHOTO COURTESY OF LIBBY JAMES

Libby James, 62 years young, continues to lead multiday hiking and cycling tours.

heart rate and lactate threshold training intensities would be incorrect for masters women cyclists.

Other studies in other sports have also found the traditional method of "220 - age = maximum heart rate" to be incorrect. This is why it is important to base training intensities on individual lactate threshold heart rates and perceived exertions and not use estimates from age-graded charts. A method to do this is discussed in the next chapter.

One of the theories on aging is that it is a result of the accumulation of mitochondrial DNA mutations. These mutations interfere with respiratory ATP production, which impairs cell function. When the cell is unable to go about its business of utilizing oxygen and producing energy, tissue dysfunction becomes a problem, leading to decline, and eventually death. One study looked at the muscle mitochondria of test subjects who were matched for levels of physical activity. Interestingly, the study found exercise improved and may mask mitochondrial "aging" in muscle. Exercise appears to have multiple benefits for both younger and older women.

BRIEF THOUGHTS

If you have been fearful of growing older, perhaps a different view of the path ahead is in order. Women can age beautifully and minimize some discomforts if they are armed with knowledge. Many older women will have freedom from menstrual cycles, child rearing and the financial burdens that are common to younger women. These freedoms allow older women to be more active and carefree.

For people who remain active as they age, research has found they tend to lead overall healthier lifestyles. Exercise has helped people lose weight, increase strength, quit smoking, and has encouraged them to eat better. Exercise can also significantly help with the symptoms of menopause and osteoporosis.

It seems the synergistic effects of wellness are changing how we age and our paradigm of what is typical of the aging process. Perhaps you can find a role model like the seventy-four-year-old German woman swimmer.

REFERENCES

Anderson, O., Young Versus Old, Running Research News, Volume 11, Number 1, January-February, 1995.

Balch, J. F, M.D., Balch, P. A., C.N.C., Prescription for Nutritional Healing, Avery Publishing Group, 1997.

Bierley, E.J., et al., Effects of physical activity and age on mitochondrial function, QJM, Monthly Journal Of The Association Of Physicians, 89 (4), April 1996, pp. 251-258.

Bortz, W. M. 4th, Bortz, W.M. 2nd, How fast do we age? Exercise performance over time as a biomarker, Journal Gerontology: Biological Sciences, 51 (5), September 1996, pp. 223-225.

Cairo, B., Ph.D., CryoGam Colorado, personal interviews with the author, May—July, 1998.

Friel, J., Cycling Past 50, Human Kinetics, 1998.

Ganong, W.F., Medical Physiology, Lange Medical Publications, 1979.

Kujala U.M, et al., Hospital care in later life among former world-class Finnish athletes, Journal of the U.S. Medical Association, 276 (3), July 1996, pp. 216-220.

Lutter, J. M. and Jaffee, L., The Bodywise Woman, Second Edition, Human Kinetics, 1996.

Marieb, E. N., Human Anatomy and Physiology, Third Edition, The Benjamin/Cummings Publishing Company, 1995.

Nichols, J.F., et al., Relationship between blood lactate response to exercise and endurance performance in competitive female athletes, International Journal of Sports Medicine, 18 (6), August 1997, pp. 458-463.

Pollock, M. L., et al., Twenty-year follow-up of aerobic power and body composition of older track athletes, Journal of Applied Physiology, 82 (5), May 1997, pp. 1508-1516.

Smith, E., Therapeutic Herb Manual, published by Ed Smith, 1997.

Spirduso W. W., Physical Dimensions of Aging, Human Kinetics, 1995.

Scialli, A. R., Zinaman, M. J., Reproductive Toxicology and Infertility, McGraw Hill, 1993, pp. 133-186.

The U.S. Heritage Dictionary, Second College Edition, Dell Publishing Company, New York, New York, 1983.

The U.S. Medical Women's Association, The Women's Complete

Handbook, Delacorte Press, Bantam Doubleday Dell Publishing Group, Inc., 1995.

Vickery, D. M., MD, Fries, J.F., MD, Take Care of Yourself, Addison-Wesley Publishing Company, 1994.

Yen, Jaffee, Reproductive Endocrinology, Third Edition, W. B. Saunders Company, 1991.

CHAPTER SEVEN

Periodization, intensity, testing and progress

"Success is a journey, not a destination."
—Ben Sweetland

More than likely, one of the major reasons you are reading this book is because you want to ride your bicycle faster or farther. It doesn't matter if you are intending to try a time trial for the first time—you want to keep up with the weekend group ride or a cycling buddy; the road to each goal has similarities. But there are some common mistakes many cyclists make:

- Riding the same speed all the time
- Having no goals and no plan
- Having a sloppy nutrition and hydration routine

RIDING FAST ALL THE TIME

It makes sense that if you want to get fast, you have to ride fast. It is true to some extent, however, you can't ride fast all the time. The problem becomes mediocrity. A cyclist who is trying to ride fast all the time ends up riding one, mediocre,

FIGURE 7.1

[POLAR HEART RATE MONITOR]

speed. They are too tired to go really fast, yet they feel enough spunk to pedal a decent pace. Not too fast, and not too slow . . . hence, a mediocre speed. This chapter will help you avoid that rut and cover riding intensities, self tests to estimate training zones and ways to find out if you are actually making progress. Goal setting, planning and nutrition are covered in later chapters.

The heart rate monitor is one of the best tools available to estimate exercise intensity. It comes in a variety of models and price ranges. The least expensive model simply reads heart rate, and the more expensive models have the capability to store several hours worth of data, then download that data into a computer for analysis.

The heart-rate-monitor system consists of a transmitter belt worn below the breasts, strapped around the chest, and a receiver worn on the wrist or mounted on the handlebar of the bike. The transmitter belt picks up electrical impulses from the heart and relays the information via an electro-magnetic field to the receiver. The receiver then displays heart rate. It's like having a tachometer for your body, similar to the one on a sports car.

Heart rate is used in conjunction with perceived exertion to determine riding intensity. Perhaps you have been on a group ride where speeds were sizzling from the start. For a few moments, you were right there with the pack. Moments later, you dropped off the back and withered like a balloon's escaping air. Your heart was pounding, your legs were burning, and you were giving it all you had. That intensity, or speed, was obviously too fast for you to sustain. But other people were riding that fast, so it is humanly possible to keep such a pace. What are they doing that you aren't?

Perhaps you decide to ride with a different group. This group starts slowly, rides slowly and ends slowly. It seems you barely broke a sweat and maybe feel as if you could have ridden for days at this speed. It couldn't be worthwhile to ride this slowly while you're trying to get faster, could it?

Building and improving fitness is analogous to building a house. The first part, the foundation, must be constructed properly or the rest of the house won't hold up. After the foundation is laid, a strong frame and roof can be built. The best results come from an orderly process in the initial stages of the construction. When it comes to some of the finishing details, their order can be changed somewhat in order to accommodate construction schedule needs. Once the house is constructed, it must be maintained. If the house is properly maintained, improvements can be made to suit the needs and wants of the owner. These improvements are typically done a few at a time.

So it goes with fitness. A solid base is needed before speed or long duration is added. Once a certain level of fitness is achieved, it needs to be maintained. Each season, further improvements can be made to well-kept fitness. It can take years to build a world-class cyclist.

PERIODIZATION

You may or may not be striving to be world class. Either way, a periodization plan will be helpful to guide your journey to faster or longer rides. Briefly, a periodization plan is a plan that manipulates exercise volumes and intensities over the course of weeks, months and years. A periodization plan for an Olympic athlete will span the course of several years. This type of plan is designed to have the athlete at peak fitness for the Olympic Games. No athlete, even an Olympic-caliber athlete, can maintain peak fitness year-round. Peak performances are planned and can occur about two to three times per year.

The training plans in Chapter 10 are periodization plans. They intentionally stress the body, then allow it to rest, so the fitness level after the rest is greater than before the stressful workout. This concept is called "over compensation."

Supercompensation, however, is a fine line to ride. Too much stress and the body will break down, resulting in illness or injury. Too little stress and no progress is made. Getting yourself into peak condition will require science and art. Science comes from laboratory studies. Art is knowing when to follow a plan exactly and when to make deviations. Chapter 10 will help by giving guidance on science and art.

INTENSITY

So how do you know how fast to ride? We will use heart rate intensity zones and perceived exertion levels to guide the training in this book. Table 7.1 lists seven heart rate training zones, the percent of lactate threshold heart rate those zones are, the Borg Scale of Perceived Exertion, a col-

TABLE 7.1				
TRAINING AND RACING INTENSITIES BASED ON LACATE THRESHOLD HEART RATE				
Zone (Intensity)	% of Lactate Threshold Heart Rate (Bike)	Rating of Perceived Exertion	Breathing	Purpose
1	65-81	6-9	Hardly noticeable	Recovery
2	82-88	10-12	Slight	Aerobic
3	89-93	13-14	Aware of breathing a little harder	Tempo
4	94-100	15-16	Starting to breathe hard	Subthreshold
5a	100-102	17	Breathing hard	Superthreshold
5b	103-105	18-19	Heavy, labored breathing	Aerobic Capacity
5c	106+	20	Maximal exertion in breathing	Anaerobic Capacity

From "The Cyclist's Training Bible" by Joe Friel, 1996. Adapted by permission.

umn that correlates breathing to the various levels of exertion, and the purpose of each training zone.

ENERGY PRODUCTION

Before discussing each training zone, it is important to understand energy production within the body. Our bodies need to have a continuous supply of energy, even to sleep. Energy is supplied by complex chemical reactions. The end result of these chemical reactions is a rich compound called adenosine triphosphate or ATP. The potential energy within the ATP molecule is utilized for all energy-requiring processes of the cells of your body.

There are two basic methods your body uses to produce ATP. One method is aerobically—with oxygen—and the second method is anaerobically or without the presence of oxygen. The method of energy production your body uses depends on the rate of demand for energy, or intensity, and the length of demand for energy, or duration. Short bursts of high speed utilize the anaerobic system of energy production to fuel the muscles. For longer efforts, fat and glycogen are burned in the presence of oxygen to create ATP.

A small amount of energy is readily available to be utilized "on demand." For example, when you sprint to make it through an intersection before the light changes, a small amount of energy is needed instantly. The majority of the energy necessary for this sprint was created anaerobically. After you've made it through the intersection, a slower speed is resumed and energy is created mostly by aerobic means.

For short sprints, energy is created anaerobically and uses ATP stored in the muscle cells to complete the work. ATP is stored in the cell in limited quantities and is readily available, but is used quickly. Aerobically produced ATP, on the other hand, takes more time for the body to produce, but it is available in huge quantities. These large quantities of energy allow a cyclist to ride for several hours at easy to moderate speeds.

The energy production system within the body is quite complex. It is important to note that although a cyclist may be riding along at a moderate pace, some of the energy it takes to do so is produced anaerobically. In other words, both systems are working at the same time. As the intensity of riding increases, energy production and utilization is needed at an elevated pace. Recall that the aerobic system needs time to produce energy; it is not as quick as the anaerobic system.

So, as the riding pace increases, the more the body relies on anaerobic energy production.

One of the byproducts of one of the anaerobic energy production systems is lactic acid. Lactic acid is often viewed as an evil demon, but in fact, it is an energy source for the body. When given enough time, the body can process and use lactic acid to produce ATP. Lactate is present in the blood at rest. Even while sitting and reading this book, there are low levels of lactate circulating in your blood stream.

At low levels, lactic acid is not a problem. As you continue to increase your workout intensity, your body increases energy production, relying more heavily on anaerobic metabolism. More reliance on anaerobic metabolism means the lactate level in your blood begins to increase. When your body can no longer process lactic acid fast enough, and lactate begins to accumulate at an increasing rate in the blood, the condition is called onset of blood lactate accumulation (OBLA), or lactate threshold. This accumulation is closely correlated with heart rate and ventilitory rate. Athletes can often tell when they have reached lactate threshold because their breathing becomes labored and they begin to feel "burning" in their muscles.

If athletes exceed lactate threshold pace, they can only sustain the increased pace for a few minutes before the discomfort forces them to slow down. The margin by which lactate threshold is exceeded is inversely proportional to the time the athlete is able to sustain that pace. In other words, if an athlete's lactate threshold heart rate is 162 and they push their heart rate to 172, they will be able to hold that pace for a shorter period of time than if they were working at a heart rate of 164. Lactate threshold and its correlating average heart rate is roughly the pace that can be held for approximately one hour when participating in a single sport. For example, lactate threshold for cycling is approximately the pace and average heart rate that can be held by a highly fit athlete for a 40km time trial on the bicycle.

Lactate threshold typically occurs at 55 to 65 percent of VO_2 max in healthy, untrained people. In highly trained endurance athletes, lactate threshold is often greater than 80 percent of VO_2 max. Lactate threshold is trainable. In other words, you can train your body to process lactate at higher percentages of your VO_2 max, which means increased levels of speed before the onset of discomfort forces you to stop.

Studies have shown lactate threshold to be a reliable predictor for endurance race performance. However, VO_2 max is not nearly as reliable. So, if you have been tested for VO_2 max and your numbers weren't stellar, don't panic.

TESTING

There are various ways to estimate lactate threshold. One way is to go to a laboratory for a graded exercise test. In this test, the exercise work load is incrementally increased and blood samples are taken at specific intervals to measure the level of lactate in the blood. Also at a laboratory, during a graded exercise test, the ratio of oxygen to carbon dioxide being expelled from your respiratory system can be measured and used to estimate lactate threshold.

Keep in mind that lactate threshold and corresponding

1 ZONE	2 ZONE	3 ZONE	4 ZONE	5a ZONE	5b ZONE	5c ZONE
Recovery	Aerobic	Tempo	Sub-Threshold	Super-Threshold	Aerobic Capacity	Anaerobic Capacity
90-108	109-122	123-128	129-136	137-140	141-145	146-150
91-109	110-123	124-129	130-137	138-141	142-146	147-151
91-109	110-124	125-130	131-138	139-142	143-147	148-152
92-110	111-125	126-130	131-139	140-143	144-147	148-153
92-111	112-125	126-131	132-140	141-144	145-148	149-154
93-112	113-126	127-132	133-141	142-145	146-149	150-155
93-112	113-127	128-133	134-142	143-145	146-150	151-156
94-113	114-128	129-134	135-143	144-147	148-151	152-157
95-114	115-129	130-135	136-144	145-148	149-152	153-158
95-115	116-130	131-136	137-145	146-149	150-154	155-159
97-116	117-131	132-137	138-146	147-150	151-155	156-161
97-117	118-132	133-138	139-147	148-151	152-156	157-162
98-118	119-133	134-139	140-148	149-152	153-157	158-163
98-119	120-134	135-140	141-149	150-153	154-158	159-164
99-120	121-134	135-141	142-150	151-154	155-159	160-165
100-121	122-135	136-142	143-151	152-155	156-160	161-166
100-122	132-136	137-142	143-152	153-156	157-161	162-167
101-123	124-137	138-143	144-153	154-157	158-162	163-168
101-124	125-138	139-144	145-154	155-158	159-163	164-169
102-125	126-138	139-145	146-155	156-159	160-164	165-170
103-126	1267-140	141-146	147-156	157-160	161-165	166-171
104-127	128-144	142-147	148-157	158-161	162-167	168-173
104-128	128-142	143-148	148-158	159-162	163-168	169-174
105-129	130-143	144-148	149-159	160-163	164-169	170-175
106-129	130-143	144-150	151-160	161-164	165-170	171-176
106-130	131-144	145-151	152-161	162-165	166-171	172-177
107-131	132-145	146-152	153-162	163-166	167-172	173-178
107-132	133-146	147-153	154-163	164-167	168-173	174-179
108-133	134-147	148-154	155-164	165-168	169-174	175-180
109-134	135-148	149-154	155-165	166-169	170-175	176-181
109-134	135-148	149-154	155-165	166-169	170-175	176-181
109-135	136-149	150-155	156-166	167-170	171-176	177-182
110-136	137-150	151-156	157-167	168-171	172-177	178-183
111-137	138-151	152-157	158-168	169-172	173-178	179-185
112-138	139-151	152-158	159-169	170-173	174-179	180-186
112-139	140-152	153-160	161-170	171-174	175-180	181-187
113-140	141-153	154-160	161-171	172-175	176-181	182-188
113-141	142-154	155-161	162-172	173-176	177-182	183-189
114-142	143-155	156-162	163-173	174-177	178-183	184-190
115-143	144-156	157-163	164-174	175-178	179-184	185-191
115-144	145-157	158-164	165-175	176-179	180-185	186-192
116-145	146-158	159-165	166-176	177-180	181-186	187-193
116-146	147-159	160-166	167-177	178-181	182-187	188-194
117-147	148-160	161-166	167-178	179-182	183-188	189-195
118-148	149-160	161-167	168-179	180-183	184-190	191-197
119-149	150-161	162-168	169-180	181-184	185-191	192198
119-150	151-162	163-170	171-181	182-185	186-192	193-199
120-151	152-163	164-171	172-182	183-186	187-193	194-200
121-152	153-164	165-172	173-183	184-187	188-194	195-201
121-153	154-165	166-172	173-184	185-188	191-195	196-202
122-154	155-166	167-173	174-185	186-189	190-196	197-203
122-155	156-167	168-174	175-186	187-190	191-197	198-204
123-156	157-168	169-175	176-187	188-191	192-198	199-205
124-157	158-169	170-176	177-188	189-192	193-199	200-206
124-158	159-170	171-177	178-189	190-193	194-200	201-207
125-159	160-170	171-178	179-190	191-194	195-201	202-208
125-160	161-171	172-178	179-191	192-195	196-202	203-209
126-161	162-172	173-179	180-192	193-196	197-203	204-210
127-162	163-173	174-180	181-193	194-197	198-204	205-211
127-163	164-174	175-181	182-194	195-198	199-205	206-212

TABLE 7.2

heart rate will vary by sport. For example, triathletes typi-cally experience lactate threshold heart rates on the bicy-cle that are five to ten beats lower than their running lactate threshold heart rates.

There are also ways to estimate lactate threshold in the field. In order to get the best estimates for lactate threshold, you will need to be rested and highly motivated. If you do the test when tired, the results may be skewed. These tests are not intended to find your maximum heart rate. If you have any con-cerns about doing such tests, seek the advice of your physician first. It is not wise to conduct the tests as some of your first workouts, after being inactive for a long period of time. For all

of the tests, you'll need a wireless heart rate monitor.

Before beginning the tests to estimate lactate threshold, have a look at Table 7.1. It has a column titled "Rating of perceived exertion (Borg Scale)" and a column titled "Breathing." The Borg Scale was originally designed to correlate with heart rate for young athletes by adding zero to all the Borg numbers. For example, easy exercise at a perceived exertion value of six was intended to correlate to a heart rate of sixty. Although the numbers do not always correlate exactly to heart rate, the perceived exertion scale can be very valuable and is still widely used.

When trying to determine your own lactate threshold, the perceived exertion rating, breathing, and heart rate will be the numbers you will want to record. When doing the test, keep a copy of the Borg Scale handy, so you can refer to the exertion rating and the correlated breathing rate.

INDOOR TEST FOR ESTIMATING LACTATE THRESHOLD

To estimate lactate threshold, a preferable method involves using a CompuTrainer. The newer models of CompuTrainers have a calibration feature so that the instrument can be calibrated for each test, and accurate retesting can be done at a later date. The use of the CompuTrainer method makes it easy for a coach or assistant to note ventilatory threshold (VT) and perceived exertion for the athlete by standing next to them. Exertion and noticeable change in ventilation are best recorded while the test is in progress, instead of trying to recall the information later.

COMPUTRAINER TEST FOR ESTIMATING
LACTATE THRESHOLD

For those of you who already have a CompuTrainer, you'll note this test is different than the one using ergometer-calibration software in the instruction manual. Many athletes use this test because the athlete controls the power output, instead of the assistant.

Equipment and assistance

Recruit an assistant with clipboard, paper, pencil and a CompuTrainer. You can create your own data sheet, using the piece of paper, or make a copy of Appendix D.

Warm up on the CompuTrainer for about ten minutes and calibrate according to the instructions in the manual. Re-insert the Nintendo stereo jack into the handlebar control unit.

Set "Program" to "Road Races/Courses," program 70.

Program the course to ten miles, although you won't use the entire distance.

Input your body weight plus the bike weight and record this test data on your log sheet for later reference.

Turn "Drafting" off.

Procedure

During the test, you will hold a predetermined power level—plus or minus 5 watts—as displayed on the monitor. Begin the test at 50 watts and increase by 20 watts every minute until you can no longer continue—meaning you can't sustain the power plus or minus 5 watts, or your perceived exertion is too high. Stay seated throughout the test.

FIGURE 7.2

NAME   BG

DATE   9/6/96

BIKE AND RIDER WEIGHT   128 + 23 = 151

LACTATE THRESHOLD TEST DATA SHEET

WATTS	HEARTRATE	RATING OF PERCEIVED EXERTION
50	106	6
70	109	7
90	118	7
110	125	9
130	130	10
150	134	10
170	142	12
190	147	12
210	154	13
230	157	14
250	159	15
270	164	16
290	165	16 *NOTED VT
310	166	17
330	169	19
350	170	19
370		
390		
410		
430		
450		
470		
490		
510		
530		
550		
570		

ZONE	RPE	BREATHING
1	6-9	Hardly noticeable
2	10-12	Slight
3	13-14	Aware of breathing a little harder
4	15-16	Starting to breathing hard
5a	17	Breathing hard
5b	18-19	Heavy, labored breathing
5c	20	Maximal exertion noted in breathing

NOTES ABOUT BIKE SET-UP, CURRENT TRAINING STATUS, HOW YOU FEEL:

1) BG FELT GOOD AND WELL RESTED

2) VT SEEMED TO OCCUR AT 290 WATTS

FIGURE 7.3

Heart rate data plot for BG

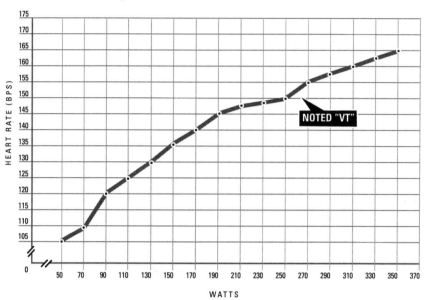

You can change gears any time.

At the end of each minute, tell your assistant how great your perceived exertion is for the particular wattage completed. Use the Borg Scale shown on Table 7.1. In other words, on a scale of six to twenty—six being very easy and twenty being very, very hard—how hard does holding each particular wattage feel to you? Keep the scale easily visible, so you can grade your exertion.

The assistant will record your exertion rating and heart rate at the end of the minute and instruct you to increase power to the next level. She or he can also encourage you to keep power at the designated intensity. If you have a heart rate monitor such as the Polar Accurex, XTrainer Plus, and no assistant, you can keep your own heart rate stored at each "lap" minute. You will have to mentally note the perceived exertion, or try to jot it down on the form in Appendix D.

Your assistant will listen closely to your breathing to detect when it becomes labored and deep. She or he will note the associated heart rate with the beginning of labored breathing and note "VT."

Continue until you can no longer hold the power level for at least fifteen seconds, or you feel you do not want to go on.

The data should look similar that shown on Figure 7.2. VT heart rate and power is usually comparable to a perceived exertion rating in the range of fifteen to seventeen and closely estimates lactate threshold. To help confirm this, realize that athletes are seldom able to go more than three to five minutes beyond their lactate threshold on this test.

Create an "XY" graph with the vertical coordinate representing heart rate and the horizontal coordinate as wattage. Plot the data points from the test onto a chart and connect them, similar to the chart shown on Figure 7.3. Lactate threshold can be estimated by using three references:

a.) Note the heart rate at which point breathing becomes labored—ventilitory threshold—which is quite subjective.

b.) Lactate threshold is usually between fifteen and seventeen on the Rating of Perceived Exertion scale.

c.) Lactate threshold is usually no more than five data points from the end of the test—when the test subject wishes to stop.

If ventilitory threshold, found in (a) does not agree with (b) and (c), disregard it.

You can use this chart, the power you achieved at lactate threshold and your current body weight for benchmarks of

145

improvement, which is discussed later in this chapter.

Now that you have an estimate for lactate threshold heart rate, use Figure 7.2 to calculate your training zones. The training zones will need to be confirmed. Compare the heart rates and perceived exertion you achieved during the test with your exertion levels and heart rates during workouts and races. Your training zones may need slight modification. Be aware that lactate threshold can change with improved fitness, particularly for beginners.

OUTDOOR TEST FOR ESTIMATING
LACTATE THRESHOLD

Find an eight-mile course you can ride, in which there are no stop signs and limited traffic. After a good warm up, do a time trial on the course. This means "all out," as fast as you can go for eight miles. You will need to either mentally notice the average heart rate during the time trial, or use a heart rate monitor with an average function. It is best to have the averaging function. Do not use the maximum heart rate you saw during your test as the average. After the test, recall your average heart rate for the eight-mile test. This average heart rate is approximately 101 percent of lactate threshold. For example, if your average heart rate for the test was 165, 165 divided by 1.01, which equals 163 for lactact threshold heart rate.

If you happen to do an eight-mile time trial in some sort of a race, use 105 percent as your multiplier. In the example mentioned in the last paragraph, you would use 165 divided by 1.05, which equals 157. Why use a different multiplier if the time trial was an actual race compared to

TABLE 7.3		
PREDICTING LACTATE-THRESHOLD PULSE RATE FROM AN INDIVIDUAL TIME TRIAL AVERAGE HEART RATE		
Distance of ITT	**As Race**	**As Workout**
5K	110% of LT	104% of LT
10k	107% of LT	102% of LT
8-10 miles	105% of LT	101% of LT
40k	100% of LT	97% of LT

a workout? Because we are typically able to push ourselves much harder in a race than a workout.

What if your optimal course is shorter than eight miles? Can that be used? Yes. A list of time trial distances and their various multipliers are listed on Table 7.3. If you are in the beginning stages of improving your cycling, you may be better off to use one of the shorter time trial distances, such as 5km. As you improve season after season, you can increase the time trial distance or continue to use a distance in the 3.1 (5km) to 4-mile range.

TRAINING ZONES

You are now armed with an estimated lactate threshold and seven training zones. Here is more information about each zone:

ZONE 1

Zone 1 riding is used for recovery purposes. It is also used in conjunction with Zone 2 to build volume of riding hours and base fitness.

ZONE 2

Zone 2 riding is used for building base fitness and maintaining current levels of fitness.

ZONE 3

Zone 3 riding is used for early season tempo riding to begin lactate threshold improvement. Zones 1 through 3 are used extensively for events lasting longer than about three hours.

ZONE 4

This zone is used in conjunction with intervals, hill riding and tempo rides to improve lactate threshold speed and muscular endurance. It is common for the intervals in this zone have a work to rest ratio of 3 or 4:1.

ZONE 5A

This zone is used in conjunction with intervals, hill riding and tempo rides to improve lactate threshold speed and muscular endurance. It is typically used after some Zone 4 work has already been done.

ZONE 5B

The major use for this zone is to improve speed endurance. The intervals in this zone have a work to rest ratio of 1:1. This zone is also used in hill work.

ZONE 5C

Zone 5c is fast, really fast, powerful riding. Climbing hills out of the saddle elicit heart rates in 5c zone. Riding in Zone 5c cannot be maintained for long periods of time. It is common for the intervals in this zone have a work to rest ratio of 1:2 or more.

The comments for each zone are not all-inclusive, but give an idea of the uses for each particular training zone.

TESTS TO CHECK FOR PROGRESS

How do you know if your training plan is working? Because race or tour conditions, group tactics, and sometimes event courses can change from season to season, your event results can be a misleading measure of fitness and training. For these reasons, I suggest athletes measure training progress on regular intervals such as every four, six or eight weeks with each test preceded by reduced volume and rest.

Chapter 10 has more information on periodization plan construction and the use of rest weeks. Athletes should take a rest week every three to four weeks. During the rest week, volume is reduced and intensity is kept in some of the workouts. Some of the intense, or fast workouts can be fitness testing. I like to use standard tests that can be repeated each rest week. It is best if the tests are done under circumstances that are repeatable.

In order to know if you are improving or not, reduce as many external variables as possible such as wind, rain, temperature extremes and course changes. The easiest way to do this is on an indoor trainer.

AEROBIC TIME TRIALS

Early in the fitness-building plan, do aerobic time trials. As mentioned previously, these are done during the rest week. An aerobic time trial is done at a particular heart rate. In this case, it is Lactate Threshold Heart Rate (LTHR) minus nine to eleven beats. For example, if your cycling LTHR is one hundred sixty-three, your aerobic time trial is done at a heart rate between 152 and 154.

If you have access to a CompuTrainer, with the calibration mode, you can ride a five-mile time trial and be reasonably sure the resistance against your tire will be repeatable for the next time trial. You need to make certain, however, that you calibrate the trainer each time you test.

Procedure for aerobic time trial on CompuTrainer

Select a gear you can turn the cranks at eighty-five to one hundred twenty revolutions per minute (rpm) for the entire time trial. You won't change gears during the test. Before the time trial, warm up in heart rate zones 1 and 2 for twenty to thirty minutes.

Toward the end of the warm-up, elevate your heart rate into the aerobic time trial zone.

Go right into the time trial, not stopping to rest or stretch out. Ride five miles steadily in the designated heart rate zone.

After the time trial, spin easily in order to cool down and stretch.

In your workout journal record the date, the gear used, time for the five-mile time trial and any comments. Keep all your cycling time-trial data in a single location so the information can be referenced and compared at a later date.

What if you don't have a CompuTrainer? A regular trainer will work, if you have a cyclometer with a rear wheel pick-up. Understand that this test will not be as accurate as a test completed on equipment that can be calibrated. Do your best to set-up the trainer and bicycle exactly the same, each time you do the test. For example, make certain the tire pressure is the same each time. Take as many measurements as you can, to ensure your tire puts the same amount of pressure on the roller as it did the last time you tested. You will not be able to measure tire or roller wear, but you can measure physical distances between the bicycle and the trainer. For example, use the distance from the center of the rear skewer to the roller surface. Keep the measurements in the same notebook as your results, so they can be used on future tests.

Procedure for aerobic time trial on a wind trainer

Select a gear and trainer tension you can turn the cranks at eighty-five to one hundred twenty rpm for the entire time trial. You won't change gears during the test. Before the time trial, warm up in heart rate zones 1 and 2 for twenty to thirty minutes.

Toward the end of the warm-up, elevate your heart rate into the aerobic time trial zone.

Go right into the time trial, not stopping to rest or stretch out. Ride five miles steadily, in the designated heart rate zone.

After the time trial, spin easily in order to cool down and stretch.

In your workout journal record the date, the gear used, time for the five-mile time trial, any special bike set-up notes, and any comments. Keep all your cycling time trial data in a single location so the information can be referenced at a later date.

When you did the test in subsequent sessions, did the test seem easier, but your time didn't improve? Did the test seem too easy? Did you have trouble getting your bike set up on the trainer? Did you just change tires? Did you have trouble getting your heart rate into the aerobic zone? Comments like these may tell you if your set-up contributed to poor results.

AS-FAST-AS-YOU-CAN-GO TIME TRIALS

Another method to chart progress involves the lactate threshold heart rate testing outlined earlier in the chapter. If you used the eight-mile, outdoor time trial to estimate lactate threshold, use that test again to measure training progress. Did your average heart rate change? Were you able to ride the course in less time? Jot notes in your training journal about the weather conditions and how you felt.

Eight-mile time trials can also be done on an indoor trainer. Some people find an all-out time trial done indoors to be self-inflicted torture; but if the time trials are done on a trainer that can be calibrated, variable weather is eliminated and the time trials tend to have more reliable information.

You can also use the CompuTrainer lactate threshold test as another indicator of fitness. In this case, you will compare your heart rates at the various power levels. Riding at the

FIGURE 7.5

Example of improvements made in a year

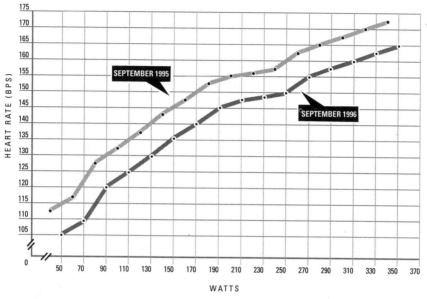

same wattage increments, with a lower heart rate marks progress. You can also use the data to compare your fitness levels, year after year. Figure 7.5 shows BG's fitness improvements. BG measured fitness in September of 1995 and '96. As you can see in 1996, BG was able to produce higher wattages for the given heart rates, compared to '95. Or, another way to look at it, BG was able to ride any particular wattage at less cost—a lower heart rate. The 1996 improvements also allowed the achievement of a higher maximum wattage.

Another marker of improvement using the CompuTrainer lactate threshold test is the ability to achieve a higher wattage at lactate threshold in relation to body weight. Some people lose weight only to lose muscle mass and power. If your lactate threshold power (LTP) was 300 watts and your body weight (BW) was 128 pounds, your lactate threshold power as a function of body weight (LTP/BW) equals 2.34. If you maintained 300 watts as your LTP, but lost 10 pounds, your LTP/BW would equal 2.54. If you lost that 10 pounds and your LTP also decreased to 250 watts, your LTP/BW would be 2.12. So, if you lost weight in an effort to go faster and also lost power, the weight reduction did not improve speed.

BAD TEST RESULTS

What happens if your test data shows no improvement, or worse yet, shows that fitness or speed is degrading? Does that mean your season is heading down the tubes? Is your training completely off? Not necessarily. Some athletes may do poorly in one of their tests and within a week have a personal best performance in a race. What's that all about?

Sometimes, test data will show no improvement, even when you know you are getting stronger. The data may show slow numbers because you were on the edge of becoming ill, you were tired from a restless night, or you were unmotivated to do the test. I suggest athletes pay close attention to their subjective test and training comments in addition to raw test results. If one test turned up slowly, but other workouts show you are making significant progress, don't make drastic changes to your training just yet.

By doing time trials and data collection, you can chart your progress throughout the season and from one season to the next. You can use the data to make changes in your training or as reinforcement that your training is going well. This information can be more accurate and timely than a race situation in order to help you shape your training for the season.

BRIEF THOUGHTS

The utilization of training intensity zones is important to fitness improvement. A heart rate monitor is a valuable tool that can give immediate feedback on exercise intensity. Exercising heart rate, in conjunction with regular time trials, can measure training progress. Time trials, exercise journal information, and subjective feelings are all tools to evaluate training progress.

REFERENCES

Burke, E. R., Ph.D., Serious Cycling, Human Kinetics, 1995.

Edwards, S., The Heart Rate Monitor Book, Polar Electro Oy, 1992.

Friel, J., The Cyclist's Training Bible, VeloPress, Boulder, CO, 1996.

Janssen, P. G. J. M., Training Lactate Pulse-Rate, Polar Electro Oy, 1987.

Martin, D. E., Ph. D., Coe, P. N., Better Training for Distance Runners, Second Edition, Human Kinetics, 1997.

McArdle, W., et al., Exercise Physiology, Energy, Nutrition, and Human Performance, Third Edition, Lea & Febiger Publishing, 1991.

CHAPTER EIGHT

Strength
training *and*
stretching

She came to cycling from a running background. Standing 5-feet 1-inch, 105 pounds, her physique was one of a distance runner: slight upper body, thin arms and powerful legs. When she first began to cycle she didn't have the upper-body strength to pump her tires past 80 pounds per square inch (psi); they required 120 psi. She credits a weight training program for her gains in upper- and lower-body strength. She is now capable of pumping her own tires to 120 psi. She enjoys other sports such as hunting and backpacking. Her husband noticed her strength gains on backpacking trips because she is capable of handling heavier loads for longer periods of time. She notices her strength because she's capable of doing many things she couldn't do before her weight training program, and she likes the look of those new muscles.

More athletes are turning to strength training to enhance their performance in endurance events. Others are still holdouts, fearing the gym may turn them into hulking-human specimens, capable of power-lifting small cars. Not to worry, though, cyclists shouldn't weight train like a power lifter or body builder because their fitness goals are different.

Consider that our natural maximal, muscular strength is achieved sometime in our twenties or early thirties. For this reason, anyone over thirty years old should invest some time into a strength training program. The older you are, the more you need the gym.

Women tend to be approximately 50-percent weaker in the upper body and 30-percent weaker in the lower body than men. This measure is for average men and average women, and is in terms of absolute strength. Athletic women are generally stronger than non-athletic women; however, they are generally not as strong as athletic men in the same sport. Much of this strength difference is due to hormonal factors, which give males greater muscle mass. Although women may not have goals to be as strong as men within their sport, they can, however, use a weight training program to increase their strength per pound of body mass and lean muscle mass.

Some of the adaptations that occur when we strength train are increased muscle fiber size; increased muscle contractile strength; and increased tendon, bone and ligament tensile strength. These changes are thought to improve physical capacity, economy, metabolic function; decrease injury risk; and help you look darn good.

"I may look good, but will I be faster?" There have been studies on trained and untrained sedentary cyclists, with both groups experiencing positive results. In one study, untrained cyclists who strength trained for twelve weeks improved their cycling endurance by 33 percent and lactate thresholds by an average of 12 percent, while their control group, who did no training, made no gains.

In a separate study on trained cyclists, the addition of a strength-training program increased their cycling endurance by 20 percent, allowing them to pedal fourteen minutes longer, before fatigue set in. They also increased short-term, high-intensity endurance performance in the four- to eight-minute range, by 11 percent.

In addition to performance increases, a weight training program can prevent bone loss and even increase bone mass, as has been mentioned in previous chapters, which is critical to the prevention of osteoporosis. How important a weight training program may be to endurance athletes is not quantitatively known at this time.

STARTING A STRENGTH TRAINING PROGRAM

The benefits of strength training are sending more women to the weight room to pump iron. The large men who train to be body builders, powerlifters, or simply train to be large may intimidate some women. Most of these men are courteous, helpful and willing to share the equipment. If uncomfortable in your own gym, perhaps it's time to change gyms. Find a place where you can be comfortable exercising on any piece of equipment.

It's also comforting to know no one was born with the knowledge to use all the pieces of equipment in the gym nor were they born with perfect weight-lifting form. When you're just beginning a weight-training program, ask for help. This book is a guide, but it is also worthwhile to ask one of the trainers at the gym to help with setting up weight-training machines and with proper lifting form. When seeking help, ask someone you trust to recommend a trainer and ask the trainer for his or her credentials.

The strength-training exercises in this book are intended to augment your cycling program. If you desire more body sculpting, consult a trainer or a book written for that purpose. Because many cyclists are trying to juggle fitness, family and job responsibilities, this particular strength-training program minimizes weight room time while maximizing the benefits to a cycling program. Some guidelines for this program are to:

• focus on the muscle groups that do the majority of work on the bike.

• make multijoint exercises the priority, and do single-joint exercises as time allows. For example, squats, which are described later in the chapter, use three joints: the hip, knee and ankle. Knee extensions use only the knee joint.

• when appropriate, mimic positions and movements of cycling as close as possible.

• always include abdominal and lower back exercises to strengthen your torso. Although cycling primarily uses legs, it takes a strong torso to climb hills, sprint, maintain balance, and bridge a gap to the cyclists ahead.

Strength-training fitness precedes on-bike fitness. Some of the training programs outlined in Chapter 10 do not include all of the strength-training phases listed on Table 8.1. Generally speaking, the more time you have to prepare for an event, the greater variety of training you can do and achieve greater levels of fitness.

• Separate strength training sessions by at least 48 hours.

• Maintain good postural alignment whenever possible. This means when standing in a normal, relaxed position, the head is supported by the neck, which has a normal curvature. The neck, which is part of the spine, also has a curvature that is normal for you. For example, when doing squats, the head and neck should be in a position that allows the curvature of your neck to be in a normal position—head not craned toward the ceiling, or chin at the chest.

• Always, always, always maintain control of the weight on the concentric and the eccentric actions. This means using muscles, not momentum, to lift the weight. It means lowering the weight, using muscles to control the speed, not allowing gravity to do all the work and only using your muscles to stop the weight at the end of the motion.

THE PROGRAM IN DETAIL

Table 8.1 is in a format that can be copied and taken to the gym, along with the Strength Training Data Sheet in Appendix E. Whether or not you use Appendix E to track strength gains and training program is a personal choice, however a journal of some sort is recommended.

STRENGTH TRAINING PHASES

AA—Anatomical Adaptation

This is the initial phase of strength training that is included at the beginning of a racing season or when someone is just beginning a strength-training program. Its purpose is to prepare tendons and muscles for greater loads in the next strength-training phases.

MS—Maximum Strength

This phase is used to teach the central nervous system to recruit high numbers of muscle fibers. During this phase, it is best to begin the first set with a weight that is much lighter than you think you can handle. Add additional weight on subsequent sets, being careful not to overload and risk injury.

Many athletes find this phase fun because strength gains come quickly as loads increase. Be cautious not to extend this phase beyond the recommended number of weeks. Continuation of this phase for several weeks may result in muscle imbalances, particularly in the upper leg, which could lead to hip or knee injuries.

PE—Power Endurance

This phase develops the capacity to quickly recruit muscle fibers for movement and sustain their operation. Power is the ability to apply a large force over a distance in a short amount of time. In this phase the speed of the lifting motion is fast and, for experienced weight lifters, may be done with an explosive movement. The weight is lowered with a slower movement and under control. Safety and proper lifting technique should never be compromised for speed of movement.

ME—Muscular Endurance

The ME phase of strength training teaches the body to manage fatigue at moderately high load levels by increasing capillary density and the number and size of mitochondria. This phase is beneficial to those who lack race endurance.

PM—Power Maintenance

For the experienced weight lifter, this phase maintains gains made in the PE phase of strength training. These athletes can use the fast movements they used in the PE phase.

For the novice weight lifter, or for someone crunched for time, this phase resembles a more traditional form recommended by many health professionals. The movements are moderate and controlled—no explosive movements. Repetitions are in the ten

TABLE 8.1

STRENGTH TRAINING

Phase	AA	MS	PE	ME	PM	EM
Weeks per phase	4-10	3-6	3-6	2-8	2+	2-3
Days per week	2-3	2	2	1-2	1	1
Exercises *(in order of completion)*	Circuit 123456789	12[35][67]	1[27][63]	1[27][63]	1[27][63]	1[27][63]
Load *(% of 1 rep max)*	40-60	80-95	65-85	30-50	65-85	40-60
Sets	3-5	3-8	3-5	2-4	1-3	1-2
Reps per set	20-30	3-6	8-15	40-60	10-15	30-40
Speed of movement	slow	slow-mod.	fast	mod.	mod.-fast	mod.
Minutes of recovery (between sets)	1-1.5	2-4	3-5	1-2	3-5	1-2

AA phase *Anatomical adaptation*—use this as part of your preseason or base training. This phase helps prepare your body for harder work to come. Complete the exercises in a circuit—complete one set of each exercise, in order, then repeat the circuit.

MS phase *Maximum strength*—this phase follows AA and precedes any significant hill work. It is not recommended to do MS training and racing at the same time. Complete all reps and sets of exercise one before going to exercise two, and so on.

PE phase *Power endurance*—it is a combination of strength (measured as force), distance moved, and the time it takes to move the weight. (Distance covered in time is velocity.) The PE phase follows the MS phase.

ME phase *Muscular endurance*—it follows the PE phase, increases the capillary density, the number and size of mitochondria (energy production sites within the muscles).

PM phase *Power maintenance*—Can be done through the remainder of the season or alternated with EM.

EM phase *Endurance maintenance*—can alternate this with PE through the remainder of the season or it can be eliminated.

Exercises: 1. Hip extension (squat, leg press, step-up); 2. Seated row; 3. ***Back extension; 4. Hip extension (different from No.1); 5. Chest press (bench press or push-up); 6. Personal weakness option***: heel raise, knee extension, or leg curl (time allowing, you can do all of these); 7. ***Abdominals; 8. Dead lift (this is an optional exercise for the experienced strength trainer); 9. Lat pull.

***Continue to use AA load, sets, reps, rest and speed for these exercises.

Before each strength training session, warm up with ten to twenty minutes of aerobic activity. Cool down with ten to twenty minutes of easy spinning on the bike. Do not use running to cool down.

DO NOT do any exercise that causes pain. This includes joints that "pop" or "crack" and sharp pain occurring during the exercise or lasting for days after the lifting session.

Reprinted and modified with permission from Joe Friel's The Cyclist's Training Bible, 1996.

163

to fifteen range, and rest between sets is around three minutes.

EM—Endurance Maintenance

Depending on the needs of the particular athlete, this phase can be used to maintain gains made in the ME phase, by rotating it with the PM phase. Some athletes chose to eliminate EM if endurance is not an area that limits their ability to become a better rider. Other athletes might choose to use EM one day of the week and PM a second day of the week. Athletes who have a job that requires them to travel extensively find this option to be helpful.

WEEKS PER PHASE

For each phase, Table 8.1 recommends the number of weeks per phase. Strength training needs to be blended into an endurance program and should enhance the endurance program, not adversely affect it.

EXERCISES

The recommended exercises are listed at the bottom of Table 8.1 and are shown later in the chapter. Some exercises have more than one option shown. While it is not possible to show all available options for each exercise, it is advantageous for athletes to have more than one choice for each exercise. For the times when the gym gets busy, it is nice to have more than one option. Additionally, exercises that are slightly different, such as the squat and leg press, stimulate muscles in different manners. The end result is a greater number of muscle fibers stimulated by slightly varying the routine either within a week, or from week to week. For example, if you lift on Tuesday and Thursday, during the PM phase, use squats on Tuesday and leg press on Thursday.

In the AA phase, lifting can be completed in a "circuit," meaning that you complete the first set of all the exercises before completing the second set. Sometimes this is a problem in a busy weight room, particularly for hip-extension exercises. If a crowded weight room is an issue, go ahead and complete all of the sets of hip extension, for example, before moving to the next exercise.

The order of completion of exercises in the other phases is such that all sets and repetitions of each exercise are completed before moving on to the next exercise. The exceptions are the exercises in [brackets] that can be completed in "superset" format. Superset means alternating between the exercises within the brackets before moving on to the next exercise.

LOAD

The load estimates are given in terms of 1 Rep Max, or the maximum weight you could lift only once. It is not recommended that you attempt to find your 1 Rep Max—rather estimate it by finding the amount of weight you can lift ten times, then divide that number by 0.75. For example, if you can leg press 150 pounds ten times, maybe eleven, but no more, divide 150 by 0.75 to estimate your 1 Rep Max as 200 pounds.

Another way to estimate load is to begin with a weight that is embarrassingly easy. Slowly keep increasing the weight until you can only lift the number of repetitions listed for any particular phase.

SETS

The number of repeated lifting bouts done at any particular exercise.

REPETITIONS PER SET

This is the number of repetitions done within each set at any particular exercise. For example, during the PM phase, the athlete will do a hip extension exercise one to three times and each time they do the exercise, they will lift the weight ten to fifteen times.

SPEED OF MOVEMENT

The recommended speed is subjective; however, the weight must be controlled in both directions of movement. The phase carrying the biggest concern is the PE phase. Novice athletes—those in their first two years of strength training—should not try for highly explosive moves.

MINUTES OF RECOVERY

Each phase has recommended recovery times between sets. These times are important for each phase. For example, the MS phase is compromised if the athlete shortens the two- to four-minute recovery times. A shortened recovery time means the athlete would have to reduce the weight, not making full use of the MS phase.

During the recovery time, stretch. Stretching exercises are outlined later in the chapter.

RECOVERY WEEKS

As part of your periodization plan, some weeks you will reduce the volume of your training to rest and recover. This can be applied to strength training by reducing the number of strength training days that week, reducing the time spent

start position   *movement/finish position*

[SQUATS]

in each strength session by reducing the number of sets within a workout, slightly reducing the weight lifted on each exercise, or a combination of any of the three items mentioned.

STRENGTH EXERCISES

SQUATS

Start position

Stand with toes pointing forward about shoulder width apart from inside edge to inside edge.

Movement and finish position

Keeping normal curvature of your back and head forward, squat until your upper thighs are about halfway to being parallel to the floor, around the same angle as the knee bend at the top of the pedal stroke.

- Knees and feet remain pointed forward the entire time.
- Knees remain over the feet, not wandering in or out.
- Return to the start position.

Common errors

- Looking at the floor and bending at the waist, loosing the normal curvature of the spine at the bottom of the lift.
- Squatting too low.
- Placing the feet about 20 inches apart and toes pointing out.
- Knees rock inward on the way up.

Stretches

- Stork stand and triangle

STEP-UP

Start position

- Use dumbbells or a bar loaded with weight.
- Place your left foot on a sturdy platform about mid-shin high, with toes pointing straight ahead.

Movement and finish position

- Step up, using the muscles in your left leg and touch the platform with your right foot, pausing only a moment and

start position   *movement/finish position*

[STEP UP]

return to the starting position

- Knees and feet remain pointed forward the entire time.
- Return to the start position.
- Complete all repetitions working the left leg, then repeat with the right leg.

Common errors

- Looking at the floor and bending at the waist.
- Allowing the toes to point out.
- Allowing the knees to sway in or out.
- Toeing off the bottom leg. In the example above, it would be pushing off of the right leg to make the step, instead of using the

start position

movement/finish position

[LEG PRESS]

muscles in the left leg to make the motion.

Stretches

Stork stand and triangle

LEG PRESS

Start position

• If the seat is adjustable, make the angle of the seat to

the floor twenty to thirty degrees.

• Place your feet flat on the platform about 8 inches apart with toes pointing forward.

Movement and finish position

• Press the platform away from you, until your legs are straight, knees almost locked.

• Lower the platform until your upper and lower leg form an eighty- to ninety-degree angle.

• Knees and feet remain pointed forward and about 8 inches or shoulder width apart the entire time.

• Keep your knees aligned with your hips and ankles during the entire motion up and down.

• Return to the start position.

Common errors

• Placing feet too high on the platform, such that the ankles are in front of the knee joint.

• Placing feet too low and heels hang off the platform.

• Raising heels off of the platform during the lift phase.

• Lowering the platform so that your knees touch your chest. This generally relaxes some of the muscles that should be working, lifts your butt off the seat pad, rocks your pelvis forward, and eliminates the normal curvature of the spine.

• Not controlling the weight in both directions.

Stretches

Stork stand and triangle.

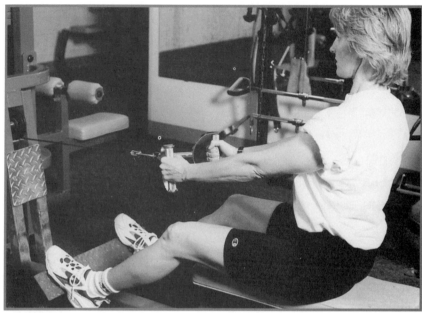

start position

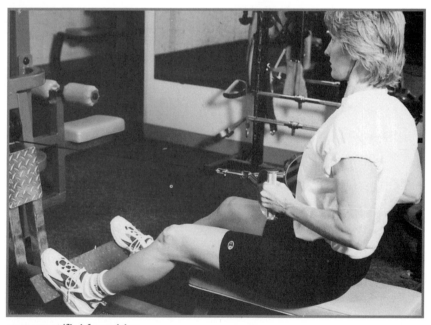

movement/finish position

[SEATED ROW]

SEATED ROW

Start position

• Use a handle that puts your hands in a position similar to holding the hoods of your bicycle handlebars. At many gyms there will be two handles available, use the widest one. Or use one of the short bars available at most gyms and put your hands the same distance apart as holding the handlebar top.

• Seated, with your torso and legs forming close to a ninety-degree angle, place your feet flat on the footplates.

• Head and neck are upright, eyes looking forward.

• Elbows are nearly straight when handles are held at arm's length and there is tension in the cable.

• Shoulder blades are relaxed and separated (abducted.)

Movement and finish position

• The pull is initiated by retracting the shoulder blades together, then pulling the bar toward the chest, leading with your elbows.

• After a brief pause at the chest, return the handle to the start position by moving first at the elbows, then the shoulders.

• After the elbows are nearly straight, allow the shoulder blades to separate slightly, returning to the start position.

• The back should remain still throughout the entire exercise, only flexing to return the bar to the floor when the exercise is complete.

• Abdominal muscles remain contracted to stabilize the torso.

Common errors

• Flexing or bending at the waist and using the back to

start position

movement/finish position

[BACK EXTENSION (FLOOR)]

initiate the movement.

• The shoulder blades must be abducted first, in order to train the muscles of the upper back.

Stretches

• Pulldown

BACK EXTENSION (FLOOR)

Start position

• Lying face down on the floor, place your hands next to

your armpits, fingers pointing forward.

Movement and finish position
• Using your back muscles, raise your chest off the ground, keeping pelvic bones on the floor.
• Your neck remains aligned with your spine, maintaining it's normal curvature.
• Your arms are used minimally.
• Pause for a moment.
• Keeping your back muscles contracted, lower your chest back to the starting position.

Common errors
• Attempting to use your head and momentum to get your chest off of the floor.
• Using your arms to push your chest off of the floor.
• Totally relaxing the back muscles when returning to the start position.
• Hyperextending the neck, pushing the chin towards the ceiling.

Stretches
• Squat or pretzel

BACK EXTENSION (PEDESTAL)—FOR THE EXPERIENCED LIFTER

Start position
• Adjust the heel pad, if possible, so it holds your legs

 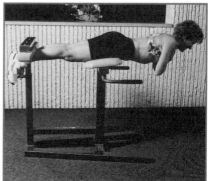

start position   *movement/finish position*

[BACK EXTENSION (PEDESTAL)]

parallel to the ground.

• Begin with your head in the lowest possible position.

• Arms crossed across the chest—a weight can be held across your chest to increase resistance.

Movement and finish position

• Contract the muscles in the back, butt and the back of the legs to raise your head until your back is parallel with the floor.

• Pause for a moment.

• Maintaining body control, lower your head only as far as you can maintain a stable body. When you feel your muscles "give out" and your back relaxes, you've gone too far down.

Common errors

• Not pausing at the top and bottom the exercise.

• Using momentum and swinging the torso up and down.

• Relaxing all muscles when returning to the start position.

start position   *movement/finish position*

[DUMBELL CHEST PRESS]

Stretches

• Squat or pretzel

DUMBBELL CHEST PRESS

Start position

• Lie on your back on a bench with your back in a neutral position, one that allows the normal curvature to be present.

• Feet touching the floor or on the bench, whichever position is most comfortable.

• Weights are held in the hands, aligned with the elbows and shoulder joints—a barbell can be used when going to heavier weight.

Movement and finish position

• Retract the shoulders and squeeze your shoulder blades together.

• Lower the weight, by leading with your elbows, until

your elbows align with your shoulder joints.

• Your upper arm remains perpendicular to the floor throughout the movement.

• Pause for a moment and return to the start position by keeping your hands directly above your elbows throughout the movement.

Common errors

• Allowing the dumbbells to drift toward the centerline of the body or away from the body on the upward movement.

• Arching your back when lifting heavier weights.

• Not retracting the shoulders.

Stretches

• Pulldown

PUSH-UP

Start position

• Begin with hands slightly wider than the shoulders, fingers pointing forward or slightly in.

• The floor contact points will be the hands and either the knees or toes.

Movement and finish position

• Keeping the body rigid, tight abdominal muscles, push your chest away from the floor until your elbows are extended and nearly locked.

• Lower the body back toward the floor, in a controlled

start position

movement/finish position

[PUSH UP]

manner, until the angle between the upper and lower arm is between 90 and 100 degrees.

• Pause for a moment before pushing back up again.

• Keep the head aligned with the body, as if you were in a standing position.

• Repeat the action until all repetitions are complete.

Common errors

• Relaxing all muscles on the downward motion.

 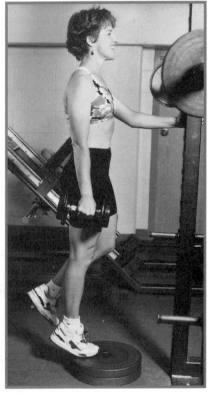

start position   *movement/finish position*

[HEEL RAISE]

• Allowing the body to sag in the middle, arching the back.

Stretches

• Pulldown

HEEL RAISE

Start position

• Use a standing calf raise machine or a riser block.

• Using a standing calf machine, you can work both

legs at once or one at a time.

- Using a riser block, you can either use your body weight or hold a dumbbell.
- Doing single-leg heel raises, point the toe of the working leg forward.
- The ball of your foot is on the platform and heel is as low as possible, allowing you to maintain an eccentric contraction in the calf muscle—calf muscle is not totally relaxed.
- Knee is straight but not locked out.

Movement and finish position

- From the heel down position, contract your calf until you are on the ball of your foot, as high as you can go.
- Pause for a moment at the top position.
- In a controlled manner, return to the start position.
- Complete all repetitions in a set with one leg, then switch legs.

Common errors

- Not going as high as possible.
- Going too low and losing tension on the calf muscle.
- Relaxing the muscles on the down motion.

Stretch

- Wall lean

KNEE EXTENSION

Start position

- Begin with both legs fully extended, with a weight you

 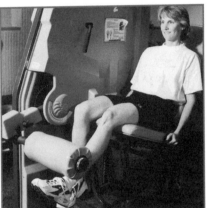

start position   *movement/finish position*
[KNEE EXTENSION]

can lift with a single leg.

• The seat should be adjusted so you have back support and the center of your knee joint aligns with the pivotal joint on the exercise equipment.

• Keep knees and hips aligned throughout the exercise.

Movement and finish position

• Use one leg to lower the weight about 8 inches or just before the point where your quadriceps muscles lose contraction—do not go all the way down.

• *Return to the starting position and pause for a moment.*

• Complete all repetitions in the set, with one leg before switching to the other leg.

Common errors

• Lowering the weight past the point of keeping the quadriceps muscles contracted—you can put your hand on your quadriceps and feel when they are contracted and tight and when they are relaxed.

• Using momentum to swing the weight up and down, instead of using a controlled motion.

    • Arching the back in the lift phase.

    • Allowing your butt to lift off the seat pad.

    • Allowing your knees to rotate in or out.

Stretches

    • Stork stand

LEG CURL

Start position

    • Begin with the support pad a few inches above the heel.

    • Align the center of your knee joint with the pivot point on the equipment.

    • Relax your foot; don't try to flex it.

Movement and finish position

    • Curl one leg up as far as possible.

    • Pause for a moment.

    • Return the rotating arm to the start position, keeping the hamstring muscles contracted.

    • Complete all repetitions in a set, with one leg, before switching to the other leg.

Common errors

    • Not curling the leg as far as possible, stopping short.

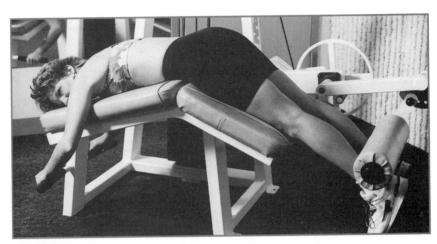

start position

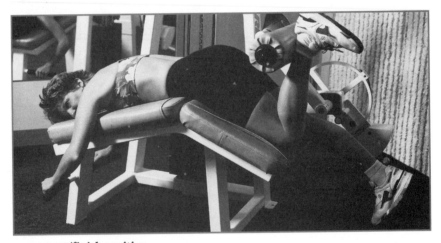

movement/finish position

[LEG CURL]

- Relaxing the hamstring muscles when lowering the weight.
- Arching the back to complete the lift.
- Using momentum to complete the lift.

Stretches
- Triangle

ABDOMINAL CRUNCH

Start position

- Lying on your back, bend your knees so your feet rest comfortably on the floor.
- Hands are behind the head for support—do not pull on the head—or crossed across the chest.
- Feet flat on the floor.

start position

movement/finish position

[AB CRUNCH]

start position   *movement/finish position*

[DEAD LIFT]

Movement and finish position

• Contract your abdominal muscles, bringing your bottom ribs toward your hipbones.

• Your shoulders, neck, and head follow.

• You are as far as you can go when your feet begin to rise off of the floor.

• Pause for a moment, keeping your feet on the floor.

• Slowly lower yourself until you are just before the point of losing the contraction on your abdominal muscles. In other words, don't relax on the floor before the next repetition.

Common errors

- Pulling on the head with the hands.
- Using a rocking motion and momentum, instead of controlling the movement.

Stretches

- While lying on the floor on your back, stretch your hands and feet in opposite directions along the floor.

DEAD LIFT

Start position

- Stand with feet about shoulder width apart and point your toes forward.
- Grasp the barbells with your hands just outside of your thighs.

Movement and finish position

- Keeping your head up and looking straight ahead, use your legs and butt to stand erect, lifting the weights off of the floor—do not straighten the legs and then use your back muscles to lift the weights.
- In the erect position arms are locked straight and knees are slightly bent.
- Again using your leg and butt muscles, lower the weight to near the floor, until your upper legs have about

the same bend as they do at the top of your pedal stroke when you are cycling.

• Complete all repetitions before returning the weights to the floor.

• As you become more experienced, a bar and weight-plates can be used instead of dumbbells.

Common errors

• Straightening the back or the legs separately, instead of simultaneously.

• Bending at the waist and pointing the chest toward the floor.

Stretches

• Stork stand and triangle

LAT PULLDOWN

Start position

• Grasp the bar with arms fully extended and hands about shoulder width apart, palms facing forward.

• Sit down on the bench, feet flat on the ground, and knees bent at about a nienty-degree angle.

• Adjust the thigh pads so they help keep you seated.

Movement and finish position

• Leaning slightly back, pull the bar toward the upper chest, by first depressing the shoulders away from your ears, then retracting the shoulder blades—pulling them together.

start position   *movement/finish position*

[LAT PULLDOWN]

- Follow by pulling with the arms.
- Pause for a moment.
- Return the weight moving the arms, then the shoulders.

Common errors

- Jerking the weight and using a lot of torso movement.
- Leaning back to get the weight started—using your body weight instead of your muscles to move the weight.

Stretches

- Pulldown

STRETCHING

It seems you are either a stretcher, or you are not. Those who stretch are religious about their routine, while those who don't stretch don't see any benefit to doing so, nor do they associate any negative consequences with not stretching.

First let's address two basic types of flexibility: static flexibility and dynamic flexibility. Static flexibility is the range of motion relative to a joint, with little emphasis on speed of movement. An example is hamstring, back and upper back flexibility for people trying to ride in a time-trial position or for those enduring a long ride. Dynamic flexibility is resistance to motion at the joint and involves speed during physical performance. An example of dynamic flexibility is a cyclist jumping out of the saddle to aggressively climb a hill or sprint to catch an opponent. A good cyclist must have both types of flexibility.

Flexibility has been shown to improve neuromuscular coordination, improve physical efficiency, increase blood supply and nutrients to joint structure, improve balance and muscular awareness, improve performance, and improve strength. Improve strength?

A study on swimmers, football players and runners had them do contract-relax flexibility training for the knee extensors and flexors. Contract-relax flexibility training involves a passive stretch of a muscle after an isometric contraction. The athletes did flexibility training for eight weeks, three days per week. The researchers found flexibility training to increase the range of motion of the knee joint by about 6 percent. The scientists also found the stretching to improve knee joint torque. Eccentric knee extension torque increased between 19 and 25 percent, depending on particular velocity of measurement. Eccentric knee flexion torque increased by 16 and 18 percent, again depending on the velocity of measurement. Concentric knee flexion torque increased between 8 and 10 percent, while knee flexion isometric torque increased by 11 percent.

In summary, the contract-relax flexibility training increased the strength of the knee flexors and extensors—hamstrings and quadriceps, respectively, to name some of the major muscles—during eccentric actions. The training also increased the strength of the knee flexors during concentric actions.

HOW TO STRETCH

There are many methods to stretch. The one recommended in this book is called "proprioceptive neuromuscular facilitation" (PNF). There are also many variations on this technique. One easy-to-follow version is:

• static stretch, stretch and hold the muscle for about eight seconds—and remember to breathe.

• contract the same muscle for about eight seconds—leave out the contraction step when stretching during the rest interval of strength training and hold static stretches for about fifteen seconds.

• stretch and hold the stretch, again, for about eight seconds, breathe.

• continue alternating muscle contractions and stretches until you have completed between four and eight static stretches. End with a stretch and not a contraction.

You should find that you are able to stretch farther, or increase your range of motion, each time you repeat the stretch.

STRETCHES FOR CYCLING AND WEIGHT ROOM

The stretches listed in this chapter are ones that can be done while standing up because usually people don't want to sit on the ground in a hot, dirty parking lot after riding their bike in a race or a touring event. Some of the exercises stretch multiple muscles, so they can save time for the hurried athlete. It is best if they are done in the order they are listed. Some of these stretches may or may not work for you. If you want further ideas for stretching exercises, a couple of good resources are "Sport Stretch" by Michael J. Alter, and "Stretching" by Bob Anderson.

STORK STAND: STRETCHES THE QUADRICEPS MUSCLES

While balancing against something—your car, a fence, a wall or your bike—grasp your right foot behind your butt.

Static stretch by gently pulling your foot up and away from your butt.

- Stand erect and keep your hip, knee and ankle in the same plane. In other words, don't allow your knee to drift out from your body.
- Contract by pushing against your hand with your foot. Begin with a gentle force.
- Repeat with the other leg.

Common errors
- Pulling the foot against the butt and compressing the knee joint.

[STORK STAND]

• Bending over at the waist.

TRIANGLE: STRETCHES THE HAMSTRING MUSCLES

• Bend over at the waist and balance yourself against something.

• Place the leg to be stretched forward and place your other leg behind the front leg about 12 inches, toes pointing forward.

• With your weight mostly on the front leg, press your chest toward the front kneecap and relax your back muscles.

• A stretch should be felt in the hamstring muscles of the front leg.

[TRIANGLE]

• Contract the front leg by trying to pull it backward against the floor—there is no movement.

• Repeat with the other leg.

Common errors

• Allowing the toes to point out.

• Not relaxing the back muscles.

PULLDOWN

Stretches the latissimus dorsi, trapezius, pectoralis, and triceps muscles.

• Hold onto something for support, hands placed slightly wider than shoulder width, feet about shoulder width apart, and

[PULL DOWN]

knees slightly bent.

• Allow your head to relax between your arms.

• For the contraction phase push against the support with your arms, contracting the muscles in your upper back.

Common errors

• Not relaxing all the muscles in the arms, chest and upper back.

SQUAT: STRETCHES THE LOWER BACK, CALVES, QUADRICEPS AND GLUTEAL MUSCLES.

• This particular exercise stretches several muscle groups at once. Some people find it puts uncomfortable pressure on

[SQUAT]

their knees. If you are one of those people you can sit on the ground and do the pretzel.

• Using something for support and balance, squat down keeping your heels on the ground. It's best done with cycling shoes off.

• Allow your butt to sag close to your heels as you press your body weight forward. Hold the stretch for 15 to 30 seconds.

• There is no contraction exercise to activate all the muscles involved in this stretch.

Common errors

• Allowing your heels to come off the ground.

• Keeping leg and back muscles tense.

PRETZEL: STRETCHES THE GLUTES AND LOWER BACK

• Sit on the ground with your legs extended in front of you and your hands behind your hips.

• Cross your right foot over you left leg and slide your right heel towards your butt.

• Place your left elbow on the outside of your right knee.

• Look over your right shoulder while turning your torso. Gently pushing on your knee with your left elbow will increase the stretch.

• Hold the stretch for 15 to 30 seconds.

• There is no contraction exercise for this stretch.

• Repeat with the other leg.

[PRETZEL]

start position   *movement/finish position*

[WALL LEAN]

Common errors

Keeping shoulders, back, and butt muscles tense—take a deep breath and relax.

WALL LEAN: STRETCHES THE CALVES

• Lean against an immovable support object, with the leg to be stretched straight behind you and your other leg is forward supporting most of your weight.

• Toes are pointing forward.

• Press the heel of the back leg into the ground and move your hips forward, keeping your back knee locked and straight. The farther forward you press you hips, the more stretch you should feel in the back leg's calf muscles.

• Slightly bend the back knee to stretch different calf muscles.

• Contract the calf muscles by pushing against the support object as if you were pushing it away using your back leg.

Common errors

- Pointing the toes in or out.
- Not putting most of your weight on the back leg.

Brief thoughts

A strength training and stretching program supplement a cycling program. A strength-training program may be beneficial to holding osteoporosis at bay or even building precious bone. Not to mention it can make you ride faster and more powerfully. In addition to the performance benefits already mentioned, stretching can also be a nice way to relax.

REFERENCES

Anderson, B., Stretching, Shelter Publications, Bolinas, California, 1980.

Alter, M. J., Sport Stretch, Human Kinetics, 1998.

U.S. Council on Exercise, Personal Trainer Manual, Published by The U.S. Council on Exercise, 1992.

Bell, F., B.S., C.S.C.S., C.P.T., Program Director of Colorado Acceleration Program, McKee Medical Center Sports Medicine, Loveland, CO, personal interviews with author July 1998.

Friedlander, A. L., et al., A two-year program of aerobics and weight training enhances bone mineral density of young women, *Journal of Bone and Mineral Research*, April 10 (4), 1995, PP. 574-585.

Friel, J., The Cyclist's Training Bible, VeloPress, Boulder, CO, 1996.

Handel, M., et al., Effects of contract-relax stretching training on muscle performance in athletes, *European Journal of Applied Physiology*, 76 (5), 1997, pp. 400-408.

Hickson, R. C., Potential for strength and endurance training to amplify endurance performance, *Journal of Applied Physiology*, November 65 (5), 1988, pp. 2285-2290.

Kerr, D., et al., Exercise effects on bone mass in postmenopausal women are site-specific and load-dependent, *Journal of Bone and Mineral Research*, February 11 (2), 1996, pp. 218-225.

Kraemer, W. J., Ph.D., Fleck, S. J., Ph.D., Exercise Technique Seated Cable Row, *Strength and Health Report*, Volume 1, Number 3, June 1997.

Kraemer, W. J., Ph.D., Fleck, S. J., Ph.D., Exercise Technique Classic Lat Pull-Down, *Strength and Health Report*, Volume 1, Number 6, June 1997.

Kraemer, W. J., Ph.D., Fleck, S. J., Ph.D., Exercise Technique Machine Standing Calf Raise, *Strength and Health Report*, Volume 2, Number 1, March 1998.

Marcinik, E. J., et al., Effects of strength training on lactate threshold and endurance performance, *Medicine and Science in Sports and Exercise*, June 23 (6), 1991, pp. 739-743.

McArdle, William D., Katch, Frank I., Katch, Victor L., Exercise Physiology, Energy, Nutrition, and Human Performance, Third Edition, Lea & Febiger, 1991, pp. 457.

Puhl, J., et al., Sport Science Perspectives for Women, Human Kinetics, 1988, pp. 7.

McCarthy, J. P., et al., Compatibility of adaptive responses with combining strength and endurance training, *Medicine and Science in Sports and Exercise*, March, 27 (3), 1995, pp. 429-436.

Pearl, B., Morgan, G. T., Ph.D., Getting Stronger, Shelter Publications, 1986.

Tanaka, H., Swensen T., Impact of resistance training on endurance performance. A new form of crosstraining?, Sports Medicine, March 25 (3), 1998, pp. 191-200.

Wallin D., et al., Improvement of muscle flexibility. A comparison between two techniques, *American Journal of Sports Medicine*, July-August, 13 (4), 1985, pp. 263-268.

CHAPTER NINE

Goal
setting

*"If you don't know where you're going, you will
probably wind up somewhere else."*
—Dr. Laurence J. Peter

In our fast-paced lives, often we accomplish tasks and move on to new tasks before the old accomplishment is hours old. Go, go, go . . . do, do, do . . . faster, faster, faster. It seems that we are all trying to fit a few more items into that nonexistent extra hour each day. One good reason to set goals is that their accomplishment provides us with an opportunity to recognize accomplishment and celebrate. It is important to pause, take a look at what we have done, and feel good about it. These moments of recognition are very reinforcing and encourage us to press forward or shoot for a new goal.

Setting a major goal allows us to work backward and design a plan to reach the ultimate goal. If we set a goal that is weeks or months away, it is nice to have subgoals to recognize progress and, of course, celebrate.

Although goal setting seems simple, without some basic characteristics, a goal can be vague or unachievable. Characteristics of good goals include:

• State goals in positive terms: They explain what you want to achieve, as opposed to what you don't want to happen.

• Goals need to be challenging: The goals should be challenging enough so you aren't 100 percent certain you can achieve them.

• Goals need to be achievable: If your goals are so challenging that they become impossible, you will easily be discouraged. Goals need to be within reach.

• Goals need to be under your control: Your goals should be based on your performance and within your control, not someone else's.

• Make your goals specific and measurable: Instead of saying, "I want to ride fast," consider stating, "I want to improve my speed for a five-mile time trial from fifteen miles per hour." In this case, any time improvement is acceptable.

Let's look at each category in more depth

STATE GOALS IN POSITIVE TERMS

Goals are best stated in a positive sense. For example, "I don't want to be dropped on Sunday group rides" is a goal stated in negative terms. It says what you don't want to happen. Instead, try "Stay with the group on the Sunday ride" as your major goal. This means that even if you have to draft someone the entire time, you want to stay with the pack.

GOALS NEED TO BE CHALLENGING

If you are already staying with the group on Sunday rides, to make "Stay with the group on the Sunday ride," as your major goal will be too easy and boring. There is no challenge in that goal. If you are already staying with the group, perhaps a goal could be "Go to the front and lead for part of a group ride." This goal is stated in positive terms and it's challenging.

GOALS NEED TO BE ACHIEVABLE

One of the most common mistakes is to make goals too challenging. If a goal is impossible to achieve, it is easy to get discouraged and quit. For example, an eager rider may make a goal to ride every day for the next six months. Missing one day the second week of the plan makes achieving the goal impossible as missing one day the fifth month also makes the goal unreachable. This goal is too restrictive.

A goal that is more achievable and still provides health benefits is to "Ride bike and strength train between five and seven times a week for the next six months." You may even add an illness disclaimer if you'd like: "Being ill will not count against me." This kind of goal statement encourages the healthy behavior of constancy and exercise, while giving you room for unforeseeable interruptions.

GOALS NEED TO BE UNDER YOUR CONTROL

It is best to set goals based on you and your performance. Setting goals based on someone else can be disappointing. For example a goal stated, "Ride faster than Susan on next Sunday's ride" may prove disappointing. What happens if you do ride faster than Susan, and in the post-ride chat session you find out Susan was sick with the flu for the past three days and is still trying to recover? Will you feel good about "riding faster than Susan?" Will you feel success, or a shallow victory?

You can use other people as benchmarks for your fitness goals, but there is no way for you to control their training or how they ride. If you want to use Susan for benchmarking performance, fine, but also have other ways to measure your success, such as "Improve my five-mile time trial speed from sixteen miles per hour." If you improve your speed, perhaps you will ride as fast or faster than Susan. Measure success based on you.

MAKE GOALS SPECIFIC AND MEASURABLE

This is always a tough one. I have a questionnaire for riders seeking my coaching help. One of the questions is, "At the end of our first season together, how will we know if we were successful?" Often a response will be, "If I'm a better rider." How will we know when you are a better rider? What does a better rider look like? Below is a list of more specific goals describing a better rider:

• Improve my average speed on the dump-loop from the current seventeen miles per hour.

• Ride fifty miles in a single day.

• Improve my hill riding such that I can ride Carter Lake Hill without walking.

• Complete a 40km time trial.

• Ride one hundred miles in a single day.

• Complete a three-day tour, averaging three hours of riding each day.

• Feel strong on the group rides.

Notice some of the goals are number-specific. In other words, anyone could look at your performance and measure your average speed changing from seventeen mph to seventeen-and-a-half mph on the dump-loop. Other goals are more behavioral and subjective. While other people may notice that you are riding the hills faster, only you will know if you are feeling strong or not. Although the measurement is subjective, you can still measure your success. For example, on a scale of one to seven—one being best—how would you rate your hill climbing today? Ask yourself that same question every couple of weeks. Can you see progress?

Another example of a behavioral goal is, "I will begin hills conservatively and plan to finish each one stronger than I started." You can subjectively judge the difference between blasting up the bottom half of the hill and fading at the top versus beginning with a smooth, relaxed cadence and fininishing the hill strong. Although the goal seems subjective, you may also measure success by looking at average speed for the last quarter of the hill climb.

SUBGOALS

Chapter 10 gives specific training plans to complete specific goals, such as "Ride fifty miles, averaging 14.3 mph, at the end of twelve weeks." Since it will be three months before you complete the goal, I suggest you look at the training plan and make between one and three subgoals each week. Your subgoals can come from the training plan, they can be nutritional in nature, recovery oriented, or another area you need to work on. For example, your goals for one week may be:

- Complete the Saturday two-hour ride.
- Drink at least eight glasses of water each day.
- Get between seven and eight hours of rest each night.

If you were to add up the accomplishment of three goals each week for thirteen weeks, there would be thirty-nine reasons you made it to your ultimate goal. So, each week, jot down three things you want to accomplish. As you complete each one, give it a check mark and celebrate.

CELEBRATIONS

Kids are, by far, leading authorities on celebrating small successes. Their celebrations include jumping up and down, excited chatter, letting other people close to them know what they've accomplished, victory-twist dancing, and various other energizing moves. The best part is, they celebrate when they have accomplished even the smallest objective. They may celebrate if they are the first one of the playgroup to simply get on their bike and on the road.

Adults, on the other hand, are usually boring celebrators—if they celebrate at all. It is the celebration of each small success that will help propel you toward a goal. Whether others are told of your accomplishments or they are kept private, take a moment to recognize success—and perhaps do a victory dance.

BRIEF THOUGHTS

Goals and subgoals are handy tools for achieving success. Goals are more likely accomplished if they are written down, instead of allowing them to float in your head. Take time to celebrate success before pressing on to the next goal.

R E F E R E N C E S

Bernhardt, G., Reflections and Goals, *Triathlete*, November, 1997.

Daniels, A. C., Performance Management, Performance Management Publications, Tucker, Georgia, 1989.

CHAPTER TEN

Training
plans

---

*"Unless you try to do something beyond
what you have already mastered, you will
never grow."*   *—Ralph Waldo Emerson*

For the busy athlete, it is often frustrating to purchase a book on training because many of them give guidelines for preparing a plan—but there are no training plans already written within the book. Perhaps your life is already complicated enough and it would be helpful if someone just gave you an outline of what to do because you don't have time to sit down and write a plan for yourself. If it's plans you want, this chapter is for you.

Within this chapter are five training plans. Because each training plan is titled and has a specific goal, you will know what you should be able to do when you complete the plan. All the plans have an athlete profile, a description of whom the plan was designed for, and, at the end, are some typical questions and answers.

If you find the training plans offered here to be appetizers and you want to take a stab at designing your own training plan, "The Cyclist's Training Bible," written by Joe Friel, and published by VeloPress Books, would be a good book to purchase.

All of the plans at the end of this chapter follow a periodization format. Simplified, that means your body will be introduced to training stresses in a planned and controlled manner. At the same time, rest is planned to allow your body to repair, recover, and achieve a higher level fitness. A written plan helps athletes see the future and be patient. Those without a plan often train like maniacs for two weeks—when enthusiasm is high—then become ill, injured or burned out and give up.

Sometimes, people have a plan, but it may be faulty. A good example is the ever-increasing riding plan. A decision is made three months prior to a group tour that a tour would be a fun thing to do. The athlete begins with what seems to be a reasonable idea: increase volume each week to prepare for the event. And so it goes; the riding volume increases each week so that by the time the tour comes, the athlete is fried and has no desire to ride. Those athletes needed to schedule some rest weeks within their plan.

Okay, there are periods of work and rest—and what else? The plans are divided into periods of Base, Build and Event. Generally speaking, the base period builds volume and adds some intensity near the end. The build period, for the plans having a build period, adds some more intense training.

Strength training is blended into each plan, so heavier weights precede hill work or fast intervals on the bike. The twelve- to thirteen-week plans are pared down to provide minimal amounts of training necessary to complete the goal. You will notice the plans that span six months offer more variety and will yield a higher level of fitness.

SPECIFIC WORKOUTS

All of the workouts are based on the training heart rates you determined for yourself by doing one of the tests in Chapter 7. So, that is step one, if you haven't done it yet. Do one of the tests in Chapter 7 to estimate your lactate threshold heart rate. If you have zero fitness you should not do the lactate threshold test, and you should consult a physician before beginning an exercise program. If you have any special health conditions, it would be wise to consult a physician about any special restrictions they may place on your exercise intensities.

WARM UP AND COOL DOWN

Before beginning intervals, tempo rides or races be certain to get a good warm-up. A warm-up needs to be between ten and thirty minutes, depending on the particular workout and how much time you have assigned. This means beginning in 1 zone and slowly increasing speed, so that your heart rate is close to the zone in which you will be doing the work intervals. If you can't get your heart rate into the specified zone by the third interval, quit trying, spin easily, and head home; it wasn't your day.

After each workout and race, spin easily to cool down. By the end of your cool-down, your heart rate should be 1 zone or less. Stretch your muscles shortly after a cool-down.

WORKOUT CODES

Endurance workouts

E1

Ride in the small chain ring on a flat course, keeping your heart rate in the 1 zone.

Some of the plans allow for E1 cross-training. Keep in mind the target heart-rate zones will be different for each sport. If you do aerobics or cross-country ski as cross-training, you can use perceived exertion to gauge your intensity level.

E2

This level is used for aerobic maintenance and endurance training. Your heart rate should stay primarily in the 1 to 2 zones. How much time is spent in each zone depends on how you feel that day. The goal of E2 rides is not to see how much time you can spend in the 2 zone. Ride on a rolling course if possible, with grades up to 4 percent. For reference, most highway off ramps are 4-percent grade. Remain in the saddle on the hills. If you ride with a group and have an E2 ride to do, you must have the inner discipline to let the group go if they want to hammer.

E3

This workout is used for endurance training and the beginning of lactate threshold training. Ride a rolling course in 1-3 zones. Stay seated on the hills to build and maintain hip power. Ride a course and use gearing that allows you to work intensity into 3 zone, but not so hard that you dip into 4 and 5 zones.

E4

This is a multifaceted workout that is for building endurance, speed and strength. The first time you do an E4 workout, keep your heart rate in the 1 to 4 zones. As you continue to do more E4 workouts, you can spend some time in the 5 zone. The final progression is to spend larger amounts of time in the 4 and 5 zones. This progression is not detailed in the plans and is left to the individual athlete.

Speed workouts

S1

Spin step-ups. This workout is intended to work on pedaling form and neuromuscular coordination. On an indoor trainer: Warm up with low resistance and a pedaling cadence of 90 revolutions per minute. After fifteen to twenty minutes of warming up, increase the cadence to 100 rpm for three minutes, 110 rpm for two minutes, and more than 120 rpm for one minute. If time allows, spin easy for five minutes to recover, and repeat a second time. If you are just beginning to increase pedaling speed, you may have to cut all of the times in half in order to maintain the recommended speeds. It is important the resistance is low to allow you to focus on the speed of your feet and not force on the pedals.

This workout can be done on the road if the road is flat or slightly downhill.

S2

Isolated Leg. This workout helps work the dead spot out of your pedal stroke. After warming up with light resistance on an indoor trainer do 100 percent of the work with one leg while the other leg is resting on a stool. You can do this on the road, outdoors by relaxing one leg while the other leg does 90-percent of the work. Change legs when fatigue sets in or set an interval to prevent excess fatigue. Work up to a work interval of thirty to sixty seconds per leg. After doing a work segment with each leg, spin easily with both legs for a minute, and then go back to single leg work.

Do not continue to pedal with one leg when you become sloppy. Do not worry about achieving any particular heart rate, smooth pedaling form is most important. Begin with a total of three to five minutes on each leg and build time, as you become stronger. The plans included in this chapter suggest times of work for each leg.

S7

Accelerations. This workout is intended to work on leg speed and the neuromuscular pathways. Warm up well, then do the specified number of thirty-second accelerations, spinning an easy two minutes and thirty seconds between each acceleration. The end of the thirty seconds should be faster than the beginning. On the plans, it looks something like 4-6 x 0:30 (2:30 RI), which means do four to six times thirty-second accelerations, with two-and-a-half-minute rest intervals between each one.

• Why did I go from S2 to S7? As mentioned previously, this book is intended to dovetail with "The Cyclist's Training Bible," and it uses more codes than I will use in this book.

Muscular endurance workouts

M1

Tempo. This workout is the beginning of lactate threshold speed work. After a warm up, on a mostly flat course, ride in the 3 zone for the time indicated on the plan.

M2*(3Z)

Cruise intervals. These intervals will also begin work on lactate threshold speed in the early season. On a mostly flat course or indoor trainer, complete the number of intervals given on the plan, allowing your heart rate to rise into the 3 zone over the course of the interval. For example, 4-5 x 4:00 (1:00 RI) means after your warm-up ride four or five times four minutes, allowing your pulse to rise into the 3 zone and no higher. After your heart rate is in the 3 zone, try to hold it there until the end of the interval. Begin timing the interval as soon as you begin an increased effort—do not wait to begin the clock when your heart rate is in 3 zone. (All work intervals begin when effort is increased and rest intervals begin when effort is decreased.) Spin easily and recover for one minute between efforts.

M2*(4/5A)

Cruise Intervals. These intervals are for lactate threshold speed, as the season and your fitness progress. On a mostly flat course or indoor trainer, complete the number of intervals given on the plan, allowing your heart rate to rise into the 4 to 5a zone over the course of the interval. For example, 4-5 x 4:00 (1:00 RI) means after your warm-up, ride four or five times four minutes, allowing your pulse to rise into the 4 to 5a zone and no higher. After your heart rate is in the 4 to 5a zones, try to hold it there until the end of the interval. Take 1 minute to spin your legs and recover, between work intervals.

M3*(3Z)

Hill Cruise Intervals. Same as M2*(3Z) except on a long, 2- to 4-percent grade.

M3*(4Z)

Hill Cruise Intervals. Same as M2*(4/5a) except on a long, 2- to 4-percent grade.

M6

Tempo. This workout is for lactate threshold speed. After a warm up, on a mostly flat course, ride in the 4-5a zone for the time indicated on the plan.

Speed-endurance (anaerobic) and taper workouts

Some of the workouts specify a rolling course or a hilly course. That becomes relative to where you live. In general, a rolling course has grades up to about 4 percent and a hilly course has steeper grades. If you live in Flat City, simulate hills by shifting up a gear or two to make the pedaling seem like a hill.

A1ᴀ

Easy group ride. This particular workout is not anaerobic, but is part of a series of group rides. Ride with a group and stay mostly in the 1-3 zones.

A1ʙ

Faster-paced group ride. Ride with a group and stay mostly in the 1-4 zones. Some time can be spent in 5 zone, but keep it minimal.

A1ᴄ

Fast, aggressive group ride. Ride with a group and ride in all zones. Be aggressive and power up the hills, chase riders who might have been faster than you in the past, have fun.

A1ᴅ

Ride as you feel. If you're feeling great, ride aggressively with some time in all zones, if you're tired, take it easy.

A2*(5ʙZ)

Speed-endurance intervals. After a good warm-up on a mostly flat course, do the specified number of intervals, allowing your heart rate to climb into the 5b zone. The intervals may be done on a flat course or slightly uphill. For example, 4-5 x 3:00 (3:00 RI) means do four or five times three minutes getting your heart rate into 5b zone and keep it there until the end of the interval. Take three minutes between intervals.

A6*(5B-cZ)

Hill Reps. After a good warm up, go to a 6- to 8-percent grade hill and complete the specified number of hill repetitions. Stay seated for the first sixty seconds as you build to 5b zone, then shift to a higher gear, stand, and drive the bike to the top, allowing your heart rate to climb into 5c zone. Recover completely for three to four minutes between repetitions.

A7

Taper Intervals. After a good warm-up, do the specified number of ninety-second accelerations, getting your heart rate in the 4 to 5a zones. Take three full minutes to recover and get your heart rate back to 1 zone before going to the next interval. On the plans, the intervals will look like 4 -5 x 1:30 (3:00 RI). These intervals help keep your legs feeling fresh and speedy while volume is tapering prior to a race or important ride.

Test workouts

T1

Aerobic Time Trial (ATT). This is best done on a CompuTrainer or a trainer with a rear-wheel computer pick-up. It can also be done on a flat section of road, but weather conditions will affect the results. After a warm-up, ride five miles with your heart rate nine to eleven beats below your lactate threshold heart rate. Use a single gear and don't shift during the test. Record the gear you used, your time, and how you felt in your training journal. Each time you repeat the test, try to make your testing conditions the same. As aerobic fitness improves, the time should decrease.

T2

As-fast-as-you-can-go Time Trial (TT). After a fifteen- to thirty-minute warm up, complete a five- to eight-mile time trial, as fast as you can possibly ride. If you are a novice, use five miles. You may need to use a distance somewhere between five and eight miles because your course dictates the exact distance. Your course needs to be free of stop signs and heavy traffic. You can use a course with a turn-around point. Use any gear you wish and shift any time. Each time you repeat the test, try to make testing conditions—wind, temperature, subjective feelings, outside stressors—as similar as possible.

Cross-training

XT

Some of the plans show an option of cross-training such as aer-obics, cross-country skiing, and in-line skating, to name a few. Keep in mind your cross-training sport heart rates will not match your cycling heart rate. Use perceived rating of exertion to estimate correct training zones. These workouts should be mostly easy.

PLANS

All of the plans assume you have some level of current fitness. They are not written for someone just beginning an exercise program. Most of the plans have at least an aerobic time trial and perhaps an all-out time trial included somewhere within the plan.

As one measure of your fitness gains, you can do a baseline time trial before beginning one of the plans. Use the five-mile aerobic time trial for this.

So, before beginning any of the plans, determine your lactate threshold heart rate from one of the tests in Chapter 7 and then do and aerobic time trial (T1) before beginning the plan.

PLAN 1

GOAL: Ride fifty miles, averaging 14.3 mph at the end of twelve weeks.

PROFILE: This plan is for cyclists who are currently riding about four hours per week and looking for a new challenge. They have between three and seven hours available to train each week.

PLAN 2

GOAL: Ride one hundred miles, averaging 16 mph at the end of twelve weeks.

PROFILE: This plan is for a cyclist who is currently riding at least four hours per week and doing some strength training. This person doesn't have a lot of time to train, but would like to successfully complete a century.

PLAN 3

GOAL: Ride a three-day tour at the end of thirteen weeks, averaging three hours each day.

PROFILE: The person this plan was designed for is busy. She or he needs Tuesdays and Thursdays without exercise, due to other commitments. Fridays she is often tired, but can do some type of exercise and it needs to be easy. Weekends are open to exercise hours. She is currently doing five to seven hours of exercise each week, at least three hours of which, is cycling.

The weekday workouts are structured such that they can be done on an indoor trainer or at a gym.

PLAN 4

GOAL: Ride a 40km time trial, or ride faster on the weekend group rides.

PROFILE: Person 1: This plan was designed for a person who has been cycling for a few years, mostly in the summertime. She or he wants to try a race and a time trial seems like a good way to start. She may be doing the 40km cycling leg for a triathlon team or doing a USA Cycling-sponsored time trial. Either way, she wants to be fast on race day.

They are cycling about three hours each week and strength training one to two times per week, prior to beginning this plan.

PROFILE: Person 2: This plan also works for a person who has cycled for years, mostly in the summer time, and has been frustrated when joining group rides. It seems just when she is getting in shape in August or September, the group rides are dwindling.

She is cycling about three hours each week and strength

training one to two times per week, prior to beginning this plan.

If you are looking to increase your cycling speed beyond a recreational level, it will require more than the three months summer can offer. More than likely, the faster cyclists in your club or group ride are those who maintain some type of cycling fitness year round. If you want to be in reasonable shape for spring group rides and progressively get faster as summer approaches, this plan is for you.

PLAN 5

GOAL: Ride hills faster, or improve speed on hilly weekend group rides.

PROFILE: This plan is also written for people who have cycled for years, mostly in the summer time, and have been frustrated when trying to climb hills and join group rides—particularly when the course is hilly. They are cycling about three hours each week and strength training one to two times per week, prior to beginning this plan.

To measure progress, since this plan is specifically for hills, you can make your five-mile time trial—not the aerobic time trial—on a section of road that includes a climb. The other way you can measure progress on this plan is to subjectively note how you feel climbing hills, compared to years past.

The group rides are specified as hilly or rolling. The plan tapers and keys on a group ride at the end of twenty-four weeks of training. Your group rides will be getting progressively stronger from weeks seventeen to twenty-four; however, the group ride at the end of the plan should be a humdinger. You'll be rested and ready to climb like a goat.

It is important to note that hill climbing requires technique as well as aerobic stamina and strength. If you begin a hill too fast, you will fizzle and fade by the end. Try to begin the hill repeats and hilly group rides a bit conservatively. Plan to finish each hill stronger than you began it.

QUESTIONS AND ANSWERS

1. Should I always shoot for the highest number when a range is given?

No. A range is given on some workouts, to allow you to customize the workout for how you feel. Also, if you are in a time crunch and have to cut the workout short, go for fewer repetitions.

2. If a workout prescribes two hours and I'm feeling great, can I just go ahead and do three hours?

Generally speaking, on two-hour rides, try not to go over or under more than about fifteen minutes. On three-hour-and-longer rides, shoot for plus or minus twenty to thirty minutes. On shorter weekday rides, aim for around ten minutes, plus or minus.

3. What happens if I get in a real time crunch and can only do thirty minutes of a sixty-minute workout, or I have to skip it altogether?

Realistically, you will probably miss a few workouts. If you're going to skip a workout, start with an E1 that's an hour or less. The priority workouts are usually the long weekend rides that are continuously building volume, weekday intervals, and strength sessions.

4. What if I can ride faster than the goal paces for fifty and one hundred miles?

You can adjust the weekend rides accordingly. In other words, if you can average 18 mph instead of 16 mph, you can adjust the weekend ride time by about 13 percent (18 divided by 16.) The adjustment isn't much and is within the guidelines in answer No. 2. For example, 13 percent of a three-hour ride is about twenty-three minutes.

5. Can I rearrange the workouts within the week? I work weekends.

Rearranging the workouts is fine, with a few guidelines: Keep at least forty-eight hours between strength training sessions; try to keep high-intensity sessions separated by forty-eight hours—unless otherwise called for in the original plan; do not try to make up missed weekday workouts on the weekend. In other words, don't try ride for six hours on Saturday if you missed three one-hour workouts during the week and you have a three-hour Saturday ride scheduled.

6. I can only make it to the gym once per week. Is one strength training session really worth it?

Once per week is better than none.

7. I want to use the three-day tour plan, but the ride I'm going on doesn't go three hours each day. My tour is approximately two hours, four hours, and three hours. will Plan 3 still work for me?

Yes.

8. What if I get sick, can I still train?

If your symptoms are above the neck and minimal—runny nose, headache, scratchy throat—go ahead and workout if you feel up to it. Cut your intensity to zones 1 and 2. Reduce the total workout time or stop altogether if you feel bad once you get the workout started.

If your symptoms are below the neck or intense—cough, chills, vomiting, achy muscles, fever, sore throat—don't even start the workout. A virus likely causes these symptoms. Ignoring the symptoms and trying to train through the illness carries the risk of a more serious illness that can have you literally sidelined for months. Missing a few days of training to get well is your best investment of time.

9. What happens if I miss some training days due to illness?

If you miss one to three days, resume your training as shown on the plan, skip the workouts you missed. If you miss a week or more, consider pushing your goal forward and depending on how you recover, you may want to repeat a week or two of training, to get you back on track. Whatever you do, take it easy coming back—you don't want another set back.

10. I want to be a faster group rider, but I can only train five hours in any given week. Will I get results if I just reduce Plan 4 to accommodate my life?

If your group rides are going between two and three hours, it will become very difficult to keep improving on only five hours of training per week.

BRIEF THOUGHTS

Recall from Chapter 7, "In working with cyclists, the most common mistakes are: **riding the same speed all the time, no goals and no plan, sloppy nutrition and hydration.**"

This chapter suggested goals, gave you plans, and varied the riding speeds within the plans. Most athletes tell me that not having to design their own plan is great. They can come home, look at what they're supposed to do and get on the bike.

At first glance, the codes and plans may seem confusing. Perhaps after a short period of time, you will find they are easy to decipher.

It is important to know these plans aren't gender-specific. Any adult, male or female, old or young, can use the tests in Chapter 7 and the plans here in Chapter 10. Again, the plans are not intended for people who are doing no exercise, rather for those looking for a new level in their cycling or the next step. Perhaps after following one of the plans, you'll find new speed or new strength on the hills, allowing you to take your riding up a notch, use a bigger gear.

Plan 1
Ride 50 miles

Week		Monday	Tuesday	Wednesday	Thursday	Friday	Saturday	Sunday	Weekly Total
1	Time / Workout / Specific	1:00 Strength AA	Day off	1:00 Strength AA	0:30 Bike — S7 4x30"(2' 30"RI)	Day off	0:30 Bike — E1	1:00 Bike — E2	4:00
2	Time / Workout / Specific	1:00 Strength AA	Day off	1:00 Strength AA	0:30 Bike — S2 3-5 min ea. leg	Day off	0:45 Bike — E1	1:00 Bike — E2	4:15
3	Time / Workout / Specific	1:00 Strength AA	Day off	0:30 Bike — E2 4x30' (2' 30"RI)	0:30 Bike — S7	Day off	Day off	1:00 Bike — E2	3:00
4	Time / Workout / Specific	1:00 Strength AA	Day off	1:00 Strength AA	0:30 Bike — S2 3-5 min ea. leg	Day off	0:45 Bike — E1	1:15 Bike — E2	4:30
5	Time / Workout / Specific	1:00 Strength AA	Day off	1:00 Strength AA	0:30 Bike — S7	Day off	1:00 Bike — E1	1:30 Bike — E2	5:00
6	Time / Workout / Specific	1:00 Strength PM	Day off	1:00 Strength PM	0:45 Bike — S7 4-5x30"(2' 30"RI)	Day off	1:00 Bike — E1	1:30 Bike — E2	5:15
7	Time / Workout / Specific	1:00 Strength PM	Day off	0:45 Bike — T1 5 mile ATT	0:30 Bike — S7 5-6x30'(2' 30"RI)	Day off	0:30 Bike — E1	1:00 Bike — E2	3:45
8	Time / Workout / Specific	1:00 Strength PM	Day off	1:00 Strength PM	0:30 Bike — S2 5-6 min ea. leg	Day off	1:00 Bike — E1	2:00 Bike — E3	5:45
9	Time / Workout / Specific	1:00 Strength PM	Day off	1:00 Strength PM	0:45 Bike — E2	Day off	1:00 Bike — E1	2:15 Bike — E3	6:00
10	Time / Workout / Specific	1:00 Strength PM	Day off	1:00 Strength PM	0:45 Bike — E2	Day off	1:15 Bike — E2	2:30 Bike — E3	6:30
11	Time / Workout / Specific	1:00 Strength PM	Day off	0:45 Bike — T1 5 mile ATT	Day off	Day off	1:00 Bike — E2	1:15 Bike — E1	4:00
12	Time / Workout / Specific	1:00 Strength — PM lighten weights	Day off	0:45 Bike — E2 4x30"(2' 30"RI)	0:30 Bike — S7	Day off	Day off	3:30 Ride 50 miles	5:45

Plan 2
Ride 100 Miles

Week		Monday	Tuesday	Wednesday	Thursday	Friday	Saturday	Sunday	Weekly Total
1	Time	1:00	1:00	1:00		Day off		1:30	6:30
	Workout Specific	Strength AA	Bike — E2	Strength AA	Bike — S7 4 x 30" (2' 30"RI)		Bike — E1	Bike — E2	
2	Time	1:00	1:00	1:00		Day off	1:00	2:00	7:00
	Workout Specific	Strength AA	Bike — E2	Strength AA	Bike — S7 6-8 x 30" (2' 30"RI)		Bike — E1	Bike — E2	
3	Time	1:00	Day off	1:00	Day off	Day off	0:45	1:30	4:15
	Workout Specific	Strength AA		Strength PM			Bike — S7 4-6x30" (2' 30"RI)	Bike — E2	
4	Time	1:00	1:00	1:00	Day off	Day off	0:45	2:30	6:15
	Workout Specific	Strength PM	Bike — E2	Strength PM			Bike — S2 3-5 min ea. leg	Bike — E3	
5	Time	1:00	Day off	1:00	1:00	Day off	1:30	3:00	7:30
	Workout Specific	Strength PM		Strength PM	Bike — M1(3Z) 4-5 x 3' (1' RI)		Bike — E1	Bike — E3	
6	Time	1:00	0:30	0:45	1:00	Day off	1:30	3:30	8:30
	Workout Specific	Strength PM	Bike — S2 3-5 min ea. leg	Bike — E2	Bike — M1(3Z) 5-6 x 3' (1' RI)		Bike — E2	Bike — E3	
7	Time	1:00	Day off	0:45	Day off	Day off	1:00	1:30	4:15
	Workout Specific	Strength PM		Bike — E2			Bike — T1 5 mile ATT	Bike — E3 (mostly 1-2Z)	
8	Time	0:45	Day off	1:00	Day off	1:00	Day off	4:00	6:45
	Workout Specific	Strength EM		Bike — M1(3Z) 4-5 x 4' (1' RI)		Bike — E2		Bike — E3	
9	Time	0:45	Day off	1:00	0:30	Day off	1:15	4:30	8:00
	Workout Specific	Strength EM		Bike — M1(3Z) 3-5 x 5' (1'30" RI)	Bike — E1		Bike — E2	Bike — E3	
10	Time	0:45	Day off	1:15	0:45	Day off	1:00	5:00	8:45
	Workout Specific	Strength PM		Bike — M1(3Z) 3-4 x 6' (2' RI)	Bike — E1		Bike — S7 4-8 x 30" (2' 30"RI)	Bike — E3	
11	Time	0:45	Day off	0:45	Day off	Day off	0:45	2:00	4:15
	Workout Specific	Strength PM		Bike — E2			Bike — T1 5 mile ATT	Bike — E2	
12	Time	1:00	Day off	0:45	Day off	0:30	Day off	6:00	8:15
	Workout Specific	Bike — E2		Bike — S7 4-5 x 30" (2' 30"RI)		Bike — S7 2 x 30" (2' 30"RI)		Ride 100 miles (16mph)	

Plan 3

Ride 3 days, Average 3 Hours of Riding each day

Week		Monday	Tuesday	Wednesday	Thursday	Friday	Saturday	Sunday	Weekly Total
1	Time / Workout / Specific	1:00 / Strength / AA	Day off	1:00 / Bike — S2 / 3-5 min ea. leg	Day off	1:15 / Bike — E1	1:15 / Bike — E2	1:15 / Bike — E1	5:45
2	Time / Workout / Specific	1:00 / Strength / AA	Day off	1:00 / Bike — S1 / Spin Step-ups	Day off	1:15 / Bike — E1	1:45 / Bike — E2	1:30 / Bike — E1	6:30
3	Time / Workout / Specific	1:00 / Strength / AA	Day off	1:00 / Bike — S2 / 4-6 min ea. leg	Day off	1:15 / Bike — E1	2:00 / Bike — E2	1:30 / Bike — E1	6:45
4	Time / Workout / Specific	0:45 / Strength / PM	Day off	1:00 / Bike — T1 / 5 mile ATT	Day off	Day off	1:30 / Bike — E2	1:00 / Bike — E2	4:15
5	Time / Workout / Specific	1:00 / Strength / PM	Day off	1:00 / Bike — S1 / Spin Step-ups	Day off	1:15 / Bike — E1	2:30 / Bike — E2	1:30 / Bike — E2	7:15
6	Time / Workout / Specific	1:00 / Strength / PM	Day off	1:00 / Bike — S1 / Spin Step-ups	Day off	1:15 / Bike — E1	3:00 / Bike — E2	1:30 / Bike — E2	7:45
7	Time / Workout / Specific	1:00 / Strength / PM	Day off	1:00 / Bike — T1 / 5 mile ATT	Day off	1:15 / Bike — E1	3:00 / Bike — E3	2:00 / Bike — E1	8:15
8	Time / Workout / Specific	1:00 / Strength / PM	Day off	1:00 / Bike — M3(3Z) / 4-5 x 3-4' (1'30" RI)	Day off	Day off	1:30 / Bike — E2	1:00 / Bike — E2	4:30
9	Time / Workout / Specific	1:00 / Strength / PM	Day off	1:00 / Bike — S7 / 6-8 x 30" (2' 30"RI)	Day off	1:15 / Bike — E1	3:00 / Bike — E3	2:30 / Bike — E2	8:45
10	Time / Workout / Specific	1:00 / Strength / PM	Day off	1:00 / Bike — M3(3Z) / 4-5 x 3-4' (1'30" RI)	Day off	1:30 / Bike — E1	3:30 / Bike — E3	2:30 / Bike — E2	9:30
11	Time / Workout / Specific	1:00 / Strength / PM	Day off	1:00 / Bike — S7 / 6-8 x 30" (2' 30"RI)	Day off	1:30 / Bike — E1	4:00 / Bike — E3	2:30 / Bike — E2	10:00
12	Time / Workout / Specific	0:45 / Strength / PM	Day off	1:00 / Bike — S7 / 6-8 x 30" (2' 30"RI)	Day off	Day off	1:30 / Bike — E2	1:00 / Bike — T2 / 5 mile TT	4:15
13	Time / Workout / Specific	0:45 / Bike — S7 / 4-6 x 30" (2' 30"RI)	Day off	0:30 / Bike — S7 / 3-4 x 30" (2' 30"RI)	Day off	3:00 / Bike Tour	3:00 / Bike Tour	3:00 / Bike Tour	10:15

Plan 4
40K Time Trial or Faster Group Riding

Week		Monday	Tuesday	Wednesday	Thursday	Friday	Saturday	Sunday	Weekly Total
1	Time	1:00	0:45	1:00	1:00	Day off	1:00	1:00	5:45
	Workout Specific	Strength AA	Bike — S2 5-7 min ea. leg	Strength AA	Bike — E1 or XT		Bike — E2	Bike — E1 or XT	
2	Time	1:00	0:45	1:00	1:00	Day off	1:00	1:00	5:45
	Workout Specific	Strength AA	Bike — S1 Spin Step-ups	Strength AA	Bike — E1 or XT		Bike — E2	Bike — E1 or XT	
3	Time	1:00	0:45	1:00	1:00	Day off	1:00	1:00	5:45
	Workout Specific	Strength AA	Bike — S2 6-8 min ea. leg	Strength AA	Bike — E1 or XT		Bike — E2	Bike — E1 or XT	
4	Time	0:45	0:45	1:15	1:00	Day off	1:00	1:00	6:15
	Workout Specific	Strength AA	Bike — S1 Spin Step-ups	Strength MS	Bike — E1 or XT		Bike — E2 5 mile ATT	Bike — E1 or XT	
5	Time	1:15	1:00	1:15	0:45	Day off	1:00	1:00	8:15
	Workout Specific	Strength MS	Bike — S2 7-9 min ea. leg	Strength MS	Bike — E2 or XT		Bike — E2	Bike — E1 or XT	
6	Time	1:15	1:00	1:15	1:00	1:00	1:30	1:15	7:45
	Workout Specific	Strength MS	Bike — S1 Spin Step-ups	Strength MS	Bike — E1 or XT	Bike — E1	Bike — E2	Bike — E1 or XT	
7	Time	1:00	1:00	1:00	1:00	1:00	2:00	1:30	9:00
	Workout Specific	Strength PM	Bike — S2 8-10 min ea. leg	Strength MS	Bike — E1 or XT	Bike — E1	Bike — E2	Bike — E1 or XT	
8	Time	1:15	Day off	1:00	1:00	Day off	1:00	1:00	5:00
	Workout Specific	Strength MS		Strength PM	Bike — S1 Spin Step-ups		Bike — T1 5 mile ATT	Bike — E2	
9	Time	1:00	1:00	1:00	1:00	Day off	1:15	2:00	7:15
	Workout Specific	Strength PM	Bike — E2	Strength PM	Bike — M2(3Z) 4-5x4" (1"RI)		Bike — E3	Bike — E2	
10	Time	1:00	1:00	1:00	1:00	1:00	1:30	2:30	8:00
	Workout Specific	Strength PM	Bike — E2	Strength PM	Bike — M2(3Z) 4-5x4" (1"RI)	Bike — E1	Bike — E2	Bike — E3	
11	Time	1:00	1:00	1:00	1:00	1:00	1:30	3:00	9:30
	Workout Specific	Strength PM	Bike — E2	Strength PM	Bike — M2(3Z) 3-4 x30" (2' 30"RI)	Bike — E1 OR — Day off	Bike — E2	Bike — E3	
12	Time	1:00	Day off	1:00	1:00	Day off	1:00	1:00	5:00
	Workout Specific	Strength PM		Bike — S7 4-6 x 30" (2' 30"RI)	Bike — E2		Bike — T1 5 mile ATT	Bike — E2	
13	Time	1:00	1:00	1:00	1:00	Day off	1:30	2:15	7:45
	Workout Specific	Strength ME	Bike — E2	Strength ME	Bike — S1 Spin Step-ups		Bike — E4	Bike — E2	

Plan 4
40K Time Trial or Faster Group Riding

Week		Monday	Tuesday	Wednesday	Thursday	Friday	Saturday	Sunday	Weekly Total
14	Time	1:00	1:00	1:00	1:00	0:45	2:00	2:30	9:15
	Workout Specifics	Strength ME	Bike — E2	Strength ME	Bike — E1	Bike — E1 OR — Day off	Bike — E4	Bike — E2	
15	Time	1:00	1:00	1:00	1:00	0:45	2:00	3:15	10:00
	Workout Specifics	Strength PM	Bike — E2	Strength ME	Bike — S1 Spin Step-ups	Bike — E1 OR — Day off	Bike — E4	Bike — E2	
16	Time	0:45	Day off	1:00	1:00	Day off	1:00	1:15	5:00
	Workout Specifics	Strength PM		Bike — E2	Bike — S7 4-6x30"(2' 30"RI)		Bike — T2 5 mile TT	Bike — E2	
17	Time	1:00	1:00	1:00	1:00	1:00	1:30	2:30	9:00
	Workout Specifics	Strength PM	Bike — S7 4x30"(2' 30"RI)	Bike — M2(4-5a) 4-5x3'(1'RI)	Bike — S2	Bike — E1 OR — Day off	Bike — E2	Bike — A1a Group ride	
18	Time	1:00	1:00	1:00	1:00	1:00	1:30	2:30	9:00
	Workout Specifics	Strength PM	Bike — S7 4x30"(2' 30"RI)	Bike — M2(4-5a) 4-5x3'(1'RI)	Bike — E2	Bike — E1 OR — Day off	Bike — E2	Bike — A1b Group ride	
19	Time	0:45	Day off	1:00	0:30	Day off	1:00	0:45	5:00
	Workout Specifics	Strength PM		Bike — M2(4-5a) 3-4x6'(2'RI)	Bike — E1		Bike — A1c Group ride	Bike — E1	
20	Time	1:00	1:15	1:15	1:15	0:30	1:15	2:30	9:00
	Workout Specifics	Strength PM	Bike — S7 4x30"(2' 30"RI)	Bike — M2(4-5a) 3x8"(2RI)	Bike — E1	Bike — E1 OR — Day off	Bike — E2	Bike — A1c Group ride	
21	Time	1:00	1:15	1:15	1:15	0:30	1:15	2:30	9:00
	Workout Specifics	Strength PM	Bike — S7 4x30"(2' 30"RI)	Bike — M6 25-30min (4-5a)	Bike — E1	Bike — E1 OR — Day off	Bike — E2	Bike — A1d Group ride	
22	Time	1:00	Day off	1:00	1:00	Day off	1:00	1:00	5:00
	Workout Specifics	Strength PM		Bike — E2	Bike — S7 4-6x30"(2' 30"RI)		Bike — T2 5 mile TT	Bike — E2	
23	Time	1:00	1:00	1:15	0:45	0:30	1:15	2:30	8:30
	Workout Specifics	Strength PM	Bike — E2	Bike — M2(4-5a) 3-4x10'(3'x30"RI)	Bike — E1	Bike — E1 OR — Day off	Bike — E2	Bike — A1d Group ride	
24	Time	1:00	1:00	1:00	1:00	Day off	2:00	1:30	7:30
	Workout Specifics	Strength PM	Bike — E2	Bike — A2(5b) 4-5x3'(3'RI)	Bike — E1		Bike — A1c Group ride	Bike — E2	
25	Time	Day off	1:00	0:45	0:30	0:30	1:30	1:15	5:00
	Workout Specifics		Bike — A7 4x90"(3'RI)	Bike — A7 3x90"(3'RI)	Day off	Bike — S7 3x30"(2' 30"RI)	Race 40K Time Trial	Bike — E1 OR — Day off	

Plan 5
Improve Hill Climbing

Week		Monday	Tuesday	Wednesday	Thursday	Friday	Saturday	Sunday	Weekly Total
1	Time	1:00	0:45	1:00	1:00	Day off	1:00	1:00	5:45
	Workout	Strength	Bike — S2	Strength	Bike — E1		Bike — S2	Bike — E1	
	Specific	AA	5-7 min ea. leg	AA	or XT			or XT	
2	Time	1:00	0:45	1:00	1:00	Day off	1:00	1:00	5:45
	Workout	Strength	Bike — S1	Strength	Bike — E		Bike — E2	Bike — E1	
	Specific	AA	Spin Step-ups	AA	or XT			or XT	
3	Time	1:00	0:45	1:00	1:00	Day off	1:00	1:00	5:45
	Workout	Strength	Bike — S2	Strength	Bike — E1		Bike — E2	Bike — E1	
	Specific	AA	6-8 min ea. leg	AA	or XT			or XT	
4	Time	1:00	0:45	1:00	1:00	Day off	1:00	1:00	5:45
	Workout	Strength	Bike — S1	Strength	Bike — E1		Bike — T1	Bike — E1	
	Specific	AA	Spin Step-ups	AA	or XT		5 mile ATT	or XT4	
5	Time	1:15	1:00	1:15	0:45	Day off	1:00	1:00	6:15
	Workout	Strength	Bike — S2	Strength	Bike — E2		Bike — E2	Bike — E1	
	Specific	MS	7-9 min ea. leg	MS	or XT			or XT	
6	Time	1:15	1:00	1:15	1:00	1:00	1:30	1:15	8:15
	Workout	Strength	Bike — S1	Strength	Bike — E1	Bike — E1	Bike — E2	Bike — E1	
	Specific	MS	Spin Step-ups	MS	or XT	or XT			
7	Time	1:15	1:00	1:00	1:00	1:00	2:00	1:30	9:00
	Workout	Strength	Bike — S2	Strength	Bike — E1	Bike — E1	Bike — E2	Bike — E1	
	Specific	MS	8-10 min ea. leg	MS	or XT	or XT			
8	Time	1:00	Day off	1:00	1:00	Day off	1:00	1:00	5:00
	Workout	Strength		Strength	Bike — S1		Bike — T1	Bike — E2	
	Specific	MS		MS	Spin Step-ups		5 mile ATT		
9	Time	1:00	1:00	1:00	1:00	Day off	1:15	2:00	7:15
	Workout	Strength	Bike — E2	Strength	Bike — M2(3Z)		Bike — E3	Bike — E2	
	Specific	PM		PM	4-5 x 3' (1' RI)				
10	Time	1:00	1:00	1:00	1:00	Day off	1:30	2:30	8:00
	Workout	Strength	Bike — E2	Strength	Bike — M2(3Z)		Bike — E2	Bike — E3	
	Specific	PM		PM	4-5 x 4' (1' RI)				
11	Time	1:00	1:00	1:00	1:00	1:00	1:30	3:00	9:30
	Workout	Strength	Bike — E2	Strength	Bike — M2(3Z)	Bike — E1	Bike — E2	Bike — E3	
	Specific	PM		PM	3-4 x 5' (1' 30" RI)	OR — Day off			
12	Time	1:00	Day off	1:00	7Bike — E2	Day off	1:00	1:00	5:00
	Workout	Strength		Bike — S			Bike — T1	Bike — E2	
	Specific	PM		4-6 x 30' (2' 30" RI)			5 mile ATT		
13	Time	1:00	1:00	1:00	1:00	Day off	1:30	2:15	7:45
	Workout	Strength	Bike — E2	Strength Bike — S1	Bike — E4	Bike — E2			
	Specific	ME		ME	Spin Step-ups				

Plan 5
Improve Hill Climbing

Week		Monday	Tuesday	Wednesday	Thursday	Friday	Saturday	Sunday	Weekly Total
14	Time	1:00	1:00	1:00	1:00	0:45	2:00	2:30	9:15
	Workout Specifics	Strength ME	Bike — E2	Strength ME	Bike — E1	Bike — E1	Bike — E4 OR — Day off	Bike — E2	
15	Time	1:00	1:00	1:00	1:00	0:45	2:00	3:15	10:00
	Workout Specifics	Strength PM	Bike — E2	Strength ME	Bike — S1 Spin Step-ups	Bike — E1 OR — Day off	Bike — E4	Bike — E2	
16	Time	0:45	Day off	1:00	1:00	Day off	1:00	1:15	5:00
	Workout Specifics	Strength PM		Bike — E2	Bike — S7 4-6 x 30" (2' 30"RI)		Bike — T2 5 mile TT	Bike — E2	
17	Time	1:00	1:00	1:00	1:00	1:00	1:30	2:30	9:00
	Workout Specifics	Strength PM	Bike — S7 4-8 x 30" (2' 30"RI)	Bike — M3(4-5a) 4-6 x 3' (1' RI)	Bike — E2	Bike — E1 OR — Day off	Bike — E2	Bike — A1a Group ride (hills)	
18	Time	1:00	1:00	1:00	1:00	1:00	1:30	2:30	9:00
	Workout Specifics	Strength PM	Bike — S7 4-8 x 30" (2' 30"RI)	Bike —A6(5b-cZ) 4-5 x 90" ('3'RI)	Bike — E2	Bike — E1 OR — Day off	Bike — E2	Bike — A1b Group ride (rolling)	
19	Time	0:45	Day off	1:00	0:30	Day off	2:00	0:45	5:00
	Workout Specifics	Strength PM		Bike — S7 6-8 x 30" (2' 30"RI)	Bike — E1		Bike — A1c Uphill fast, down EZ	Bike — E1	
20	Time	1:00	1:15	1:15	1:15	0:30	1:15	2:30	9:00
	Workout Specifics	Strength PM	Bike — S7 4-8 x 30" (2' 30"RI)	Bike —M3(4-5a) 4-5 x 3-4' (1' RI)	Bike — E1	Bike — E1 OR — Day off	Bike — E2	Bike — A1c Group ride (hills)	
21	Time	1:00	1:15	1:15	1:15	0:30	1:15	2:30	9:00
	Workout Specifics	Strength PM	Bike — S7 4-8 x 30" (2' 30"RI)	Bike — A2(5bZ) 4-5 x 3'uphill (3' RI)	Bike — E1	Bike — E1 OR — Day off	Bike — E2	Bike — A1b Group ride (rolling)	
22	Time	1:00	Day off	1:00	1:00	Day off	1:00	1:00	5:00
	Workout Specifics	Strength PM		Bike — E2 4-6 x 30" (2' 30"RI)	Bike — S7 5 mile TT		Bike — T2	Bike — E2	
23	Time	1:00	1:00	1:15	1:00	0:30	1:15	2:30	8:30
	Workout Specifics	Strength PM	Bike — E2 4-5 x 3'uphill (3' RI)	Bike — A2(5bZ)	Bike — E1	Bike — E1 OR — Day off	Bike — E2	Bike — A1d Group ride (hills)	
24	Time	1:00	1:00	1:00	1:000	Day off	2:00	1:30	7:30
	Workout Specifics	Strength PM	Bike — E2 4-5 x 90" (3'RI)	Bike —A6(5b-cZ)	Bike — E1		Bike — A1c	Bike — E2 Group ride (hills)	
25	Time	Day off	1:00	0:45	Day off	0:30	2:00	1:00	5:00
	Workout Specifics	4 x 90" (3'RI)	Bike — A7)3 x 90" (3'RI)	Bike — A7 3 x 30" (2' 30"RI)		Bike — S7	Fastest group ride you've ever done.	Bike — E1 OR — Day off	

REFERENCES

Friel, J., The Cyclist's Training Bible, VeloPress, Boulder, CO, 1996.

Numerous athletes I've worked with over the years, thanks for your help.

CHAPTER ELEVEN

Nutrition

Most importantly, eat!

A story of change

Windy Ann was a competitive racer, trying to get better. She wanted to lose some weight to help her edge toward faster race speeds and more podium spots. It seemed the women who were faster than her were also thinner. Maybe if she were lighter she would be able to race even faster. She was well-read on diet and nutrition. Literature throughout the 1980s told her she could lose weight by following a low-fat diet, going no lower than 1200 calories per day, and exercising. So that's what she did.

Windy carefully monitored her calories and opted for high-value foods. High-value foods were those that were chocked full of vitamins and minerals, but they also needed to be low in fat. Foods fitting this description were fruits and vegetables. She knew she needed protein, but she was also aware that the average U.S. consumes entirely too much protein. She got most of her protein from non-fat dairy products and an occasional piece of fish or poultry.

After several years of competition and training, she was unable to change her body weight. Why? She exercised between six and ten hours each week, worked between forty-eight and fifty-five hours each week, and watched what she ate. How could she not lose weight? She worked hard at her job, she was athletic and conscious of food intake; why didn't her body look like the body of a fit athlete? She had no energy, and she always had a nagging injury each year that kept her from developing her full speed potential.

In the early 1990s, frustrated with her situation, Windy sought the help of a registered dietitian, who asked her to keep food logs for a week. Keeping a food log was easy for Windy; she had meticulously counted calories for years. She could estimate portions without weighing them and would occasionally check her expertise against a measuring cup or a scale. The registered nurse found Windy's diet to be very high in vitamins and minerals; low in fat—only 10 percent of total caloric intake; low in protein—only 10 percent of total calories; and high in carbohydrates—80 percent of total calories. Her daily intake averaged around 1300 calories per day. Perfect for wanting to lose weight—well, maybe one hundred calories per day too high. It was the perfect diet for an endurance athlete and for someone trying to keep their 195-198 cholesterol from getting any higher. Yet, if this diet were so perfect, why wasn't she thinner? Why didn't her body have that svelte, strong, athletic look advertised in magazines? She would later discover that she had other problems, which she didn't even realize were diet related.

Chris, the registered dietitian, told Windy that she thought her caloric intake was too low. Based on Windy's work and exercise routine, Chris recommended Windy increase her daily caloric intake to around 2300 calories. What? Increase calories? How was Windy ever going to lose weight? Surely not by eating more food?

Chris also thought Windy's fat and protein intake was too low. Windy suspected this as well. She had read about the work that Barry Sears did with the Stanford swim team. He helped them change their diet to 30-30-40; 30 percent fat, 30 percent protein and 40 percent carbohydrates. Windy wanted Chris's opinion about a 30-30-40 diet.

Chris had also read about this new diet and they agreed to move forward and give it a try. Windy would eat more food, more fat, more protein and fewer carbohydrates. After one week, Windy returned to Chris's office to find she had lost three pounds. She physically felt better, although it felt like she was eating a ton of food.

Now convinced she should make changes to her diet, Windy continued eating more calories and the macronutrient split of those calories would include more fat and more protein.

It was November when Windy began her diet change. In the weeks and months following the change, she began to take notice of some big changes. She had more energy, was sleeping through the nights, not getting up three to five times—sometimes for a snack. Her hair was growing faster and needed to be cut more often. She simply felt good, and her menstrual cycle had resumed.

Three years before starting the new diet, Windy had quit taking birth control pills. After she quit taking birth control pills, her menstrual cycle was never regular. She just thought it was due to being on the pill for so long. Within five months of changing her diet, Windy had regularly occurring menstrual cycles.

By the time the next racing season arrived in May, Windy was feeling better than ever. She made it through a winter of training with no nagging injuries, regular menstrual cycles, no winter injuries to haunt her all race season, but still no significant weight loss. The initial three pounds was all Windy lost, but the numbers on the scale were meaning less and less to her. They meant less because she felt better and she was racing faster. The entire race season following her diet change, her racing times improved.

During the race season, she found she could consume a diet near 30-30-40, however, she needed to change that regimen during races. She found she needed to consume a sports drink during longer races, or she felt terrible. She also found she needed more carbohydrates in the hours following a hard workout or race in order to speed her recovery.

Windy had faster race times, regular menstrual cycles, no injuries, and, in general, she felt better, but she was worried about her cholesterol level. If this new diet was good for her athletics, but was putting her at risk for heart disease, she decided she would head back to the old, low-fat diet. Fourteen months after changing to a 30-30-40 diet, Windy had blood tests from which she found her total cholesterol to be improved at 160—she was surprised.

After two years of changing her eating habits, Windy lost an additional seven pounds. It was a slow process, but worth the time.

Although she no longer keeps food logs, Windy tries to balance her snacks and meals by eating some protein, fat and carbohydrates. She no longer lives on nonfat yogurt, bagels, fruits and vegetables. She hasn't given up the fruits and vegetables, but now she consumes lean meats and nuts as well. And fat is no longer an enemy.

No one mentioned, or the author, have any affiliation with Barry Sears, financial or otherwise.

The story about Windy is a story I share with many of the athletes who I coach. It is a true story and, unfortunately, it's not uncommon. The most important message of this story is that extreme calorie restriction and repeated dieting slows metabolism.

- *Rule No. 1:* Eat adequate calories to maintain weight.
- *Rule No. 2:* Do not try to lose weight with extreme calorie restrictions. Very low fat and/or very low protein diets are correlated with amenorrhea.
- *Rule No. 3:* Eat a balance of macronutrients.

A body that receives inadequate nutrition will breakdown. This can mean more frequent colds and flu, or it can be more serious physical injuries that won't heal. The ill and injured cannot train and burn calories, nor can they be competitive athletes.

On a positive note, Windy knew something was wrong and took action. She knew what it was like to feel really good and thought she should feel like that all the time. She had too many things she wanted to do and had no time for injury or illness.

The beginning of Windy's story is a familiar one. Athletes, both women and men, want to lose weight in order to increase speed. The first thing they do is cut calories from their diet. No one wants to diet for any extended time, so they cut a lot of calories for a short period of time to get this diet thing over with. When athletes cut significant calories from their diet in order to lose weight the result is often negative.

In a specific study on triathletes, dietary habits of four men and two women elite triathletes were examined. An analysis of a seven-day diet record showed their daily intake of calories and carbohydrates to be insufficient to support their estimated requirements. They were also found to be low on zinc and chromium. Researchers made diet recommendations to the athletes, and follow-up seven-day diet records found the athletes increased average daily calories; increased carbohydrate consumption; met their daily requirements for zinc, chromium and all other nutrients; and they improved their performance.

In a separate study on trained cyclists, a high-fat diet was found to increase endurance. Five trained cyclists followed either a high-fat diet (70 percent fat, 7 percent carbohydrate, 23 percent protein) or a high-carbohydrate diet (74 percent carbohydrate, 12 percent fat, 14 percent protein) for two weeks, then tested performance. The high-fat diet was associated with increased performance for endurance at 60 percent VO_2 max.

If performance isn't your only concern, and you want to live to be one hundred years old, think about the people who live in Lerik, Azerbaijan—a small mountain town near the Iranian border. This village is famous for people living to one hundred years and more. There are scores of old people living in the town, how do they do it?

The town is poorly served by medicine, most of the people are uneducated, they don't eat much, and they work like beasts of burden. Vegetables, fruit and sour cheeses make up the majority of their diet. When Azerbaijan was part of the Soviet Union, doctors visited the town and took numerous blood samples, looking for some secret to longevity. The tests were inconclusive. Researchers theorized the longevity was related to genetics and clean, stress-free living.

Confused yet? How is it that athletes, whether their discipline is triathlon, cycling or surviving, can all follow completely different diets and all increase their performance or outlive most average people? What are athletes supposed to believe? What is the perfect diet?

If there were one golden diet that worked for everyone on earth, the person who discovered that diet would be rich and famous. If we talk about diet in very general terms, perhaps there is only one good one: eat and drink enough to build and maintain a healthy body. Seems easy. The difficult part comes when people want to know exactly what to eat. How many carbohydrates, how much fat and protein? How many calories? Precisely which foods should I eat each day to guarantee optimal health? Perhaps the perfect diet is easy, but not simple. An appropriate diet depends on:

- *Genetics*
- *Activity level—past, present and future*
- *Lifestyle, including stress level*
- *Quality of food consumed*

Most of us do not have the lifestyle of the people living in Lerik, so perhaps they aren't a fair comparison. People living in modern cities deal with pollution, job-related toxins, job- and family-related stress, water and foods that have been processed. Should diet be individualized? If so, how do we know what our own optimal diet is?

The remainder of this chapter will attempt to give you information you can use to evaluate and improve your diet. A single chapter can not cover all the information necessary to understand the topic of nutrition, and as technology develops we will have more accurate and new information. In this book is an overview of macro and micronutrients, nutritional concerns common to athletes—in particular women—and the chapter gives some recommendations.

MACRONUTRIENTS

Depending on which book you read, there are either three or four macronutrients. The common macronutrients are carbohydrates, fat and protein. Some sources consider water to be a fourth macronutrient.

WATER

Between 40 and 60 percent of an individual's body weight is water. Water is typically 65 to 75 percent of the weight of muscle and less than 25 percent of the weight of fat. This water is essential to a functioning body. A body can survive many days without food; however, it can survive only a few days without water.

Many people do not stay well hydrated. Most literature recommends drinking between eight and ten glasses of water each day. If you are drinking eight to ten glasses each day and your urine is dark yellow in color and foul smelling, you aren't drinking enough. These are signals of dehydration. A general guideline is to drink enough water so that your urine is light in color and has minimal odor.

Caffeinated coffees, teas and soft drinks have a diuretic effect, which means they increase the normal urinary output. Limiting your intake of caffeine will help keep you hydrated.

Caffeine has also been shown to increase calcium losses, so limiting your intake will help preserve precious bone.

A well-hydrated athlete also performs better. Dehydration levels as low as 2 percent of body weight are thought to impair athletic performance.

• *Rule No. 4:* Drink plenty of water.

CARBOHYDRATES

Carbohydrates are almost exclusively found in plants and their processed byproducts. Fruits, vegetables, beans, peas and grains are sources of carbohydrates. The only animal products and byproducts that have significant carbohydrates are milk and yogurt.

Carbohydrates are divided into two major groups: complex and simple. Foods in the complex group include vegetables, whole grains, beans and peas. These foods include fiber and starches, and are made of long, complex sugar molecules that are more difficult for the body to breakdown into sugar than are simple carbohydrates. Some simple carbohydrates—sometimes referred to as simple sugars—include fructose (fruit sugar), lactose (milk sugar), sucrose and glucose. Notice all of them end in the suffix "ose," meaning that it is a carbohydrate. When you read the label on a food product and it has several "ose" ingredients listed separately, each ingredient is really simple sugars of different origins or combinations of sugars.

The body absorbs sugars into the blood, heart, skeletal muscle and liver—in that order. When blood sugars reach homeostasis, heart and skeletal muscles accept glucose. The always-working heart and the working muscles use glucose for energy. Skeletal muscles also have the capability to store glucose as glycogen, to use for work at a later time. The liver also takes glucose from the blood and converts it to glycogen. The glucose not immediately needed by functioning body parts is stored as fat.

The rate at which carbohydrates are digested and their effect on the rise of blood glucose is described by the food's glycemic index. Foods that are easily digested and cause a pronounced rise of blood sugar, have high glycemic-index values. This pronounced rise of blood sugar initiates an insulin surge from the pancreas and stimulates body cells to store glucose as fat.

Insulin is useful to the body when it regulates blood sugar at a moderate pace. When insulin continuously spikes, dips, or is produced in inadequate quantities, health problems arise. Some health problems include hypoglycemia (low blood sugar), diabetes (high blood sugar), and issues related to coronary heart disease.

It is preferable to maintain blood sugars and insulin response such that there are not large peaks and valleys. Foods that are more slowly digested have a lower glycemic-index value and do not cause the glucose and accompanying insulin spike. The glycemic-index value of some common carbohydrate foods is shown on Table 11.1. It is important to note foods containing fats and proteins have lower glycemic indexes because fat and protein are harder to digest.

High-glycemic foods are most valuable during exercise and for post-exercise recovery. Otherwise, they should be used in moderation or in combination with fat and protein.

TABLE 11.1

GLYCEMIC INDEX

High glycemic (80% or higher)

Apricots	Banana	Carrots	Corn
Corn chips	Corn flakes	Crackers	French bread
Grapenuts	Honey	Mango	Molasses
Muesli	Oat bran	Pastries	Potatoes
Raisins	Rice	Rye crisps	Shredded wheat
Soda pop	White bread	Whole wheat bread	

Moderate Glycemic Index (50-80%)

All-bran cereal	Baked beans	Beets	Garbanzo beans
Navy beans	Oatmeal	Oranges	Orange juice
Pasta	Pinto beans	Potato chips	PowerBar
Spagetti	Yams		

Low Glycemic Index (30-50%)

Apple	Apple juice	Apple sauce	Barley
Black-eyed peas	Dates	Figs	Grapes
Yogurt	Kidney beans	Lentils	Lima beans
Peaches	Pears	Peas	Milk
Rye bread	Sweet potatoes	Tomato soup	

Very Low Glycemic Index (less than 30%)

Cherries	Grapefruit	Peanuts	Plums	Soy beans

• *Rule No. 5:* There are no "bad" foods, however, some foods should be consumed with discretion.

FAT

Our bodies need fat; it is essential for normal body functions. Fat makes foods taste good, is enjoyable to eat, and makes us feel satisfied after its consumption. As with carbohydrates, there are some fats that should be consumed in moderation. There are three major categories of fats: saturated, polyunsaturated and monounsaturated.

Those fats that should be consumed in moderation, are the saturated variety. Excess consumption of saturated fats can raise cholesterol levels, particularly the LDL or "bad" cholesterol. They are found in animal products and some tropical oils such as coconut and palm. When some of the otherwise healthy oils are hydrogenated, a process that turns a liquid fat into a solid product, the new fat is saturated and contains trans-fatty acids. These trans-fats are not well digested by the body and are thought to contribute to coronary artery disease. Hydrogenated fats are prevalent in many processed foods such as crackers, cookies and some canned products. Read labels on food products and look for hydrogenated oils.

Polyunsaturated fats are found in corn, safflower, soybean and sunflower oils. Consumption of the polyunsaturated family may actually lower cholesterol, however, in the process of doing so, the HDL or "good" cholesterol may also be lowered.

Fats that are thought to positively influence health are the monounsaturated fats found in nuts and some vegetables. They are found in almond, avocado, olive, canola and walnut oils. Of course, the whole food itself contains these oils as well.

The fats necessary for good health are called essential fatty acids (EFAs). The body cannot manufacture these fats. EFAs contribute to a healthy body by improving hair and skin texture, reducing cholesterol and triglyceride levels, preventing arthritis, and contributing to healthy hormone levels. EFAs are found in large quantities in the brain, aiding in the transmission of nerve impulses and overall brain function. EFAs are also essential for rebuilding and producing new cells.

Omega-3 and omega-6 fats are the two EFAs. Omega-3 fats

are found in coldwater fishes such as salmon, mackerel, menhaden, herring and sardines. Omega-6 fats are found primarily in raw nuts, seeds, grape seed oil, sesame oil and soybean oil. To supply essential fatty acids, omega-6 fats must be consumed in the raw form, pure liquid or supplement form, and not subjected to heat in processing or cooking. Wild game, not subjected to current chemical-fatten-them-up-feedlot-style diets, is rich in omega-3 and omega-6 fats.

• *Rule No. 6:* Fat in the diet is essential to optimal health.

PROTEIN

Protein in the diet is absolutely necessary for growth and development of the body. Next to water, protein makes up the greatest portion of our body weight. All cells contain protein. Some food protein sources are considered "complete proteins" because they include all of the amino acids the body can't manufacture on it's own. Complete protein foods include milk, eggs, poultry, fish, cheese, milk, yogurt and soybean products.

People who chose to be vegetarians need to be well educated on combining foods because most plant products—with the exception of soybeans—are incomplete proteins, which means they are missing one or more of the essential amino acids. If a diet is missing one or more of the essential amino acids, a deficiency will develop, resulting in illness or injury.

MICRONUTRIENTS

Vitamins and minerals are micronutrients because they are needed in smaller quantities than water, carbohydrates, fat and protein. Vitamins and minerals are considered coenzymes, and enable the body to produce energy, grow and heal. Vitamins regulate metabolism and assist in the biochemical processes that release energy from digested food. Some vitamins are known for their antioxidant properties, cancer prevention, and cardiovascular disease protection. Vitamins E and C are two of the vitamins scientists believe we should supplement in our diet because we probably don't get enough of these vitamins in our diets. Some of the sources of Vitamin E include nuts, seeds, whole grains, cold pressed vegetable oils and dark green leafy vegetables. Vitamin C is primarily found in green vegetables, citrus fruits and berries.

Minerals are necessary for the correct composition of body fluids, the formation of blood and bone, the regulation of muscle tone, and the maintenance of healthy nerve function. Calcium and iron are two of the minerals of most concern to women. Adequate calcium is necessary to ward off osteoporosis, and can be found in dairy products, green leafy vegetables, and fish with bones (sardines and salmon). Iron's most important function is the production of hemoglobin, myoglobin, and the oxygenation of red blood cells. It is found in the largest quantities in the blood. Menstruating women lose blood and iron each month with their periods, and care must be taken to consume adequate iron, so as not to become anemic. Iron is primarily found in meat, fish, poultry, eggs and green leafy vegetables.

PHYTOCHEMICALS

Scientists have recognized for years that diets rich in fruits, vegetables, grains and legumes appear to reduce the risk of a number of diseases, including cancer, heart disease, diabetes and high blood pressure. Researchers have found these foods contain antioxidants that prevent cells against oxidation—a damage similar to rust on metal. More recently, scientists found phytochemicals in these same foods, and they are thought to prevent a number of diseases and aid in the repair of cells when disease strikes. Phytochemicals give plants their rich color, flavor and disease protection properties. There are literally thousands of phytochemicals. Tomatoes alone are thought to contain more than ten thousand different varieties.

Science continues to discover more and more about foods and their valuable properties. Supplements can not replace the value of whole foods; humankind's quantity of knowledge is still quite small.

• *Rule No. 7:* A healthy diet should contain a wide variety of minimally processed foods.

HOW MUCH OF WHAT?

Now things get sticky. We need carbohydrates, fat and protein, but how much of each? Eat enough calories—so how many would that be? How does one go about losing weight without compromising health? Should we take vitamin and mineral supplements? Long bouts of exercise need calorie supplementation, but how much and what kind of foods? Long or exhaustive exercise requires quick recovery—how is that best accomplished? The answer to all of these questions is a simple, "Well, it depends."

If we first establish priorities, set goals, and determine how to measure the goals, then the answers become clearer. First, let's look at priorities and goals.

Consume a diet that:

• ***Builds and maintains a healthy body in the short term, and minimizes the risk of disease in the future.*** Not only will you be able to live a full and active life, but you can spend discretionary money on items other than health care.

• ***Allows you to feel good physically and mentally.***

• ***Considers genetic predisposition.***

• ***Takes into account your lifestyle and activity level.***

• ***Enhances your athletic capabilities.***

Before getting into more detail on diet specifics, it's important to discuss disordered eating and eating disorders.

DISORDERED EATING AND EATING DISORDERS

The social pressures to be thin are advertised everywhere. Thin, beautiful models are on the covers of numerous newsstand magazines; a publisher's hope is that a consumer will like the look of the cover, pick it up and eventually purchase the magazine.

Women are becoming more educated about the visual stimuli that comes out of Hollywood, and newspaper and magazine advertisers. Often, young teens are made-up to look like adults, and that image is then used to sell products. Products are purchased, sometimes, with hopes of looking like the model. Sadly, even fourteen-year-olds can't relax and be kids. The sidebar on page 252, titled "Poison Beliefs" is a sad account of teenage girl's beliefs about food.

Even the photographs are illusionary. Technology allows us to take any photographic image and manipulate it. Got a photo where it would look nice with a few flowers in the foreground? They can be added. Is there a blemish on the model? No problem, just remove it. Too many wrinkles? No big deal, those can be softened a bit. If you have ever watched a good magician, you know illusions can be very powerful. Once the illusions are exposed, the magic is gone. So, before you attempt to imitate a model, ask yourself if the model is real or an illusion.

Perhaps illusions contribute to the estimated 65 percent of female athletes with disordered eating behaviors. Disordered eating can be the precursor to eating disorders. Some behaviors signaling disordered eating are:

- *Obsessive talk about food, calories, fat grams and body weight.*

- *Constant awareness of weight and food intake of other people.*

- *Not eating in public.*

- *Often talking of being overweight.*

- *Consistently skipping meals.*

- *Classifying some foods as "bad" and totally forbidden from the diet.*

- *Consumption of "bad" foods causes bingeing, purging or punitive behaviors.*

- *Self-diagnosed allergies to foods based on a single or few adverse reactions.* Food group elimination can cause unnecessarily restrictive eating behavior and may risk vitamin and mineral deficiencies.

Unfortunately, the desire to be thin can transform into a full-blown eating disorder. Two of the most common eating disorders

Poison beliefs

The Reporter-Herald newspaper conducted a survey on body image and received comments from seventy-seven seventh-graders and thirty-three fourth-graders. When asked how they felt about the way they looked, half of the girls didn't give positive answers. Forty-two percent of the fourth-graders and 46 percent of the seventh-graders said they wished they were thinner. At a tender, young age of ten, 42 percent of the girls are worried about gaining weight. That number climbs to 53 percent in the twelve-year-old group.

Many of the girls—90 percent—read fashion magazines, and a full 64 percent of them admire the women in the magazines, and many aspire to look like them. Considering the average model is 5 feet 11 inches and weighs 114 pounds, this is a near impossible goal for the majority of the female population,

averaging 5 foot 4 inches tall and 140 pounds. A few of the girls did believe the models were too thin, however, they were the minority.

Sadly, many of the girls are passing up opportunities to be active for fear of being ridiculed. For example, they may avoid the swimming pool altogether. Others wear heavy, bulky T-shirts at the swimming pool to cover tummies, thighs and butts. Both of these behaviors discourage girls from activity—the very thing that can help them have fit, healthy bodies.

It is apparent from this survey, done in the spring of 1998, that unhealthy attitudes about body image start at an early age. Although there is growing awareness that fit, healthy bodies and minds are valuable assets, the cultural drive to correlate thinness with self-worth is poisoning another generation of women.

are anorexia and bulimia. Anorexia is characterized by restricting food to the point of near starvation. Anorexics see themselves as fat, although their outward appearance to others is emaciated. They usually have an incredible amount of nutritional knowledge, which they use to categorize foods as either "good" or "bad." Fat and calories are evil monsters.

People with anorexic behaviors will often prepare elaborate meals for others or give food as gifts, but will not eat the foods themselves. If they do sample a forbidden food, the quantity would be too small to equal one bite.

Bulimia, on the other hand, is a disorder characterized by episodes of bingeing on high-calorie foods. A bingeing person can consume two thousand to twenty thousand calories in a single sitting. The consumption is followed by guilt and a purging behavior follows. Purging takes the form of vomiting, fasting, laxative or diuretic use, or excessive exercise.

Disordered eating or an eating disorder can lead to amenorrhea and, eventually, bone loss. When this occurs, the health of the athlete is sacrificed. No weight-loss scheme, short- or long-term, is worth your long-term health.

While on the topic of weight loss, there are a gazillion diets out there. Go into any bookstore and browse the health and nutrition section. Weight-loss schemes are abundant. But before embarking on any dietary protocol, ask yourself:

- *Who are the subjects being discussed in the dietary plan?*
- *Is my background similar?*
- *Is my lifestyle similar?*
- *Are my goals similar?*
- *How restrictive is this diet?*

A few years back, there was a popular diet circulating that involved eating a great deal of vegetable soup. The diet was designed to reduce the weight of obese patients preparing for open-heart surgery. These people probably had some genetic conditions that predisposed them to heart disease. They probably were not very fit or active. And their goal was to lose weight fast, to prepare for open-heart surgery.

Now, unless you have the same lifestyle and background as these people, and you are planning on a trip to the hospital to have surgery with constant medical attention, why would you follow their diet? To lose weight fast?

If that logic works, then anyone wanting to be a top cyclist should eat the way the Tour de France riders do. They average 5800 calories (61 percent carbohydrates, 15 percent protein, and 23 percent fat) per day. Why would few people consume a Tour de France cyclist's menu to be a stronger, faster rider—calories and all—when a larger number of people are willing to follow a diet designed for obese heart patients? Faulty logic. Following either of these diets, to the letter is inappropriate, unless you are one of the people the diet is designed for.

So, what kind of diet should you follow? Before changing, it is necessary to know where you are. If you visit a registered dietitian who specializes in sports nutrition, they will ask you to keep a food diary. If you decide to start this process on your own, you will need to do the same thing. If it turns out you have been maintaining a healthy weight and you can eat three thousand calories per day, great! If you constantly feel week and tired by eating two thousand calories per day, something needs to change.

Get yourself a reference book such as "The NutriBase Nutrition Facts Desk Reference," and look at what you are currently doing. You can begin with just calories or you can log the grams of carbohydrate, fat and protein. Of course the most helpful information is honest information. Try not to change eating behaviors just because you are keeping a food log.

Next, fill out the "Health Questionnaire" on page 319. After filling out the questionnaire, you will have information to help determine if you are healthy or not. If you are not healthy, consider changing your diet or lifestyle, or both.

BENCHMARK FORMULAS

So far, we have reviewed a set of nutrition rules, prioritized the goals of a healthy diet, determined what we are currently eating, and recorded our current health status on the "Health Questionnaire." We know where we have been and where we want to go, now how do we get there?

If you are satisfied with your current diet, it meets your needs, and is within the goals of a healthy diet, celebrate! If you think your diet needs fine tuning, or you just want more information, read on.

HOW MANY CALORIES DO I NEED TO CONSUME?

One of the common formulas used to determine daily caloric requirements to maintain body weight is the JeeJeeBoy: 30 calories per kilogram of body weight.

To find your weight in kilograms, take weight in pounds and divide by 2.2. For example, if you weigh 140 pounds, your weight in kilograms is 140/2.2 = 63.6 or 64 kg. To find your daily caloric needs, 64 x 30 = 1920 calories.

Now the modifiers:

• Add more calories if you lead a highly active lifestyle, one hundred to three hundred may be appropriate.

• Add about four to six hundred calories per hour of cycling.

• Add about three hundred calories per hour of weight lifting.

• Subtract calories if your lifestyle or job is sedentary, one hundred to three hundred may be appropriate.

So, the 140-pound person in our example would need to consume somewhere between 1620 and 2820 calories to maintain her weight. For weight maintenance, she needs to consume more calories on days when she is very active and training, then consume fewer calories when her body doesn't need them.

WHAT IF I WANT TO LOSE WEIGHT?

Since, from the food logs, you know how many calories it takes to maintain your current weight, decrease your daily intake by two hundred to three hundred calories, not dropping total caloric intake below 1500. This slow approach to weight loss reduces the risk of compromising your health through reduced food intake.

WHAT KIND OF CALORIES?

There is a range for macronutrient consumption that will maintain or improve health and athletic training:

Carbohydrates	40 to 65 percent of total calories
Fat	15 to 30 percent of total calories
Protein	15 to 30 percent of total calories

Exactly how much of each macronutrient you should eat depends on the answers you gave on the health questionnaire and your current mode of training. Everyone needs to change their diet to meet their current health and athletic training needs. Those needs are constantly changing. Nutrition needs on a heavy training day are not the same as when you are resting and exercising very little. Consider the following suggested diet modifiers:

• *Carbohydrate consumption on the higher end* when training fast miles (Zones 4 and 5) or long miles (ninety minutes or more.)

• *Carbohydrate consumption on the lower end* when doing training in Zones 1 to 3.

• *Protein consumption between 1.5 and 2.0 grams per kilogram of body weight, on the higher end* when training hard, trying to build muscle mass, or to maintain trying muscle mass when dieting.

Notice there are different ways to estimate calorie and nutrient needs. Some sources reference macronutrient breakdown, while other sources talk about consuming a certain number of grams of each macronutrient. It can get confusing when the measuring systems are talked about interchangeably. To help clarify, it is important to know that not all food grams have equal energy value:

• *1 gram of carbohydrate contains about 4 calories of energy*

• *1 gram of protein contains about 4 calories of energy*

• *1 gram of fat contains about 9 calories of energy*

• *1 gram of alcohol contains about 7 calories of energy*

Nutrition Rules

Rule 1: Eat adequate calories.

Rule 2: Do not try to lose weight with extreme calorie restrictions.

Rule 3: Eat a balance of macronutrients.

Rule 4: Drink plenty of water.

Rule 5: There are no "bad" foods, however, some foods should be consumed with discretion.

Rule 6: Fat in the diet is essential to optimal health.

Rule 7: A healthy diet should contain a wide variety of minimally processed foods.

The following are some values for replacement energy and recovery energy needs:

For exercise longer than about an hour, consume

• 30 to 60 grams of carbohydrate per hour of intense or long exercise. This can be fluid or solid sources of energy.

• And be certain to consume adequate fluids as well. Hydration needs to be around 4 to 8 ounces every fifteen to twenty minutes.

For exercise that's more than about three hours, anecdotal evidence says athletes prefer to include fat and protein. Exact quantities for optimum performance are not clear, however many ultraendurance athletes prefer more balanced foods, not as heavily loaded with only carbohydrates. Hydration needs to maintained at 4 to 8 ounces every fifteen to twenty minutes.

To speed recovery, post-long or exhaustive workouts,

consume liquid or solid fuel within twenty to thirty minutes after exercise containing:

- 1.5 to 1.6 grams of carbohydrate per kilogram of body weight
- and 0.4 to 0.5 grams of protein per kilogram of body weight

Some examples of foods some athletes consume include milkshakes; chocolate milk; bagels and cottage cheese or lean meat; fruit and protein powder smoothies, yogurt smoothies with fruit; and beef jerky combined with a sports drink.

To speed recovery, post-long or exhaustive workouts, consume liquid or solid fuel over the twenty-four hours after exercise containing:

- 6 to 8 grams of carbohydrate per kilogram of body weight

Some studies indicate regular snacks of approximately 50 grams of carbohydrate, every two hours may optimize recovery. Of course, an evening meal containing adequate carbohydrates will be necessary to get an athlete through a night complete with sleep. In other words, don't try to set an alarm to wake up every two hours to eat.

Back to our 64-kilogram athlete, let's say she is doing a big day of training. Her total calories need to be about 2800. If her protein intake were 1.8 grams per kilogram of body weight, that would be 115 grams of protein, or about 460 protein calories.

On her long ride of three hours today, she will consume 200 carbohydrate calories per hour—or 600 calories total. And she will consume a post-ride recovery food containing

1.5 to 1.6 grams of carbohydrate per kilogram of body weight. So, say 1.6 x 64 = about 90 grams of carbohydrate, or 90 x 4 = 360 carbohydrate calories. These 960 carbohydrate calories meet her cycling needs.

Since her ride was a very fast group ride, she will need to consume between 6 and 8 grams of carbohydrate per kilogram of body weight, over the next twenty-four hours, to restore her glycogen levels. At 6 grams, she would need 384 grams of carbohydrate (including the post ride recovery drink) and at 8 grams per kilogram of body weight, she would need 512 grams of carbohydrate. Choosing 512 grams, she needs to consume about 2000 carbohydrate calories— over 24 hours—to restore her glycogen. She can consume some of those calories today and some tomorrow.

If today's caloric needs are about 2800:

• *Protein calories are 460* or 16 percent of the total (460/2800)

• *Carbohydrate calories at 60 percent* of the total mean, 1680 calories (420 grams) need to be carbs.

• *The remaining calories are fat: 2800 - 460 - 1680 = 660 calories* (about 73 fat grams) or about 30 percent fat.

This example was done to show you how to calculate calorie needs and macronutrient requirements. Modifiers were given to help you decide when to go on the high side and when to go on the low side. Again, you will need to decide what works for you. If you change your diet, know where you started before the change, know what the changes were, and take good notes about your health. Use the "Health Questionnaire" as a guide.

NUMBERS, NUMBERS, NUMBERS

Now that you have formulas to estimate caloric needs, macronutrient breakdowns, fueling during a long ride, and post-ride fueling strategies, here are some words of caution:

The word "estimate" is critical. Don't worry about getting the exact numbers when you are consuming calories. There is a margin of error on food product labels and there is a margin of error when estimating personal nutrition needs. Again, refer to the "Health Questionnaire" to determine if your nutrition program works for you.

If you've determined that you need 100 grams of carbohydrate and 33 grams of protein for post-ride recovery and a food source has 115 grams of carbs and 25 grams of protein, no problem.

Try not to become a food-log-addict. Use food logs as spot checks to see what's going on with your diet. It is possible to drive yourself nuts weighing and counting everything. Let food logs serve their purpose, and then give them a rest.

Body weight is a number and simply that. Do not weigh yourself every day and look for changes. At most, weigh weekly. In fact, if you lose several pounds from one day to the next, you are probably dehydrated and should try to remedy the situation by drinking like a camel and putting some numbers back on the scale. How do you feel? How is your health? These are better measures of success.

SUPPLEMENTS AND ERGOGENIC AIDS

The "U.S. Heritage Dictionary" defines the word supplement as, "Something added to complete a thing or to make up for a deficiency." Notice it does not say, "Substitute for...." No amount of vitamin and mineral supplementation will make up for a crummy diet, something people don't seem to understand. As case in point, I was talking with a young person sacking my groceries recently. The young man was inquiring about the volume and variety of vegetables I was purchasing, "Are you a vegetarian or something?"

"No, at our house," I replied. "We eat lots of different vegetables because they taste good and their vibrant colors make an exciting plate."

"Oh, I don't eat vegetables," he said, "so I just eat meat and potatoes and take vitamins. Anyway, one vitamin has all the stuff I really need, so I don't have to worry about it."

His thought process is all too common. While he continued sacking the groceries I explained about fiber, phytochemicals and probable unknown substances contained in real food. I explained how young the discovery of phytochemicals was and that although we humans are pretty smart, we are a long way from knowing everything. Supplements are meant to compliment a diet high in whole foods. With that said, no supplementation plan will make up for a diet high in processed foods, saturated fat, sugar and salt, low in fiber, and low in variety. I don't know if he will change his habits, but at least he's thinking. He asked if I would let him take my groceries to the car, so he could ask more questions. "You bet!"

Researchers are continually finding more information about vitamin and mineral supplementation. A survey among top researchers, asked what they, themselves, take

for vitamin and mineral supplementation and answers were not uniform. Some supplements worth discussing are:
- *Multivitamin and mineral tablets*
- *Vitamin C*
- *Vitamin E*
- *Calcium*
- *Iron*

MULTIVITAMINS

Most experts agree a multivitamin and mineral supplement is recommendable. Some experts still hold a strong belief we should be able to meet all of our vitamin and mineral needs from food, but more research is telling us it just doesn't happen for most folks. U.S. Department of Agriculture data indicates that at least 40 percent of the people in the U.S. routinely consume a diet containing only 60 percent of the Recommended Daily Allowances (RDA) of only ten of the selected nutrients. We would likely fair worse if more nutrients were evaluated.

There continues to be controversy as to whether or not athletes' requirements for vitamins and minerals exceed that of the average population. If athletes are consuming a balanced and varied diet, and taking a multivitamin, perhaps that is enough.

VITAMINS C AND E

The current a recommendation is to supplement a multivitamin with 1000 milligrams of vitamin C and 400 IU of vitamin E. Both of these are antioxidants, substances that block oxidative damage to the cells of our body.

CALCIUM

In several chapters thoughout the book, calcium has been mentioned in the prevention of osteoporosis. The current recommendation is to consume somewhere between 1000 and 1500 milligrams of calcium daily. In order for calcium to be well-absorbed vitamins C, D, E and K all play a role. Several of the minerals also play important roles in calcium absorption. For example, too much magnesium and/or phosphorus—found in many soft drinks and processed foods—can inhibit the absorption of calcium.

Just supplementing the diet with calcium isn't the cure-all. Weight-bearing exercise also plays an important role and more is not necessarily better. Even men, who seem to be less prone to bone loss, can suffer when exercise levels are excessive. One study found Tour de France racers had bone mass densities between 10 and 17 percent lower than those of age-matched counterparts did. One can conclude that cycling is not a weight-bearing exercise and attribute the loss to cycling. But not so fast....

A second study on University of Memphis basketball players found players were losing about 3.8 percent of their bone mass from preseason to midseason of a single year. Bob Klesges, the head scientist, determined the ballplayers were losing substantial amounts of calcium in their sweat. He concluded this by collecting the sweaty T-shirts of the players and carefully wringing out their contents to be analyzed. He found the players gained back some of their bone mass during summer, but that 1.1 percent wasn't enough because they lost an additional 3.3 percent when practices resumed, and the total losses were now at 5.8 percent.

With supplemental calcium, they were able to regain the losses.

In summary, try to get 1000 to 1500 milligrams of calcium from your diet. If you are not getting enough, consider a supplement. The superior supplement is calcium citrate malate, which is found in many juices. On average, people absorb 35 percent of the calcium in calcium citrate malate, compared to 30 percent of the calcium in other supplements. Currently, only General Nutrition Centers are licensed to make supplements containing calcium citrate malate.

IRON

Iron is essential in the production of hemoglobin and myoglobin and the oxygenation of red blood cells. Women can have problems with low levels of iron and develop anemia. One of the common causes of anemia is excessive menstrual flow. Aggravating the blood loss situation, some women consume inadequate iron. Good sources of iron are fish, meat, poultry, green leafy vegetables, whole grains, and enriched breads and cereals.

Iron is one of the supplements you should not self-medicate without the help of a physician. Constant fatigue is one the common symptoms of anemia. Low iron can be easily identified with a simple blood test. In fact, a simple blood test can detect many problems associated with diet. For athletes who are serious about wellness and competition, an annual blood test—in the off- or restorative-season—is an excellent source of information. This baseline test can then be used to diagnose changes to blood chemistry when a competitive season seems to have gone awry.

ERGOGENIC AIDS

A lot of people question the use of sports drinks, food or energy bars, and caffeine.

SPORTS DRINKS

The simple rule of thumb here is to drink the one that tastes best to you. If you select a drink that tastes good, and use it for workouts over an hour long, generally, it will be beneficial. If you purchase a drink spiked with all sorts of vitamins and minerals, but think it tastes funny or makes fur grow on your teeth during a long, hot day, it's not the best drink for you.

ENERGY BARS

Energy bars are useful for long rides, snacks for pre- and post-workouts, and pre-race snacks. They are not, however, one of the major food groups. Some athletes use them as a major source of calories, choosing them over fruits and vegetables because they are an easy food to acquire and prepare. Eat minimally processed foods. Whenever possible chose them first.

CAFFEINE

Caffeine is feasibly the most widely used drug in the world. It stimulates the central nervous system, the adrenal system, and the muscular system. It has also been shown to influence the metabolic system by stimulating fat metabolism during aerobic exercise. The results include lowered levels of perceived pain at a given pace and the sparing of glycogen as a fuel. Additionally, when used in conjunction with exercise, it appears not to have the diuretic effect that it has when consumed in a non-exercising situation.

A dose of 5 to 7 milligrams of caffeine per kilogram of body weight, given one hour prior to exercise, has been the typical protocol for the studies. Additional studies, in which the focus is on the measurement of free fatty acid metabolism, show the response to fat-burning may not be optimized until three to four hours after ingestion.

There can be negative side effects. Some people do not tolerate caffeine well and become shaky, jittery and unable to focus. It also is bothersome to some people's stomachs. Caffeine is a banned substance by the U.S. Olympic Committee when it reaches levels measuring 12 micrograms per milliliter of urine. To reach this level would require ingesting somewhere near 1200 milligrams of pure caffeine.

If you decide to use caffeine, experiment with it during a training ride and don't wait until a race or big event to test your tolerance and advantage levels. Major sources for caffeine are:

PRODUCT	CAFFEINE	MILLIGRAMS
Coffee	(8 ounces)	100-250
Espresso	(1 ounces)	35-60
Cappuccino	(8 ounces)	35-60
Caffe latte	(8 ounces)	35-60
Mountain Dew	(12 ounces)	55
Pocket Rocket, chocolate	(one packet)	50
No-Doz, regular	(1 tablet)	100
Excedrin	(2 tablets)	130

BRIEF THOUGHTS

It is critical to overall good health to consume enough calories and a wide variety of foods to ensure adequate absorption of macro and micronutrients. Not consuming enough calories can slow metabolism and cheat the body of nutrients needed for normally functioning menstrual cycles and the repair process essential for good health and athletics.

While my grandmother called me Gale Ann, my great-uncle called me Windy Ann. The story about Windy Ann at the beginning of this chapter is my story. If I can prevent other women from repeating my journey or shortening the time it takes them to consider changing their diet, I would be pleased. Women, don't be fooled into thinking this is only a problem for females. The majority of people I coach are men, and highly competitive male athletes are also prone to extreme calorie restriction.

Hopefully, this brief touch on nutrition will encourage you to learn more about the subject. Read information and recommendations carefully. Determine if the recommendations being made by the author apply to you and your situation. If you have special needs or deficiencies that weren't discussed in this chapter, take care of them and learn as much as you can about their treatment.

Eat. Eat often. Eat variety. When cycling long, eat early, don't wait. Most importantly, eat.

REFERENCES

Balch, J. F, M.D., Balch, P. A., C.N.C., Prescription for Nutritional Healing, Avery Publishing Group, 1997.

Book, C., RD, McKee Medical Center, Loveland, Colorado, personal interview with author, July 7, 1998.

Burke, L., Dr., "The Complete Guide to Food for Sports Performance," Allen & Unwin, 1995.

Coleman, E., RD, MA, MPH, Eating for Endurance, Bull Publishing Company, 1997.

Colgan, M. Dr., "Optimum Sports Nutrition," Advanced Research Press, 1993.

Correll, D., Young girls attempt to mimic model bodies, Sunday *Loveland Reporter-Herald*, June 21, 1998.

Eades, M. R., M.D., Eades, M., M. D., "Protein Power," Bantam Books, February 1996.

Frentosos, J.A., Baer, J.T., "Increased energy and nutrient intake during training and competition improves elite triathletes endurance performance," *International Journal of Sports Nutrition*, March 7 (1), 1997, pp. 61-71.

Friel, J., "The Cyclist's Training Bible," VeloPress, Boulder, CO, 1996.

Klesges, R. C., "Changes in bone mineral content in male athletes. Mechanisms of action and intervention effects," *Journal of the American Medical Association*, 276 (3), July 1996, pp. 226-230.

Lampert, E.V., et al., "Enhanced endurance in trained cyclists during moderate intensity exercise following two weeks of adaptation to a high fat diet," *European Journal of Applied Physiology*, 69 (4), 1994, pp. 287-293.

Liebman, B., "Avoiding the fracture zone. Calcium: Why get more?" *Nutrition Action*, Center for Science in the Public Interest, April 1998.

Liebman, B., "3 Vitamins and a mineral. What to take," *Nutrition Action*, Center for Science in the Public Interest, May 1998.

Lutter, J. M. and Jaffee, L., "The Bodywise Woman," Second Edition, Human Kinetics, 1996.

McArdle, William D., Katch, Frank I., Katch, Victor L., "Exercise Physiology, Energy, Nutrition, and Human Performance," Third Edition,

Lea & Febiger, 1991.

Mountain Biker, The big jolt. Mountain Biking's love affair with coffee, February 1998.

Ryan, M., RD, "Less is more, taking the sensible approach to shedding weight," *Inside Triathlon*, July 1998.

Sabo, D., et al. "Modification of bone quality by extreme physical stress. Bone density measurements in high-performance athletes using dual-energy X-ray absorptiometry," *Z Orthop Ihre Grenzgeb*, January-February, 143 (1), 1996, pp. 1-6.

Sears, B., "The Zone," HarperCollins Publishers, 1995.

Sharkey, B. J., Ph.D., "Fitness and Health," Human Kinetics, 1997.

Shulman, D., Ph.D., RD, *Exercise Physiologist*, personal interviews with author, July 1998.

The "U.S. Heritage Dictionary," Houghton Mifflin Company, 1983.

Ulene, A., Dr., "The NutriBase Nutrition Facts Desk Reference," Avery Publishing Group, 1995.

"USA Cycling Elite Coaching Clinic Manual," *USA Cycling*, February 17-19, 1997.

CHAPTER TWELVE

Mental
tools

*"Courage is resistance to fear, mastery of fear—
not the absence of fear."*   —Mark Twain

D o you have a little voice in your head that talks to you? We all do. If you haven't paid much attention to that little voice before now, perhaps it's time to take notice of what that voice is getting you into or helping you avoid.

Your little voice is talking to you when you are stuck in traffic. It says, "Great, stuck here and I have a five o'clock appointment. Now I'm going to be late."

When you stand in front of the mirror on a good day the voice says, "I look good in this color; lookin' good today."

On the bike, on a bad day the voice comments, "Oh God, I hate hills. I'm the worst hill-climber, everyone is going to leave me in their dust."

Yes, that little voice can talk you into and out of a variety of situations. If you get nothing else out of this chapter, it is important that you begin to take notice of what your little voice is saying to you and the pictures it creates in your mind. That is the first key concept of this chapter:

KEY CONCEPT 1

Notice what the little voice inside your head is saying, and the pictures it creates.

I encourage the athletes I coach to "play to win." This means to go as far as you can using all that you have. Directly opposite of play to win is "play not to lose," which is a defensive strategy attempting to maintain security and comfort. The sidebar outlines some of the differences between the two strategies.

When you play to win, it means as long as you do your best on that given day, in those given circumstances, you are a winner—no matter what place you finish the race. After all, if you have given the race or the event all there is give, you owe no one any apologies. Your focus is on you, your performance, and what you have control over.

As you train to be a faster cyclist, it is going to be uncomfortable. There are going to be times when your legs are burning and you feel like you can't go another second, but then you will go ten; you played to win. This type of discomfort, tolerating it physically and mentally, is part of becoming a faster cyclist. As you increase your level of fitness, tolerance levels for discomfort will increase, and embracing discomfort is part of growth and improvement.

There is, however, a real difference between discomfort and

Play to win	Play not to lose
• Show up and do your best	• Don't show up if you can't do well at a race or be one of the leaders on a group ride
• Focus on yourself and your performance	• Focus on others and their performance
• Take responsibility for the controllable—be accountable	• Blame your performance on the weather, equipment, other people—be a victim
• Embrace discomfort for growth	• Stay in your comfort zone
• Stretch your skills	• Avoid new situations

pain. The physical discomfort I'm referring to is typically muscular in nature and goes away by decreasing intensity. A second type of physical discomfort is the kind that shows up a day or two after a hilly ride or a tough weight-room workout. This is called delayed onset of muscle soreness or DOMS. These types of physical discomforts are common to athletic training.

Pain, on the other hand, comes in various levels, some of which need the attention of a physician. Pain that surfaces after a ride, such as a kink in your neck, but goes away either the same day or within twenty-four hours is probably nothing to worry about. Treatments including gentle stretching, icing the injured area, and taking anti-inflammatories—aspirin, ibuprofen and naproxen sodium—may help.

Pain that occurs during the ride, but doesn't force you to stop, can be treated the same way as after ride pain. In this case, you might consider taking a day or two off the bike to reduce further injury.

Pain that occurs throughout the ride, interfering with your ability to complete the ride, or pain that persists when you are off the bike needs attention. You are injured. You need to take a few days off the bike, you can stretch and ice the injured area, and take anti-inflammatories, but you also need to seek professional medical attention. Too often athletes try to train through an injury, only making it worse. It is important for you to be able to distinguish between discomfort, minor pain and injury.

Some sources of mental discomfort come from doing something you've never done before, something that may scare you a bit, or something that puts your ego at risk. What happens if you don't meet your goal? What happens if you can't keep up with the group? What will people say? I propose you are the one who really determines the definition of success or failure. Stretching yourself, taking some risks, will move you toward new levels of skill and confidence.

KEY CONCEPT 2

Play to win. The key to this concept is practice. Just as you practice and improve on physical aspects of cycling, you will need to practice the mental aspects of training. Seek new sources to increase your mental skills and keep adding to your capabilities.

KEY CONCEPT 3

Mental skills, like physical skills, must be practiced and improved.

TOOLS

In addition to the three key concepts there are some extra tools for your mental training toolbox. These concepts and tools are multipurpose; you can use them in other aspects of your life, as well as athletics.

TOOL NO.1: SET

- S—Stop the little voice
- E—Evaluate the situation
- T—Take a course of mind

There are times when the little voice can be so helpful and encouraging. It can urge us to go on when we are struggling. Unfortunately, there are also times when the little voice is negative. It may say, "This wind is horrible. You ride poorly in the wind. Why even start the ride?"

When the little voice begins to say negative things, it's time to stop the voice and evaluate the situation. The little voice is also a protective voice, letting us know about danger. If your little voice cautions you not to travel through a dark, wooded park at night, perhaps you should listen. Stop the voice and decide if the unlit park is a safe situation. If not, change your mind and pick an alternate route.

On the other hand, if the voice is telling you how horrible the wind is and you are not a good rider, stop and evaluate. Okay, there is wind, but everyone else has wind, too. Maybe you can use the wind to simulate hills and enhance your training? If you are riding with other people, how about a paceline to rotate a lead position, rotating work and rest? How about riding out in a head wind and back in a tail wind? Wouldn't it be fun to see how fast you can go on the way back?

When that little voice starts talking to you, pay attention. If the talk is negative or makes you feel fearful, evaluate all options and then take a course of mind. Is there really something to fear, or can you make lemonade out of lemons. Whatever your mind decides, your body will follow. The wind and hills can be valuable training tools, if you let them.

TOOL NO.2: KILL MONSTERS

When I was younger, I would get into bed by taking a running start from the hallway. A good running start allowed me to jump into bed, clearing the "Monster Zone." The monster lived beneath my bed and had an arm reach of approximately three feet. He was a large, brown, hairy creature, with dust bunnies stuck to his fur. He lived beneath the bed, hated light and was very active at night. He would try and grab my leg if I allowed it to dangle over the edge of the bed. If, however, I cleared the three-foot zone surrounding my bed, got my feet under the covers, and laid in the center of my bed, I was safe.

The monster was closely related to the "Closet Ghost," who stared at me if I left the closet door open at night. The closest ghost was a transparent creature with glowing eyes. Sometimes, the eyes were between hanging clothes and other times they seemed to float near the top shelf of the closet. I remember fearing both of them and making rules of behavior, which would keep me safe.

I'm not sure how I came to realize they weren't really there, but I can now admit I made the whole thing up —so vividly full of details; if I close my eyes I can still see both of them. I can also admit I still make things up, sometimes with rules to keep me safe. Maybe you make things up too? Don't worry; it's a common phenomenon.

I make things up about other people and myself. For example, some days I look in the mirror and think my hair is out of control and that I look weird. In fact, I look no different than yesterday when I thought I looked fine.

Some days I get on the bike and think I will never be a hill climber. Using Tool No.1, I ask, "Will I never be a hill climber?" If I never ride the hills and work to get better, I'll probably not be a good hill climber. On the other hand, if I work at being a better climber and make myself stronger, perhaps I can improve. Maybe that hill isn't as big as I make it out to be?

Common stories to make up are about other people. "They are thinner, faster, stronger, better, taller, shorter and more athletic than I." Before long, this other person is on a giant pedestal, out of reach of human hands. Only Gods are privileged enough to converse with them.

Really? Is that true? Or have you imagined this person, perhaps your competition in a race, to be larger than life?

Again, ask yourself if what you and your little voice are saying is true? Are those monsters real, or imagined? If you can't completely eliminate monsters, at least, turn on the light and have a good look at them. Maybe you will find they are no more than small, harmless trolls with blue hair.

TOOL NO.3:
CELEBRATE SMALL SUCCESSES EVERY DAY

This tool ties in with goal setting and was mentioned in Chapter 9. Set subgoals to mark your progress toward the larger goal. Close each day by recalling at least one good thing about your day. This sort of positive self-recognition builds self-esteem and confidence.

TOOL NO.4: HANG OUT WITH POSITIVE PEOPLE

Have you ever noticed that spending time with a positive person helps you feel better? How about when you are around a negative person? Does keeping company with a negative person wear on your nerves? Research has found that a simple grimace will raise the level of adrenaline and lower the level of serotonin in your system, producing all the physical symptoms of fear. Those symptoms include an elevated pulse, shallow breathing and slowed digestion. Negative thoughts turn into negative emotions, which turn into negative physical symptoms.

A positive outlook on any situation will more readily contribute to a healthy physical and emotional state than any negative outlook will. So, surrounding yourself with positive, supportive people is an advantage. There is one catch, though. Positive people prefer to be around positive people as well, so they will expect reciprocal behavior from you.

TOOL NO.5: WRITE DOWN POSITIVE AFFIRMATIONS

Keep a notebook or a doodle-pad with positive comments about yourself. Are you a good hill climber? Jot it down. Are you improving your average speed? Write it down. Are you good at keeping your cool when tempers flare? Make a note. A brief review of any and all positive attributes you have can boost confidence. When the going gets tough, and no matter what you do, you can't muster a single positive thought, go back and read what you have written about yourself. They will help you reframe your thoughts.

TOOL NO.6: MEASURE SUCCESS BASED ON YOURSELF

This tool was also mentioned in Chapter 9. You cannot control anyone else's performance or their fitness level. You can use other people's performances as reference points, but don't base your entire measure of personal success or failure on others. Some good measures of personal success include aerobic and all-out time trials, average speed on a particular ride, or simply how strong you feel on the bike. Record that information on a sheet of paper, and then transfer it from log book to log book, each year. Then you can look back earlier in the season and at past years to review how your performance has improved.

TOOL NO.7: ENOUGH RULES

Many people spend their entire lives waiting for "just the right time" to try something new, stretch their wings, or take a risk. They want to wait until they are rich enough, thin

enough, strong enough, confident enough, and so on....
But really, if you have a dream, you have enough right
now to make it come true. However, you may have to
work for it.

Sometimes enough is enough. It is easy to get caught up
in goals, schedules, plans and training logs. Athletes will
ignore pain signals, risking injury, and others will ignore bad
weather such as lightning, to get those final training miles in
this week. Enough is enough. Relax, enjoy family or friends,
or take a nap and resume training tomorrow.

TOOL NO.8:
RECOGNIZE A LEARNING OPPORTUNITY WHEN IT PRESENTS ITSELF

Some of us have a tough time distinguishing the difference between doing something wrong and making a
mistake. When we do something wrong, it is with intent.
We know before we do the action or say the words that it
is not the right thing to do. Intentionally swerving the
bike and forcing someone off the road is wrong.

On the other hand, if you look over your shoulder and
steer your bike to the side as a consequence, nearly causing an accident, that is a mistake. The described chain of
events could cause you or someone else injury. Learn to
ride a straight line when looking over your shoulder. Use
errors and their corrective action to help improve performance. Too often people are hard on themselves for making an error or a mistake. Mistakes are really opportunities
to learn.

TOOL NO.9: USE MUSIC AS MOTIVATION

Music can be used to set a mood, influence thoughts, and offer a bit of solitude. Watch many of the top athletes in sports and you will see them preparing for a race by wearing headphones. They are listening to music that they find motivational or calming. Pay attention to music and see what it does for your mood. Would music help you prepare for a race?

TOOL NO.10:
FOCUS ON WHAT YOU HAVE CONTROL OVER

As you train and compete, there will be a host of things you have no control over. You can't control the weather, other people's performance or actions, or accidents such as a flat tire. You can grumble and complain all you want, but the uncontrollables won't change. The only things you have control over are your attitude, your outlook on the situation and your actions. Before thoughts become tangled in a death spiral or become physically impaired by a monster, use Tool No.1 to take a course of mind. Evaluate the situation and begin brainstorming options. Many times you have several choices. You can chose to quit and go home, which is a valid option, or continue as best you can on that given day—play to win.

BRIEF THOUGHTS

The concepts and tools presented in this chapter are mental tools I've shared with athletes and business people. I was introduced to the "play to win" concept in a business environment. It was in a learning session delivered by

Pecos River Learning Centers. I've adapted the tool to athletics and believe it is has value in sports and everyday battle. In work and in play, I encourage you to hone your mental skills. The body will follow the mind, but an unwilling mind cannot force the body to perform to it's full potential.

REFERENCES

Bean, A., "Runner' Guide to Pain," Runner's World, November 1997.

Loehr, J. E., Ed.D., Mental Toughness Training for Sports, R. R. Donnelley & Sons, Harrisburg, Virginia, 1987.

Loehr, J. E., Ed.D., McLaughlin, P.J., Mentally Tough, M. Evans and Company, New York, New York, 1986.

Pecos River Learning Centers, Playing to Win Playbook and Study Guide, Pecos River Learning Centers Inc., 1992.

CHAPTER THIRTEEN

Comfort
and Safety

---

*"We should not only use all the brains we have,
but all that we can borrow." —Woodrow Wilson*

This chapter is a collection of stuff I've found useful over the years. Hopefully, the tips can help prevent uncomfortable situations or help remedy a problem once it has occurred. Nothing in this chapter is intended to substitute for a physician's advice or treatment. You need to determine when a trip to the doctor is in order. As discussed in Chapter 12, determine if the situation is discomfort—something you can handle yourself—or pain that needs professional treatment.

SADDLE SORES

Sores in the groin, upper leg and butt area can be a nuisance—or worse, force you to take time off of the bike. The best treatment for saddle sores is preventing them. The most common sores include blocked or infected glands, which show up as lumps; pain in the pelvic bone area where your weight may be resting; and chafing problems.

PREVENTION

Be certain your bike is set up correctly by referring to Chapter 3. A saddle that is too high can cause the rider to reach too far for the pedals causing either pressure or chafing. A saddle that is too low doesn't allow the legs to support the body and puts excess pressures directly on your crotch—ouch!

To help prevent chafing, slather your genital area and upper thigh with a good emollient such as petroleum jelly. A relatively new product on the market is Sport Slick, which combines the lubrication of Vaseline with antifungal properties.

Wear padded cycling shorts without underwear. Cycling shorts are designed to reduce friction from seams and give you some padding to help reduce pressure on sensitive areas.

After the ride, get out of those dirty shorts. Good hygiene is essential. Wash your crotch and don't wear those shorts again until they have been cleaned.

Don't suddenly increase weekly or daily mileage on the bike.

If you shave the upper leg and lower torso, a light application of antibiotic ointment after shaving may help prevent red spots and infected bumps.

Be certain the bike seat isn't tilted too far up or down, causing pressure or making you constantly push back in the saddle.

If problems persist, a different saddle may help, especially one with a soft or cutout area near the nose.

SELF-TREATMENT

Soaking in comfortably hot bath water one to three times per day will help boils surface and drain.

Antibiotic ointments such as Neosporin aid healing.

Moleskin with an area cut out around the sore may help keep pressure off the sore itself.

DIARRHEA

A number of cyclists, including elite racers, put up with diarrhea and hope it will go away. If you have one loose bowel movement, it is not time to panic. If diarrhea continues, do something about it. Continued loose stools contribute to dehydration and loss of valuable nutrients. There are nonprescription remedies available at the pharmacy. Diarrhea that doesn't respond to over-the-counter remedies, or is reoccurring, needs the attention of a physician.

VAGINAL PROBLEMS

Vaginal irritations can put a woman off the bike in a flash. Several disorders related to the vaginal area are lumped under the term "vaginitis." Three of the most common problems women experience are vaginitis, sometimes referred to as crotchitis; bacterial infections; and yeast infections. Some causes of these problems include warmth, moisture, poor hygiene, over-zealous hygiene, chafing of the inner labia, oral medications such as antibiotics and allergies.

Crotchitis is irritation or inflammation of the inner labia, urethra, clitoris and the skin around the vagina. Figure 13.1 shows the anatomy of this area. Redness, itching and pain are

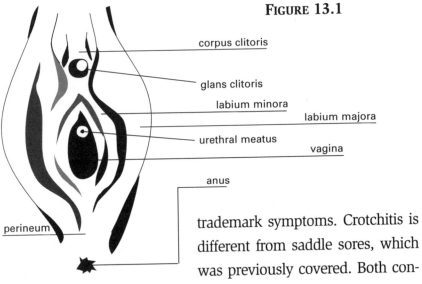

FIGURE 13.1

corpus clitoris

glans clitoris

labium minora

labium majora

urethral meatus

vagina

anus

perineum

trademark symptoms. Crotchitis is different from saddle sores, which was previously covered. Both conditions, however, share some of the same causes, such as friction, pressure, warmth and moisture. The preventative measures for saddle sores will also help prevent crotchitis.

Other preventative measures include keeping the crotch dry and ventilated when off the bike. Cotton underwear and loose fitting shorts or dresses will allow air into this area, making it less inviting for germ growth.

Removing urine, after a trip to the toilet, is best done by wiping from front to back. This reduces the chances of contaminating the vaginal area with stool. Aggressive wiping and rough toilet paper can be irritants. Patting the area dry is another option.

Once you have crotchitis, a non-prescription cream, such as Vagesil, may relieve itching and help make a bike ride more comfortable. This can be particularly helpful if crotchitis occurs during a multiday bike tour.

A second type of vaginal problem is bacterial vaginosis. Its primary symptoms include foul-smelling, profuse, watery vaginal discharge. Typical treatment includes an antibiotic prescribed by a doctor.

The third type of vaginal problem, yeast infections, often produces vaginal discharge, which is thick, cheesy and foul smelling, and is accompanied by intense itching. After a doctor confirms the condition is a yeast infection, reoccurring yeast infections can be recognized by and treated with over-the-counter medications.

The vaginal environment is a delicate balance of organisms, including normal bacteria and lubricating secretions. When normal secretions are replaced by a discharge, which is smelly, unusually thick or copious, or the vaginal area becomes inflamed or itchy, it is time to seek help. Do not allow a small problem to expand to a larger one.

TRAVEL

While we're on this crotch subject, sitting in a car or airplane seat for hours with a sweaty crotch can be the perfect environment for unwelcome bacteria to grow and cause problems. Wear cotton underwear and cotton pants, a skirt or shorts that allow the crotch to breathe. Nylon underwear and tight-fitting pants or shorts trap heat and moisture making the perfect breeding ground for bacteria.

For extra long flights, such as those overseas, take along a wash cloth and perhaps a change of underwear. Freshening up in the toilet midway through a flight can prevent problems later.

If you are prone to bacterial or yeast infections and are traveling overseas take along your regular medications. Attempting to explain vaginal problems to a pharmacist in a foreign country is one of the last things anyone wants to do on vacation.

TAMPON STRINGS

Tuck tampon strings just inside your vagina when riding your bicycle. This will keep the strings from working their way to the thigh and eventually getting tugged with every pedal stroke.

ROAD RASH

Skin damage is the nasty thing that happens when your flesh meets earth in a sliding-type accident. Softball players call it strawberries, due to the red, dotted appearance. Cyclists call it road rash. When flesh meets earth, injuries can come in various degrees, similar to a burn. Third-degree road rash, the worst condition, won't be covered here and is a condition in which the skin is entirely removed, with underlying layers of fat and other tissues exposed. This injury requires a physician and, perhaps, skin grafting.

First-degree road rash occurs when only the surface of the skin is reddened. It usually does not require active treatment, but keeping the wound clean is recommended. Second-degree road rash occurs when the surface layer of the skin is broken and a deep layer remains that will allow the skin to heal and repair itself.

The old method of treating second-degree road rash involves cleaning the area, then allowing the wound to dry, form a scab and heal on its own. Very superficial wounds can be treated with this method; however, a more active method is advised for most second-degree wounds.

The more active method of treatment involves frequent

cleansing of the wound, application of topical antibiotics, and application of protective dressings that keep the wound moist and closed to air. The wound is cleaned daily with a warm bath or compress. The superficial scabs are removed with gentle scrubbing. Pink, healthy, new skin is what you want to see. Be cautious not to get so aggressive that you cause deeper, bleeding wounds.

After cleansing, a topical antibiotic is applied. Over-the-counter antibiotics include Neosporin and Polysporin. If these are irritating to the skin, a prescription cream from a doctor may solve the problem.

Over the antibiotic cream, apply a Vaseline gauze, such as Adaptic. This gauze is nonstick in order to keep from tearing off parts of the wound, which will make the situation worse when it comes time to change bandages. Further gauze may be added for extra padding and protection. Finally, tape and tube-stretch gauze is added to keep everything in place.

Words of caution: newly pink skin recently healed from road rash is highly susceptible to sunburn. Also, exposure of this new skin to sunlight is likely to create a permanent scar. Be certain to apply sunscreen with a sun protection factor (SPF) of at least 15.

STAGES OF HEAT ILLNESS

Although you are cautious about hydration and conditioning, there may be times when either the weather suddenly becomes very hot, or you travel from a cool to a hot climate to do an event. For those reasons, it's important to know the stages of heat illness:

HEAT CRAMPS

Muscle pain and involuntary spasm often occur. Body temperature is not necessarily elevated.

HEAT EXHAUSTION

Exhaustion is often reported during the first heat wave of summer.

It is caused by ineffective circulatory adjustments compounded by a depletion of extracellular fluid, especially blood volume due to excess sweating.

Symptoms include a weak and rapid pulse, low blood pressure in the upright position, headache, dizziness, and general weakness.

To aid the situation, stop physical work or exercise, move to a cooler environment, and administer fluids. In extreme cases, intravenous therapy may be needed.

HEAT STROKE

The most serious and complex of heat-stress maladies. It requires immediate medical attention. It is the failure of heat-regulating mechanisms in the body that are brought on by excessive body temperatures. Sweating usually ceases, skin becomes hot and dry, body temperature rises to at least 104 degrees Farenheight, and excessive strain is put on the circulatory system. With some individuals sweating may be present, but heat gain by the body outstrips the avenues for heat loss. Untreated, it can result in circulatory collapse, central nervous system damage, and death. Heat stroke is a medical emergency.

PREVENTION

- Heat acclimatization takes ten to fourteen days.
- Adding a small amount of salt to food—if you do not have problems with sodium—and drinking extra water will help. This helps because with prolonged exercise in the heat, sweat loss may deplete the body of sodium.
- Avoid alcohol and caffeine, as they are diuretics.
- Frequent rests may be necessary in hot weather.
- Cold fluids are absorbed faster than warm fluids. Drink before becoming thirsty.
- Drink diluted 4 to 8 percent glucose solutions immediately before, during and after exercise in the heat. During prolonged exercise, sixty to ninety minutes and longer, drink four to eight ounces every fifteen to twenty minutes.
- Wear loose fitting, light colored clothing or fabrics that wick moisture away from your body.
- Some prescription drugs may increase heat sensitivity; be aware of the side effects of medications.

COLD-WEATHER RIDING

Cold stress on the body has four stages. It is important to recognize the early signs of trouble, so exposure to the cold doesn't become dangerous:

STAGES OF COLD STRESS, HYPOTHERMIA

Stage 1: The body shivers to exercise muscles and produce heat as core temperature drops from around 98.6 to 96 degrees F. As you will recal from Chapter 4, women's body temperatures often run lower than men's. So a two-degree drop from what is normal will probably produce shivering.

Stage 2: When body temperature drops to between 91 and 95 degrees Farenheit shivering becomes violent, speech is difficult, thinking is slow, and amnesia may occur.

Stage 3: When body temperature drops between 86 and 90 degrees Farenheit, muscles may become rigid and skin will become blue and puffy. It is a critical sign when shivering stops. The person may have poor coordination, muddled thinking, and muscle spasms that appear as jerking. The person may still be able to sit or stand unassisted.

Stage 4: Body temperatures between 78 and 85 degress Farenheit will usually result in the person becoming unconscious with reflexes depressed.

Stage 5: When body temperatures dip below 78 degrees Farenheit, the person usually experiences ventricular fibrillation and cardiac arrest.

TREATMENT

The first step in the treatment of hypothermia is to remove the affected person from the cold environment. If possible, get her out of any wet clothing and into dry gear. Heat can be added to the body with hot drinks high in carbohydrates and by electric heat or fire. Blankets or spare clothing can be used to trap air and heat next to the person's body.

In cases of extreme hypothermia, the person can be immersed in a tub of water heated to between 105 and 110 degrees Farenheit. Submerge only her torso, leaving her arms and legs out of the hot water. This allows warming of the body core and a gentle warming of the limbs. There is a condition called "after drop" that can be avoided by submerging only the torso. If the entire body is submerged, large volumes of cold blood will circulate from the extremities to the heart. This can be a shock to the system, and send the person into cardiac arrest.

There is a slim chance you will ever experience the latter stages of hypothermia on a bicycle, unless you are riding in extreme conditions. Conditions for hyperthermia may also exist during winter sports for crosstraining.

PREVENTION

In a seminar given by Papa Bear Whitmore, a noted authority on wilderness survival, he said something that struck home with me. He basically said that when the weather is cold, say 20 or 30 degrees Farenheit, people know it's cold and they prepare for it. Often, however, problems occur when the temperature is in the 40 or 50 degree range and people are unprepared for a sudden weather change. Or an accident may occur that keeps them out longer than expected. In addition to unexpected weather changes and accidents, people who travel to new places for cycling events may simply be unaware of the dangers associated with cool- and cold-weather riding.

In one possible scenario, two riders set out for a two-hour ride, beginning the ride in 40-degree temperatures. The riders expect the weather to warm up as they ride, and they each take one bottle of energy drink and one bottle of water. Halfway through a two-hour ride, one rider gets a flat and they realize the temperature is not warming up as they expected. It looks like it may rain. One of the riders realizes they only have one fluid bottle filled with water—the second one is empty. They were distracted and forgot to fill the second bottle with energy drink.

The story has two endings. In one, mechanical problems force them off the bikes again to make repairs. It begins to rain, and the wind starts to blow. They end up being out an hour longer than intended in weather they didn't expect. They shared only 150 calories of energy drink between them—after racing each other for the first hour. On the way home, they both experience hypothermia.

In the second ending, a friend happens to drive by them as the weather begins to turn from bad to worse, and gives them a lift home. It was a lucky break.

Dressing in layers when the weather gets cold is important—"cold" being a relative term. What is an acceptable riding temperature for one person may be blue-lip weather for another. It helps to understand how our bodies lose heat. Heat is lost through four primary methods: radiation, convection, conduction and evaporation.

Radiation occurs when our exposed skin loses heat to the atmosphere via electromagnetic waves. For example, radiated heat is lost when standing in cool weather, with no wind, waiting for a riding partner to arrive.

Convection heat loss is associated with air moving across the body. The body warms air molecules that come in contact with the skin, then the air molecules move away, taking precious body heat with them. This is why the air temperature can be one numerical value, and wind—such as what occurs when riding—can create a chill factor. The wind chill factor can make bearable air temperatures downright dangerous. For example, a 40 degree Farenheit ambient temperature changes to 28 degrees on your skin with ten miles per hour wind. Add a cycling speed of twenty miles per hour to that head wind and the wind chill takes the temperature to a chilling 13 degrees Farenheit

Conduction is similar to convection, except body heat is lost through a cold object, instead of the air, such as sitting on a cold surface or holding a cold handlebar with your hands. Heat is sucked from the body to warm the cold object.

Finally, evaporation is the heat loss that occurs when moisture changes to vapor. Wet skin or wet clothing loses heat several times faster than the same surface when it is dry. Also, many materials such as cotton lose their insulating properties when they become wet.

To stay warm in cold-weather riding, it is important to dress properly. The layer next to the skin of the upper body should be a material, such as propylene or Coolmax that wicks moisture away. This includes sports bra material. Fibers such as cotton retain moisture, keeping you feeling chilled. If your neck gets cold, use a moisture-wicking turtleneck as a base layer.

The second layer on the upper body, can be a cycling jersey with arm warmers or a long-sleeved jersey made of fleece, depending on the temperature. If you will be peeling layers off, down to short sleeves, go for the cycling jersey and arm warmers. If the temperatures don't allow bare-arm exposure, stick with a long-sleeve jersey or a fleece jersey. Finally, make the outer layer a breatheable, wind and moisture barrier made of a fabric such as Gore-Tex. If the weather is extremely wet, go with a totally waterproof shell.

For the lower torso and legs, there are cycling tights and pants made specifically for cold and wet weather. If it is cool and dry, usually cycling shorts and a pair of regular tights or leg warmers do the trick. For colder weather, a pair of propylene thermal underwear between your cycling shorts and tights may help. Very wet, cold-weather riding may require waterproof pants to cover the tights.

Head, ears, nose, fingers and toes seem to be the areas that get cold first. Helmet wind covers are available to protect the head. Covered helmet and ear warmers will help keep the wind chill off of sensitive areas. For the nose, a balaclava can be worn under the helmet and pulled over the nose when necessary. If your ears get particularly cold, an ear warmer can be worn under the balaclava.

There are a wide variety of gloves on the market with varying thickness of insulation for warmth. The outer coverings vary to protect from simple chill to cold and wet conditions. Layering can work for the hands as well. An inner liner of propylene next to your hands and fingers wicks moisture away, while a second glove insulates and protects from the elements.

For the feet, there are also several booties available on the market. Some booties are simply wind covers, while other booties insulate toes from cold and water. Be careful not to wear socks that are so thick they cramp your feet. Cramped feet don't have adequate circulation, resulting in cold toes. For those with toes that get cold, even with a bootie, a product called Sports Heat, purchased at a sporting goods store, can be slipped into your cycling shoe. It comes in small chemical packs that generate heat once the package is opened. They can also be very helpful in warming cold fingers.

For overall body warmth, another trick is to fill a Camelback with a warm, apple-flavored sports nutrition drink. The warm bladder against your body will help you stay toasty, and the fluid is like hot apple cider.

BRIEF THOUGHTS

Take care of yourself and your riding buddies. Prevention of problems is always better than trying to remedy a bad situation. Hopefully, you will be able to use all the preventative tips in this chapter, and not the treatment tips.

A tremendously useful resource for cycling-related injuries is "Bicycling Medicine," by Arnie Baker. It is a must-buy for the serious cyclist.

REFERENCES

Baker, A., M.D., Bicycling Medicine, Argo Publishing, San Diego, CA, 1995.

McArdle, William D., Katch, Frank I., Katch, Victor L., Exercise Physiology, Energy, Nutrition, and Human Performance, Third Edition, Lea & Febiger, 1991.

Vickery, D. M., M.D, Fries, J. F., M.D., Take Care of Yourself, Fifth Edition, Addison-Wesley Publishing Company, Inc., 1994.

Whitmore, Papa Bear, Bunstock, J., The W.I.S.E Guide to Wilderness Survival, Astonisher Press, Lincoln, NE, 1992.

EPILOGUE

Writing this book was a learning and reflection opportunity. My goal was to present information, which is supported by research data and athletes. This desire yielded volumes of wisdom from dedicated researchers and athletes alike. The process allowed me to acquire new knowledge, verify or disprove old beliefs, and I found it difficult to decide which information to leave out of the manuscript. Other authors have written entire books on the subjects, which had to be condensed into a single chapter for this text. The chapters are certainly not all-inclusive; however, further reading material can be found in the reference section at the end of each chapter.

Scientific research is discovering more about the human body and athletic performance every day. Fortunately, more research is being conducted with athletic women test subjects, and more information is being discovered about the female body. This research, in conjunction with women just getting out there and doing it, will give us all wisdom that isn't based on old wives' tales. More than likely, some of the information between the covers of this book will need to be updated within a year or so, due to further research.

In the process of searching for new research, I found myself reflecting on how I acquired past knowledge. Certainly, published information is one source of information, but there were also a few people who had significant impact on my cycling. The first person that comes to mind is David French, who helped me select my first performance bicycle. He began the process of educating me about bicycle mechanics, cycling terms and group riding techniques. He and Michael Noonan were educators and unselfish, steady riding partners for several years.

After David decided to sell his bicycle shop and patented Cycle Tote business, I had to find a new shop to frequent. I looked for someone trustworthy, eager to do a good job and found Al Killen. Al had been heavily involved in cycling with his son and professional mountain-bike racer, Jimmi Killen. He spent numerous hours volunteering as a mechanic at cycling events. A cycling family, Al's wife Rogene remains a U.S. Cycling Federation racing official. Al's expert mechanical skills and attention to detail made him an instant draw.

Each time I went into the shop, Al took the time to show me what he was doing to my bicycle and why it was important. He knew I traveled to races and believed it was important for me to be able to support myself, mechanically, for the most common equipment failures. He was right, and the information he taught me increased my confidence.

Both Al and David were very patient and willing to answer my millions of questions, even enduring the note taking. They both invested years of unselfish knowledge transfer, product and service for which I'm grateful.

In more recent years, others have been very generous with products and service support; most have been helpful for a good number of years. I can't over emphasize the importance of quality products, service, and trustworthy people who are eager to lend a hand. The following individuals, representing their respective companies have been extremely helpful:

- *TREK Bicycles*—Michael Mayer and Carolyn Meyer
- *Pearl Izumi*—Julie Washnock
- *CompuTrainer*—Chuck Wurster
- *Smith Sport Optics*—Mary Hall
- *Polar Heart Rate Monitors*—Cory Cornacchio
- *Loveland General Nutrition Center*—Kenn Howard, Rebecca Howard and Sarah Melby
- *McKee Medical Center Sports Medicine*—Marilyn Schock, Fran Bell, Brian Quale and Greg Jensen
- *Peloton Cycles*—Trent Schilousky, Robin Torres, and staff
- *Scott Barrow,* Certified Massage Therapist

There are countless others who have offered moral support and some have been tireless training partners. To them, thank you for urging me to follow my passion.

APPENDICES

Appendix A **Menstrual Cycle Chart**

Month _____

Date	1	2	3	4	5	6	7	8	9	10	11	12	13	14	15	16	17	18	19	20	21	22	23	24	25	26	27	28	29	30	31
Days since last period																															
Basal Body Temperature																															
Menstruation																															
Cervical Mucus																															
PMS Symptoms:																															
Menstrual Symptoms:																															
Treatments:																															

Menses: **S**-Spotting **L**-Light flow **M**-Medium flow **H**-Heavy flow

PMS or menstrual symptoms: **S**-Slight, hardly noticable **L**-Light, but noticable **M**-Moderate, aware of problem **H**-Problem highly aggravating, affecting activities, lifestyle

Cervical Mucus: **C**-Clear, stringy **Y**-Yellow, tacky **L**-Limited mucus **M**-Moderate mucus **H**-Heavy flow, copius mucus

Appendix B **Basal Body Temperature Chart**

Date	1	2	3	4	5	6	7	8	9	10	11	12	13	14	15	16	17	18	19	20	21	22	23	24	25	26	27	28	29	30	31
Day of Menstrual Cycle																															
Temp.> 100F record here																															
100																															
99.9																															
99.8																															
99.7																															
99.6																															
99.5																															
99.4																															
99.3																															
99.2																															
99.1																															
99.0																															
98.9																															
98.8																															
98.7																															
98.6																															
98.5																															
98.4																															
98.3																															
98.2																															
98.1																															
98.0																															
97.9																															
97.8																															
97.7																															
97.6																															
97.5																															
97.4																															
97.3																															
97.2																															
97.1																															
97.0																															

GENERAL INSTRUCTIONS:

• Before writing on the chart, make copies as needed.
• Record the month at the top of the chart.
• Record the day of your cycle in row below the date box.

• Record basal body temperature each day, before getting out of bed and before activity causes your body temperature to rise.
• Put an "X" in the date box, across from the correct temperature reading.

• If you are tracking an illness and your body temperature rises above 100 degrees Farenheight, record your temperature in the third row of the chart.

307

This list is not meant to be complete, but rather a source to help women identify problems they may have.

Acne breakouts

Alcohol cravings

Anger

Anxiety

Backache

Bloating

Breast tenderness

Clumsiness

Confusion

Constipation

Crying easily

Depression

Diarrhea

Fatigue

Forgetfulness

Headache

Increased appetite

Insomnia

Irritable

Lack of concentration

Light-headed

Mood swings

Nervous tension

Pounding heart

Salt cravings

Short temper

Sweet cravings

Swelling of feet

Swelling of fingers

Unpredictable bowel movements

Weight gain

Withdrawal from others

Yeast infection

NAME

DATE

BIKE AND RIDER WEIGHT

Lᴀᴄᴛᴀᴛᴇ Tʜʀᴇsʜᴏʟᴅ Tᴇsᴛ Dᴀᴛᴀ Sʜᴇᴇᴛ

WATTS	HEART RATE	RATING OF PERCEIVED EXERTION
50		
70		
90		
110		
130		
150		
170		
190		
210		
230		
250		
270		
290		
310		
330		
350		
370		
390		
410		
430		
450		
470		
490		
510		
530		
550		
570		

ZONE	RPE	BREATHING
1	6-9	Hardly noticeable
2	10-12	Slight
3	13-14	Aware of breathing a little harder
4	15-16	Starting to breathing hard
5a	17	Breathing hard
5b	18-19	Heavy, labored breathing
5c	20	Maximal exertion noted in breathing

NOTES ABOUT BIKE SET-UP, CURRENT TRAINING STATUS, HOW YOU FEEL:

Appendix E **Strength Training Data Sheet**

Excercise	Weight	Sets	Reps	Weight	Sets	Reps	Weight	Sets	Reps	Weight	Sets	Reps	Weight	Sets	Reps	Weight	Sets	Reps	Weight	Sets	Reps	Weight	Sets	Reps
1. Hip extension (pick 1)																								
Squat																								
Leg Press																								
Step-up																								
2. Seated row																								
3. Back extension																								
4. Hip extension																								
Squat																								
Leg Press																								
Step-up																								
5. Chest press																								
6. Personal weakness																								
Heel Raise																								
Knee Extension																								
Leg Curl																								
7. Abdominals																								
8. Dead lift																								
9. Lat pull																								

AA-3-5 sets, 20-30 reps, RI = 60-90 sec, Slow speed, Ecercises 1,2,3,4,5,6,7,8,9
MS-3-8 sets, 3-6 reps, RI = 2-4 min, Slow to moderate speed, Exercises 1,2[3,5]
PE-3-5 sets, 8-15 reps, RI = 3-5, Fast speed, Exercises 1 [2,7][6,3]
ME-2-4 sets, 40-60 reps, RI = 1-2 min, Moderate speed, Exercises 1 [2,7][6,3]

PM-1-3 sets, 10-15 reps, RI = 3-5 min, Moderate fast speed, Exercises 1 [2,7][6,3]
EM-1-2 sets, 30-40 reps, RI = 1-2 min, Moderate speed, Exercises 1 [2,7][6,3]
*Exercises 3,6, and 7 are always done at AA load, sets, and reps
**This chart can be enlarged for more room to fill in the boxes.

313

The Health Questionnaire is intended to help you record health risks related to heredity and current health condition. This information will need to be updated as more information becomes available about family members, and as your personal health changes.

Sometimes, women unwittingly put the goal to be thin ahead of the goal to be healthy. Severely restricting calories will affect current health and will certainly affect future health if wellness does not become the No.1 priority.

Each question was designed to prompt thoughts about personal health and genetic risks, and convey the idea that nutrition affects several areas of overall health. These areas can be used as markers to determine if change in nutrition habits should be considered. Physical well being, athletic performance, mental attitude and nutrition are synergistic. They each need to be optimized in order for the athlete to perform at peak capability. A bit more detail about each question:

1. Your family health history is important when making decisions about nutrition and estrogen supplementation. Record any major health problems of your grandparents, parents and siblings in this section.

2. Record the history of any health problems you've had in past years.

3. Do you currently have any health problems? Is your overall health improving or declining?

4. Describe your current diet. It is best to have a food log, giving details, but you can also describe how you eat. Do you

eat highly processed foods? Do you eat out? If so, how many times each week? How many times each day do you eat? Do you eat because you are hungry or nervous? Do you eat a wide variety of foods, or do you tend to eat the same things each day?

5. Has your diet always been similar to how it is now, or have you made recent changes? Why did you change? Have the changes improved how you feel?

6. What does your blood-chemistry work say? Are there any items that are outside the recommended ranges? If so, can the answers to questions one through five yield any help to correcting the problem?

Questions one through six are intended to stimulate thoughts about overall health as a function of time. The answer to any one of the questions may not yield valuable information, but the answers to all the questions together may help you and your healthcare providers to flesh out solutions to problems.

Questions seven through fourteen are subtle questions that something is wrong with your health. These small details, again, when examined in total, may tell a tale of good health or pending trouble. When seeking the help of a physician, take the answers from this questionnaire along as they can give a small snapshot of your health.

Appendix F **Health questionnaire**

Questions one through six give you a health snapshot, including hereditary health.

1. What is my family history of health disorders?

2. What is my personal health history? What problems have I had in past years?

3. What health problems do I currently have?

4. What is my diet currently like? (Give a verbal description. A food log can provide more detail.)

5. Have I made recent changes to my diet?

6. What does my most recent blood-chemistry work say about my health?

If you answer "yes" to several of the following questions, your diet may not be serving your needs. Chapter 11 may help modify diet, or consider seeking the help of a registered dietitian specializing in sports nutrition.

7. Are my periods irregular, often skipping months?

8. Am I frequently awake throughout the night?

9. Is my hair dry and brittle?

10. Do I have acne or wounds that won't heal?

11. Are my nails weak and brittle?

12. Am I frequently ill or injured?

13. Am I often tired or have low energy?

14. Do I often have to skip training or reduce the intensity because I have "no legs"?

GLOSSARY

Aerobic, aerobic metabolism—Requires oxygen for energy transfer.

Aerobic capacity—A term used in reference to VO_2 max. Aerobic capacity training is in the range of 90 to 100 percent of VO_2 max pace, or 95 to 98 percent of maximal heart rate in women— and 90 to 95 percent in men.

Anaerobic, anaerobic metabolism—Energy transfers that do not require oxygen.

Anthropometry—The study of people in terms of their physical dimensions. It includes the measurement of human body parts, segment masses, centers of gravity of body segments, and ranges of motion that are used in biomechanical analyses of work.

Arteries—Blood vessels rich in oxygen that conduct blood away from the heart, to the body.

ATP—Adenosine triphosphate molecules are where potential energy is stored for use at the cellular level.

Atherosclerosis—The accumulation of fat inside the arteries.

Circulatory—Usually in reference to blood flow throughout the body.

Concentric contraction—A muscle contracts, exerts force, shortens and overcomes resistance. For example, concentric contraction occurs in the quadricep muscles when lifting the weight in a knee extension exercise.

DNA—Deoxyribonucleic acid. The units of heredity are the genes on our chromosomes. Each gene is a portion of the DNA molecule.

Eccentric contraction—A muscle contracts, exerts force, lengthens and is overcome by a resistance. For example, eccentric contraction occurs in the quadricep muscles when lowering the weight in a knee extension exercise.

Economy—When referenced in exercise, this term usually means the highest level of exercise achievable at the lowest energy cost.

Extension—Movement about a joint that increases the angle between the bones on either side of the joint.

Flexion—Movement about a joint that brings the bones on either side of the joint closer together.

Hemoglobin—The oxygen-transporting component of red blood cells.

HDL—High Density Lipoprotein, considered the "good" cholesterol that helps prevent atherosclerosis.

Isometric contraction—A muscular contraction in which the muscle exerts force, but does not change in length.

Lactate—Formed when lactic acid within the cells, enter the bloodstream, lactate ions separating from hydrogen ions.

Lactate threshold—The point during exercise where increasing intensity causes blood lactate levels to accumulate.

Lactate acid—Produced within the cell from anaerobic carbohydrate metabolism.

LDL—Low Density Lipoprotein, considered the "bad" cholesterol that contributes to atherosclerosis.

Measures—

Metric to English conversion factors: 1 kilometer (km) = 0.62 miles (mi); 1mi = 1.61km; 1 meter (m) = 1.09 yards (yd); 1yd = 0.914m; 1 centimeter (cm) = 0.934 inches (in); 1in = 2.54cm; 1 millimeter (mm) = 0.039in; 1in = 25.4mm; 1 kilogram (kg) = 2.205 pounds (lb); 1lb = 0.4536kg; 1 liter (l or L) = 0.264 gallons (gal); 1gal = 3.785L; 1L = 1.057 quarts (qt); 1qt = 0.946L

Metric conversions: 1cm = 0.01m; 1m = 100cm; 1mm = 0.001m; 1m = 1000mm.

Mitochondria—Organelles within the cells responsible for ATP generation for cellular activities.

Myoglobin—Oxygen-binding matter in muscle.

Plasma—The nonliving fluid component of blood. Suspended within the plasma are the various solutes and formed elements.

Torque—A measure of a force to rotate the body upon which it acts, about an axis. It is commonly expressed in pound-feet, pound-inches, kilogram-meter, and other similar units of measure.

Triglycerides—Often called "neutral fats," they are the most plentiful fat in the body—more than 95 percent of the body fat is in the form of triglycerides. They are the body's most concentrated source of energy fuel.

Veins—Blood vessels that return blood from the body to the heart.

Ventilation—The circulation of air through the lungs.

Ventilitory threshold—The rate of exercise in which the relationship between ventilation and oxygen consumption deviates from a linear function. Breathing rate at ventilitory threshold becomes noticeably labored.

VO$_2$ max—A quantitative measure of an individual's ability to transfer energy aerobically. The value is typically expressed in terms of milliliters of oxygen consumed per kilogram of body weight, per minute. The maximum value can be measured in a laboratory in which resistance is incrementally increased on a bicycle ergometer and the test subject's oxygen consumption is constantly measured. As the work load increases, there is a point at which the test subject's oxygen consumption no longer increases to meet the increasing demand of the work load. The maximum oxygen consumption value achieved is considered VO$_2$ max.

REFERENCES

U.S. Council on Exercise, Personal Trainer Manual, published by The U.S. Council on Exercise, 1992.

Eastman Kodak Company, Ergonomic Design for People at Work, Volume 2, Van Nostrand Reinhold Company, Inc., 1986.

Ganong, W.F., Review of Medical Physiology, Ninth Edition, Lange Medical Publications, 1979.

Martin, David E. Ph.D., Peter N. Coe, Better Training for Distance Runners, Second Edition, Human Kinetics, 1997.

McArdle, William D., Katch, Frank I., Katch, Victor L., Exercise Physiology, Energy, Nutrition and Human Performance, Third Edition, Lea & Febiger, 1991.

Oberg, E., et al., Machinery's Handbook, A Reference Book for the Mechanical Engineer, Draftsman, Toolmaker and Machinist, Industrial Press, Inc., 1980.

Vickery, D. M., MD, Fries, J.F., MD, Take Care of Yourself, Addison-Wesley Publishing Company, 1994.

INDEX

NOTES

NOTES

OTHER BOOKS IN THE VELOPRESS ULTIMATE TRAINING SERIES

Complete Guide to Sports Nutrition
By Monique Ryan

Monique Ryan has been the nutrition consultant to the Saturn Cycling Team, the Volvo-Cannondale mountain bike racing team, and many others in her 13 years as an expert in sports nutrition. Her new book is a wealth of cutting-edge information and concepts explained clearly. No other sports nutrition book places such a needed emphasis on menu and meal planning, food strategies, weight management, and other practical food-related topics.
336 pp
Charts, graphs and tables
Paperback
P-NUT $16.95

Off-Season Training for Cyclists
by Edmund R. Burke, Ph.D.

Get a jump on the competition with this VeloPress Ultimate Training Series book from Ed Burke. Burke takes you through everything you need to know about winter training — indoor workouts, weight training, cross-training, periodization and more. The best cyclists in the world are doing it; you can't afford not to.
6" x 9"
200 pp
Paperback
P-OFF $14.95

Weight Training for Cyclists
by Eric Schmitz and Ken Doyle

Written from the premise that optimum cycling performance demands total body strength, this book informs the serious cyclist on how to increase strength with weight training, as cycling alone cannot completely develop the muscle groups used while riding.
6" x 9"
200 pp
Paperback
P-WTC $14.95

COMING SOON

Sports Psychology for Cyclists, *by Dr. Saul Miller and Peggy Maass Hill*

TO ORDER, CALL 800/234-8356
OR VISIT US ON THE WEB AT WWW.VELOGEAR.COM

ABOUT THE AUTHOR

Gale Bernhardt has been instructing and coaching athletes since 1974. She has a bachelor of science degree in mechanical engineering from Colorado State University, is a Certified Personal Trainer by the American Council on Exercise, and is currently classified as an elite coach by USA Cycling. Her collegiate course work included design of artificial kidneys and hearts; however, her passion remains with the heart and soul of athletes.

Bernhardt uses her education and experience to help endurance athletes meet their race-related goals. Her athletes include Olympic and professional cyclists; top national-level masters road racers, ultraendurance cyclists and multisport racers. Her athletes have placed at Olympic Trials and National Championships. She has coached multisport athletes to podium finishes at world championship events and others have gone to the Hawaiian Ironman.

She is a regular columnist for *Triathlete* magazine, and has written columns for several other publications. She has given numerous presentations on training and mental skills. Her audiences include business and corporate groups, national and world championship teams, and regional clubs.

Living and training in Loveland, Colorado, with her husband Delbert, Bernhardt is available for seminars and personal coaching, and can be reached at galebern@ultrafit.com.